Lady Blue Eyes

Lady Blue Eyes

Barbara Sinatra

WITH WENDY HOLDEN

My Life with Frank

Published by Hutchinson 2011

1 3 5 7 9 10 8 6 4 2

First published in the United States in 2011 by Crown Archetype, an imprint of the Crown Publishing Group, a division of Random House, Inc., New York.

First published in Great Britain in 2011 by
Hutchinson
Random House, 20 Vauxhall Bridge Road,
London SW1V 2SA

www.randomhouse.co.uk

Addresses for companies within The Random House Group Limited can be found at:
www.randomhouse.co.uk/offices.htm

The Random House Group Limited Reg. No. 954009

A CIP catalogue record for this book
is available from the British Library

ISBN 9780091937249

The Random House Group Limited supports the Forest Stewardship Council® (FSC®), the leading international forest certification organisation. All our titles that are printed on Greenpeace approved FSC® certified paper carry the FSC® logo. Our paper procurement policy can be found at: www.rbooks.co.uk/environment

MIX
Paper from
responsible sources
FSC® C016897
FSC
www.fsc.org

Grateful acknowledgement is made to the following for permission to reproduce their material:
Daniel E. Kaplan: "It's Vine on the Line!" by Daniel E. Kaplan. Reprinted by permission of the author.
Shannon Moseley: "I'm Free" by Shannon Moseley. Reprinted by permission of the author.
Principle Management: Excerpt from a speech given by Bono on the occasion of Frank Sinatra's Lifetime Achievement Grammy in 1994. Reprinted by permission of Principle Management on behalf of Bono.
Frankie Randall: Lyrics from "Twenty Years Ago Today" by Frankie Randall.
Reprinted by permission of the author.

Title page photo: courtesy of the author
Book design by Barbara Sturman
Printed and bound in Great Britain by Clays Ltd, St Ives plc

Dedicated to the next generation,

and especially my granddaughter,

Carina Blakeley Marx

Contents

Preface

I have always been a private person, so the idea of writing a book about my life with Frank didn't come naturally to me. My husband was also extremely private and never wrote his memoirs, although he did consider it for a while. I think if he had, though, his reminiscences would have been much more about the music than about the life.

The decision to sit down with the writer Wendy Holden and bear witness came about because several of those closest to me persuaded me that I had a unique perspective on what it was like to live with Frank Sinatra, a man who still commands worldwide fascination years after his death. Who else but his widow could speak of him so honestly, writing an open love letter to her husband while revealing him as a fully rounded individual, brilliantly talented yet utterly human, warts and all? What really clinched the idea of a book for me, though, was the fact that Frank spent so much of his time trying to "set the record straight." He was a prolific writer of letters to editors and publishers, in which he railed against the numerous lies, innuendos, and misrepresentations about him printed in articles and books across the globe. These mistruths tend to take on a life of their own, being repeated and embellished over the years until people believe them to be true.

With Wendy's gentle coaxing, I have drawn on my memories spanning eight decades to chronicle not only my twenty-six years with Frank but the journey my life took me on before I was even by his side. It has been quite an adventure, and when I look back on it now, I sometimes cannot believe that I managed to fit all this in during just one lifetime. In sharing my memories with those who still remember and revere Frank Sinatra, I hope that I have been able to present a different view, one that is written from the heart. This book is for Frank, the love of my life, and I am confident that he would fully support me in this. Most of all, I want everyone to know what a truly wonderful man he was and how, by becoming his bride, I ended up being the luckiest woman in the world.

PROLOGUE

With my wonderful husband.

A Very Good Year

The year I married Frank Sinatra was a very good year. It was 1976, but it had taken us five years of flirting and courting to finally say "I do." It probably took another year before I grew accustomed to the idea that I now carried his iconic name. At first, I'd almost whisper when booking a restaurant reservation or beauty parlor appointment. Even to say "Mrs. Sinatra" out loud felt like bragging.

For a long time I had to pinch myself almost daily to believe that I, Barbara Ann Blakeley, the gangly kid in pigtails from the whistle-stop of Bosworth, Missouri, had somehow become the wife of Francis Albert Sinatra. Could I really be married to the singer whose voice I'd first heard at a drive-in when I was fifteen years old? *"I'll walk alone because to tell you the truth I'll be lonely. I don't mind being lonely when my heart tells me you are lonely too,"* he sang with such sincerity at the height of the Second World War. Even though he didn't make me swoon like some of the "bobby-soxers" at his concerts, the tenderness in his voice still melted my tomboy heart.

Our love affair began almost thirty years later, long before we took the wedding-day vows that were to last for more than two decades. By then I was married to Zeppo Marx, the youngest of the famous comedy brothers. Our next-door neighbor Frank Sinatra had recently divorced for the third time and was dating some of the world's most desirable women. I'd met his second wife, Ava Gardner, and Mia Farrow, his third. I'd seen Marilyn Monroe when she stayed with him not long before she died, and would meet Lauren Bacall, Kim Novak, Juliet Prowse, and Judy Garland, all of whom he'd stepped out with.

Not that I was a complete naïf. As a young model and the wife of a gambler named Bob Oliver, I'd been wooed by John F. Kennedy. As a Las Vegas showgirl, I'd resisted Frank's advances, and I'd lived with a television host named Joe Graydon. I'd been chased by some of the world's most drop-dead, knockout movie stars, none of whom had anything on Frank. He had a sexual energy all his own. Even Elvis Presley, whom I'd met in Vegas, never had it quite like that.

A big part of Frank's thrill was the sense of danger he exuded, an underlying, ever-present tension only those closest to him knew could be defused with humor. One of the greatest things about Frank was that he loved to laugh. He not only surrounded himself with comedians like Don Rickles, Tom Dreesen, Joey Bishop, and Dean Martin (the most natural comic of them all) but took great delight in devising elaborate practical jokes. Even his fieriest Italian tantrum could be extinguished with a witty one-liner.

On one of my earliest visits to Villa Maggio, his sprawling mountain home at Pinyon Crest high above Palm Springs, California, which he'd bought against the fierce summer months, I joined in a late-night game of charades. I was on the opposing team to his, which included his drinking buddies the comedian Pat Henry, the golf pro Kenny Venturi, the songwriter Jimmy Van Heusen, and Leo Durocher, the baseball manager. Having placed a large brass clock on my lap, I called time before Frank's team guessed his charade—the government health warning on a pack of cigarettes.

"Three minutes are up," I cried gleefully. "You didn't get it!"

They began to howl their protests, but the look on Frank's face as he rose to his feet silenced them all. "Who made you time-keeper anyway?" he barked, his eyes like blue laser beams.

"Why, you did!" I replied.

Frank snatched the clock from my lap and gripped it tightly in his hands. For a moment I thought he might hit me with it. Refusing to be intimidated, I stared him out until he turned and hurled the clock against the door, shattering it into a hundred pieces. Springs, coils, and shards of glass flew across the room. The clock face lay upturned on the floor, its hands forever fixed at a few minutes after 4:00 A.M.

It was Pat Henry who broke the ensuing hush. The comic who opened Frank's shows said, "I know what *that* charade is, Francis."

"What?" Frank spun round and scowled.

"It was 'As Time Goes By.'"

When Frank's face cracked into a broad grin, so did the rest of ours, none more gratefully than mine. The moment of danger had passed.

What I saw that night was a glimpse of the complex inner character of the man known as the Entertainer of the Century. This was someone who had a God-given talent, The Voice. He'd clawed his way up from a tough childhood in Hoboken, New Jersey, with an even tougher mother, Dolly, who'd alternately smacked him and pressed him to her bosom. He'd fought on the streets. He'd experienced the highs, lows, and then highs again of a performer's life. He'd had his heart broken. By the time he turned his attentions to me, he was a fifty-five-year-old living legend who'd grown accustomed to getting his own way. He had money, power, and friends, all of which helped occupy his restless mind. The one thing he didn't have, though, was love.

Having been nothing but courteous for months, Frank first came looking for it my way at a gin rummy party he hosted at his house across the fairway from ours in Palm Springs, California. My husband, Zeppo, sat a few feet away, oblivious to the drama that was about to unfold. Our twelve-year marriage had long been dead. Twenty-six years older than me, Zeppo had been successful in vaudeville and manufacturing, but once he retired he preferred a routine of golf or sailing followed by early nights. Unable to relinquish the swinging lifestyle of his fraternal youth, he also dated other women. The Marx name and financial security he'd offered me and my son, Bobby, were all that was left of our once promising romance. I was bored and lonely by the time Mr. Sinatra aimed those eyes in my direction. The spark he ignited inside jerked me from my slumbers.

Frank had been watching me all night as if he was seeing me for the first time. Sitting close, he called me "Barbara, baby" in that killer voice and flashed me a lopsided smile. He asked if anyone wanted "more gasoline" and offered to fix me a fresh martini. Taking my arm, he led me to the den. It was my turn to watch as he swirled vodka around a glass, reached for an olive and then some ice. A cigarette balanced on his bottom lip, a curl of blue smoke rising. He handed me my drink with a *Salute!* and then added softly, "Come sit with me awhile."

Thrown off guard by his sudden change of tack, I found myself directly in the path of that extraordinary force of nature. There was nowhere to run. Once he turned on the charm, my defenses rolled away like tumbleweed. Inhaling his heady scent of lavender water, Camel cigarettes, and Jack Daniel's, I could do nothing but savor the moment of intoxication, oblivious to the consequences.

As we settled onto a couch, our eyes met, and then he pulled me into his arms and kissed me. I knew with that first kiss that I was about to become another Sinatra conquest, and the thought snatched away what little breath he'd left me. Nothing more would happen that night. Not for weeks, months even. That was the way Frank liked to play his game. He'd set me spinning in his orbit, and it was only a matter of time before gravity would draw me inexorably toward him. Whatever was to follow from the discreet seduction he'd begun—and I didn't dream then that it would amount to anything more than a fling—I awaited his next move with eager anticipation.

Such was the power of the Sinatra magnetism that I didn't really have a choice.

ONE

Me on the left, aged nine, with my sister, Pat, and my cousins, Shirley Jones and Don Kelly.

The House I Live In

The lifetime members of the Spit 'N' Argue Club settled into wooden chairs around the potbellied stove in my grandfather's general store. For the next few hours they'd chew tobacco, sip coffee from enamel mugs, and complain about the price of corn.

With their smell of tobacco and dried sweat, these were men I'd known all of my nine years, hardworking farmers from Carroll County, Missouri. Skipping into the store, my brown hair in braids, I headed for the long wooden counter and reached into a glass jar full of candy. Gummy beans were my favorites, so I grabbed a handful. Grandfather Hillis, known to me as Pa, stood with an apron tied around his girth in front of floor-to-ceiling wooden shelves. As I posted the first candy between my lips, he gave me a conspiratorial wink.

"Hey, HH," one of the men called out. "You oughta use some liver tonic on that kid. She's way too skinny." *Skinny* was a word I'd heard my whole life, along with *bony* and *tall*. Like my father, I towered over my friends.

"I beg your pardon!" Pa replied. "My granddaughter's not skinny—she's *streamlined*."

My father, Willis, whose first name was really Charles, looked up from his butcher's counter and gave me a shy smile, as did my uncle Bruce, who was in a corner stacking sacks of feed. The two brothers helped run the family business, Blakeley's General Store, on Main Street, Bosworth, the only one of its kind for hundreds of "Missour-a" miles. The place that had first served the wagon trains of the pioneers sold just about everything a person might need, from sausages to nails. Homesteaders came by horse and cart to trade corn and beans for luxury goods such as coffee or shoes. For some reason, my father always insisted I wear stiff new high-tops laced tight to keep my ankles "thin as a racehorse's." It worked.

In the basement, down treacherous stairs that were eventually to kill her, my grandmother Ma did the laundry and sold feed in between loading the furnace with coal. As the Depression deepened, she and Pa had no choice but to extend credit to their customers. Each night after dinner, my barrel-shaped Pa would tally up the day's IOUs, clicking through them with a long, curved fingernail he kept especially for the task. *Click-click* it went, as I stared in fascination. After an hour or so, he'd fall asleep in his chair. Painting my mouth with Mother's reddest lipstick, I'd plant a big kiss in the middle of his bald spot, knowing that the Spit 'N' Argue Club would give him hell for it the following day.

Blakeley's General Store was the sanctuary to which I'd run three blocks almost every day after school with our bulldog, Brownie. It shielded me from my little sister, Patricia (who wanted to do everything I did), and chores such as collecting eggs, churning butter, picking fruit, or plucking chickens freshly beheaded by my ma. Within the store's aromatic walls I could pick up free candy and an easy compliment. "Someday you're gonna break boys' hearts," Pa would tell me, allowing me to hug and kiss him in a way I never could my folks.

Having had my fill of gummy beans, I wandered out onto the wide front porch that fall afternoon in 1936 and drew my cardigan around me. A farmer rode up the gravel street, jumped off his horse, and tied its reins to the rail. Reaching out, I stroked the animal's nose and pulled an apple from my pocket. Taking a bite, I offered it the rest on the flat of my palm.

"Hey, Barbara," the man said, tipping his hat. "Could be a cyclone coming. Best git home."

I gazed in dismay at the leaden sky and hoped he was wrong. I hated going to the storm cellar dug out of the dirt under our house. My mother would lift the trapdoor, push us down the wooden steps, and follow with an oil lamp. We'd huddle together in the clammy space stacked with preserved goods—wax-sealed jars of pickles and fruit, most of which I'd helped peel, pulp, and prepare. There were also bottles of sweet cider and some kind of Irish whiskey. Once a year my grandfather would disappear down the steps, shut the trapdoor behind him, and get loaded. We'd hear him hollering and singing Celtic songs and knew to keep away.

My mother hated the storm cellar too. I think it was one of the many things she disliked about what she called her "dull life." Born Irene Toppass, she was a great beauty with Rochelle Hudson looks who hungered for more than Bosworth could offer. Our town of five hundred souls was so small that only Main Street had a name and there were no numbers on any of the houses. It had a barber's shop, school, post office, drugstore, and doctor's office. A railway line split Bosworth in two, but the trains generally sped through to someplace more interesting and few in town ventured beyond the boundary sign. My grandfather owned a Model T Ford, one of the only vehicles, but he walked to work each day, leaving it to gather dust in the garage.

My mother rebelled against the dullness of her daily existence any way she could. Twelve years younger than my father, she was one of the few women in town who wore makeup and the only one who smoked cigarettes. A couple of times a month she'd dress up nice and drag my father to the Gem Movie Theater. Transfixed, she'd stare up at movies such as *San Francisco* with Clark Gable and Jeanette MacDonald, or Movietone newsreels about the reelection of Roosevelt, or the execution of the Lindbergh baby kidnapper, or the death of King George V of England. What Mother most enjoyed, though, were musicals, such as *The Great Ziegfeld* or anything featuring Ginger Rogers and Fred Astaire. The glamour of Hollywood was her only diversion from housework, sewing bees, bridge parties, and church socials.

Devoted to her younger sisters, Mary and Fontaine, who'd lived with their servicemen husbands, Kelly and Bill, in Texas and Florida before settling in Wichita, Kansas, my mother was determined to join them. "Wil-lis," she'd complain to my father. "We've got to get *out* of this place. There are better opportunities for us elsewhere." Whenever my parents had one of their fights about it (or rather whenever Mother railed at my father), I'd jump on Pansy, my pony, and take a long bareback ride until the marital storm had passed. Once, during yet another heat wave that seemed to make my mother especially fractious (even though we'd all slept out under the trees), my sister and I escaped together. After trotting around the meadows behind our house, we rode Pansy right through the front door of the Metropole Ice Cream Parlor to order a soda, inadvertently creating *the* scandal of Bosworth.

My father was a pale man of few words. In all the years they were married, I never saw my parents kiss or cuddle. I sometimes wondered why he stayed with her—except that I think he must have loved her very much. In any event, nobody divorced in our town or family, and the stigma would have been too much. Amazing as it seemed to me, Father had left Bosworth once. During the First

World War, he'd traveled to France and other European cities my mother could only dream of. When he returned home, he pulled on his butcher's apron and never spoke about what he'd seen or done. It wasn't until after he died that I was shocked to find a poem he'd written about Parisian women with their "bright red lips."

Whenever my mother sat poring over her *Harper's Bazaar* magazine, which came in the mail from New York, or listened to music that made her long for city life, my father would stare bleakly out of the window. Sometimes he'd bury his head in the family Bible and mouth a silent prayer. I'm sure she thought him weak and cold, and it's true that he was never demonstrative or playful, but I think his quiet strength lay in staying with her for over sixty years.

To be fair, neither of my parents had an easy upbringing. Both from families of five or six children, they'd survived the Depression and then a war. We weren't poor like the families scratching a living in the Dust Bowl, but we were broke. The only Sears, Roebuck catalogs we saw were old ones torn into strips for the outhouse. Our dolls and toys were made from offcuts of wood. Our clothes were run up on my grandmother's Singer and patched as they wore out. For some reason my mother dressed Patricia and me as twins and insisted we do everything together—guaranteeing us a lifelong aversion to each other.

Living as we did on the fresh produce and livestock we grew or raised in our own backyard, I never felt I had gone without. It was only later that I realized the sacrifices my parents made. "We're not hungry. You two finish this up," they'd say as they divided their leftovers between us. Ours was a strong Methodist community, so my parents said grace at every meal and attended church weekly. If Pat and I skipped Sunday school, Pa would chase us around the yard with a dose of castor oil. We received the same punishment or a mouthful of carbolic soap if we were caught smoking homemade cigarettes rolled from Pa's dried tobacco leaves in the smokehouse—especially when we accidentally set it on fire.

Although my strong-willed mother and I often clashed, she instilled in me from an early age the conviction that, if I wanted any sort of life, I had to get out of Bosworth. I'd watch her reflection in the mirror as she was applying her lipstick and fixing her hair each morning and wonder if I'd ever be as beautiful or as fearless. I could tell from her faraway expression that she fantasized what her life would have been like if she'd been born someplace less dull. As for me, I didn't know any different; Bosworth was all I'd ever known. I'd heard talk of how much more exciting things were beyond its windy plains; I'd gaped at the stylish kiss-curls and clothes of my Kansas City cousins when they came to stay. I'd inherited my mother's curiosity about the world, but at nine years old I was happy to live skipping distance from the general store and dip freely into the gummy beans. Little did I know what a candy jar my life was to become.

By the time I was ten years old, my mother had finally worn my father down. There were no more one-sided arguments or uncomfortable silences; we were off to start a new life in Wichita. Despite how he must have felt, Willis Blakeley went quietly.

With the help of her sisters, Mother rented us a house near the Little Arkansas River and enrolled me in the nearest school. That summer of 1937, I was plucked from a tiny, red-painted, six-room primary school and dropped into an enormous inner-city school where most regarded me with disdain. A stranger to cashmere in my homemade clothes, I was the tall, skinny country girl with the "twang." It had never occurred to me before that I had an accent.

Almost overnight I went from cheerful and headstrong to quiet and shy. Taller than everyone else, I developed a peculiar way of standing by bending my knees and hunching my shoulders that can't have endeared me to anyone. When a gang of girls knocked my books out of my hand one day in the playground, the only black boy in the school helped me pick them up. I'd never seen a black person before, but he was kind and thoughtful and I always made a point of speaking to him after that, even when the friends I made later warned me not to.

While I was trying hard to fit in, my mother found her niche immediately as the manager of two budget dress stores known as the Dixie Shops. My father, however, was like a catfish out of the water. He found a job selling shoes, but it lasted only a week, and after that he remained home alone, lost in his memories of Bosworth. He missed the country, his family and friends, and until the day he died he hoped Mother would agree to move back there. Years later, my mother discovered a secret stash of money he'd saved for the journey "home" just in case she ever changed her mind. She never did, of course, and he returned only for the occasional vacation and family funerals. Pa Hillis went first; then Ma fell down the basement stairs and broke her hip, dying soon afterward. My father came back to Wichita with the sad realization that there was nothing left for him in Bosworth anymore.

When my aunts Mary and Fontaine got caught up in the craze for the evangelist Billy Graham, my mother followed suit. As a "born-again" fundamentalist, she taught Bible classes and evangelized with a fervor that puzzled me. Having already been baptized as a baby, I was publicly immersed, shoulder-deep, in a huge tub. Every Sunday I was urged to go up to the preacher when the Spirit moved me to proclaim that I'd "seen the light," accepting Jesus as my "Savior." Out of sheer stubbornness, I never did.

My father, who eventually found a job he liked as a butcher in a Safeway store, played ostrich when my mother imposed tight new regulations on us. There was to be no dancing, no movies, no makeup, no jewelry, and definitely no boys. Strict curfews were set. Needless to say, by the time I was fifteen, my life seemed hopelessly drab. I'd had more fun in Bosworth. This wasn't the freedom Mother had promised when we left Missouri. She and I had terrible fights, which usually ended in us not speaking to each other for days. Feeling increasingly trapped, I knew that I had to escape—just as she had taught me.

Out in the world, war was raging. Pearl Harbor had been bombed, and President Roosevelt sent troops to Europe. People were living each day as if it might be their last. Movies and big band music had never been more popular. Prohibition was over (although Kansas remained a dry state), and nightclubs and dance halls were packed. The newspapers tempered tales of faraway conflict with stories from Hollywood, such as the premiere of the movie *Casablanca*, the death of Clark Gable's wife Carole Lombard in a plane crash, or the latest in the on-off marriage of the singing sensation Frank Sinatra.

Determined to follow the latest fashions despite the fact that I was skinny, tall, and plain, I lost my twang, acquired a cashmere "hubba-bubba" sweater, and donned a poodle skirt. I persuaded my aunts, who were both hairdressers, to dye my hair "Rita Red." With my new Miss Hayworth look, I sneaked to the drive-in after school with my friends Claudine Ramsay and Winnie Markley; a jukebox in the corner of the soda parlor played the latest tunes. We'd drink Coke and watch others dance. In the privacy of my bedroom, I'd learned how to jitterbug, but it was ages before I'd dare try it in public.

It was sitting in the local drive-in as a bored fifteen-year-old that I first heard the singer everyone was talking about. Sinatramania had gripped the country, and I'd seen Sinatra's photograph in countless teen and movie magazines. The number I first heard him sing was a romantic ballad called "I'll Walk Alone," and I shivered to the toes of my bobby sox. He sang so effortlessly it seemed. Oh, how we sighed. Bing Crosby may have been the most popular vocalist of the day, but Frank was younger and far more handsome, with his sharp cheekbones and megawatt smile. Unlike Bing, he had a full head of hair with a lick that fell down endearingly over his face.

So what if some of the gossip columnists made out he was a rogue and a womanizer? That skinny kid with the big ears, who wasn't the tallest or most handsome of men, had every woman in Hollywood after him; of course it was going to turn his head. All I knew was that there was a real yearning and romanticism to his voice that touched me deeply. From that day on, I was hooked.

The advertisement in the *Wichita Eagle* caught my eye. "Pretty Models Wanted. No Experience Necessary." Taking a pair of scissors, I snipped it out and folded it into my purse. Ever since I'd pored over my mother's *Harper's Bazaar* magazines, I'd been struck by the fact that most models were tall like me. I wasn't sure that I qualified as pretty, but I did have good skin with my pale complexion and fine mousy-brown hair. Maybe modeling was my chance for escape? I decided to go along and find out.

The auditions were at the Leyton Hotel on Union Street, opposite the Emporium Department Store, where I'd been taken on as a salesgirl at the blouse counter. Deciding not to tell anyone, I dressed with special care and took the bus downtown, arriving an hour before my shift. The manager of my store was on the same bus, but he didn't spot me, so not wanting to draw attention to myself, I shrank into my seat. Directed to a third-floor suite at the hotel, I was greeted by two men who—I quickly realized—were interested in more than my modeling capabilities. "Lift your skirt, honey," one told me with a smirk. "Let's see your legs."

Reddening and clutching my purse to my chest, I flinched when the other draped his arm around my shoulders and said, "We just want to get to know you a little, that's all." Running from the room, I smeared off the Jungle Red lipstick I'd applied and hurried across the street to work. An hour later, I was summoned to my manager's office.

"Miss Blakeley," he said frostily. "I was in the lobby of the Leyton Hotel this morning and saw you get off the elevator at a very early hour. We can't have that kind of carry-on here!" Mortified when he didn't believe my story—even when I assured him we'd been on the same bus—I quit.

World War II was coming to an end, but it didn't seem to affect us much apart from drills at school and the fact that my uncles, Kelly and Bill, had been stationed abroad with the U.S. Air Force. As my eighteenth birthday approached, I began to defy my mother's curfews more blatantly. Claudine's brother-in-law owned a roadhouse called Swingland, where recruits from the Hutchinson army base would go to drink their own hooch. I'd sneak out of my bedroom window at night and run across the alley to wait for Claudine to pick me up in her car. After a fun night at Swingland, where I finally got to try out my jitterbug, I'd creep back home without my parents ever knowing.

I started to date the local basketball hero, but my mother had forbidden me from seeing him, so when she caught me talking to him on the telephone one night we had a huge fight. Furious, I packed my bags and went to Claudine, whose parents took me in. My teen rebellion didn't last. Living with them was fun at first, but it wasn't home. I began to miss my folks, even their dull routines. I'd wanted to be free, but now that I'd had a taste of freedom, I wasn't sure the streamlined kid from Bosworth was quite ready.

My dilemma was solved when my uncles came home from abroad and were stationed in Long Beach, California. In an exact replay of our final days in Missouri, Mother was determined to follow her sisters. In the end, she simply announced, "We're going." Thrilled by the prospect of a more exciting life on the West Coast, I jumped at the chance too. My father and sister would stay on in Wichita until she graduated from high school, and then they'd join us. My boyfriend was forgotten as Mother and I flew the fourteen

hundred miles to the Golden State. Staring out at the unfamil-
iar landscape far below, I was giddy with expectation. When we
reached Long Beach and I saw the Pacific Ocean for the first time,
my knees almost gave way beneath me. I'd never seen that much
water in my life. I sat on a bench and stared at it for hours. The
ocean still fascinates me in the same way.

We moved into my aunt Mary's house in the suburb of Lakewood, and my mother secured herself a position in an elegant fashion store called Lerner's. I wasted little time too and applied to the
Robert Edward School of Professional Modeling—reputed to be
the biggest and best in Long Beach. Although I was starting to
develop some curves by the time I walked through the door in my
best dress, white gloves, and straw hat, I was as nervous as a bride.
"You're perfect!" cried a chubby, pink-faced man at the reception
desk. "Come on in." His name was Mr. Finney, and he would become my champion. His business partner was Mary Kaye, who
was mean—meaner still if she'd had a few drinks—but she taught
me so much.

In a room lined with mirrors, I learned how to show off my
full five-foot-eight-inch height. "Stand up! Don't slouch!" Miss
Kaye would bark. "The world is a stage, we are all stars, and we
must shine!" She and Mr. Finney taught me to walk like a model
by imagining a glass of water balanced on each shoulder. I learned
how to enter a room "rubber-limbed and straight-backed." In lessons twice a week for three months, they showed me how to sit,
apply makeup, walk down stairs, and model clothes. I'd always
thought of myself as skinny at 112 pounds but was instructed to
lose 2 pounds, a message that was so drummed into me I've wanted
to lose 2 pounds ever since. Having never tasted seafood before
I moved to California, I was happy to live on a diet of shellfish.
Once my silhouette was acceptable, Mr. Finney displayed an enormous photograph of me in the school's window under the banner
Model of the Month, which led to some modeling jobs in a few

local stores. Eager for the experience, I worked without pay, showing anything from fur coats to lawn mowers.

At one shop, called the Parisian, the owner's wife was an enormous and unattractive woman who wore thick glasses. She'd choose a dress and ask me to try it on. "Here, put on my glasses so I can see what I'd look like in it," she'd say, handing them to me and squinting at my reflection in a mirror at the back of the store. Even though I was her exact opposite in shape and height, and my dress was several sizes smaller than the one she'd need, seeing me in it somehow always persuaded her to take it. I learned a valuable lesson about the power of a model.

Sashaying around in fancy clothes, I knew that modeling was what I'd been put on this earth to do. After all, everything else I'd tried—playing the piano, tap dancing, cooking, or taking exams—had achieved less-than-impressive results. But when Mr. Finney entered me in the Miss Long Beach beauty pageant and I only made it into the top three, I began to fear that modeling wasn't for me after all. Undaunted, Mr. Finney persuaded me to enter the Belmont Shore Fiesta. Despite the fact that I was wearing a beautiful white strapless Calponi swimsuit, I was convinced that a curvaceous blonde with a sunshine smile named Betty Harris would win. To my great surprise, I was the one presented with the rhinestone crown, bouquet of roses, and set of Samsonite luggage. Photographers rushed forward to get their shots. This was my first-ever moment in the media spotlight, and it had a surreal quality that made me feel as if I was watching myself from afar.

As the 1948 Queen of Belmont Shore, I wandered around the resort in my swimsuit and tiara for a week. By the second or third day, while I was waving at the crowd from the top of a fire engine, I noticed a tall, good-looking young man with wavy chestnut hair driving one of the cars in our parade. "Look, there's that guy again," I called to Betty, who'd been crowned my princess. "I think he's after you." I was wrong.

His name was Robert "Bob" Harrison Oliver, and he was a twenty-year-old summer student at Long Beach College. A part-time singer and bartender at his parents' restaurant, the Rose Room on Anaheim Street, he told me he'd wanted to meet me ever since he'd seen my photo in the paper. He seemed nice enough, so when he asked me out for dinner at the most romantic setting in town, a smart supper club on top of Signal Hill, I accepted. Over steaks, Bob told me he came from a large Italian family on his mother's side called the Spanos. He loved to gamble and flew the family plane to Vegas on weekends to play blackjack, but his real passion was to sing. "People say I sound a bit like Frank Sinatra," he told me. "We have the same kinda voice."

"I love Sinatra!" I told him. "I have all his 78s, and I never miss the Lucky Strike *Hit Parade* on Saturday nights."

Bob nodded. "A jazz pianist friend of mine named Nat King Cole was on that recently. Have you heard of him?" I loved the King Cole Trio and thought how much more interesting Bob's life was than mine, but as he lit my cigarette I noticed that his hand was trembling. Just as I was about to exhale, he dropped to one knee. "Barbara, I adore you," he declared suddenly, taking my hand in his. "Will you marry me?" As everyone stared at us, I laughed smoke in his face. Crestfallen, he said, "You don't have to give me an answer tonight. I'll wait. But I must have you. I'm so in love." Then he sat back down to finish his meal.

The next day, one of the judges of the Belmont Shore Fiesta approached me after another of my parades. His name was Les Pace, and he was the head of casting at Twentieth Century–Fox. "My wife, Helen, and I think you have a wonderful look. We'd like you to come in for a screen test." My week couldn't get any more surprising. Being invited for a screen test was like winning the lottery, but I decided not to tell anyone in case I jinxed it. I claimed the script, a three-minute segment from the movie

Gilda starring Rita Hayworth, was a contract for the fiesta. Reading through the scene over and over in my bedroom, I was sorely unprepared.

"Who are you talking to in there?" Mother would ask through my locked door.

"It's the radio," I'd lie.

At six o'clock on the morning of the screen test, I arrived at the Fox lot and spent two hours in makeup before being zipped into a beautiful white satin gown. Then I was led to the set and introduced to my leading man as the crew stood waiting. The clapboard clapped, the director yelled, "Action!" and my costar held me in his arms. "I want to go with you, Gilda," he said. "Please take me. I know I did everything wrong."

My mind froze. The first line my character had to say was "Johnny, isn't it wonderful?" All I could stammer was "J-Johnny, I..." Unable to remember the rest of my line, I gulped, stared at the director helplessly, and looked to my lead for inspiration. Not only had my memory blanked but my throat felt cut.

The director told the cameras to keep rolling and tried to reassure me. "Barbara, sweetheart, you look stunning. You'll be wonderful in this. Just relax."

Each time I tried again, little more than a squeak came out, and then I broke into an unstoppable attack of schoolgirl giggles.

"Cut!"

Half-laughing, half-crying, I wanted to run from the stage, but somehow, in an endless series of retakes and hand-holding, we managed to shoot the entire scene. A few days later, I received a call from the studios. "You have no future in pictures," the voice said with practiced finality. "Don't even bother taking classes."

Grateful that I'd told no one about my screen test, I accepted with some relief that Hollywood stardom wouldn't be my future after all. What had I been thinking? I was just a farm girl from Missouri, after all. When Bob Oliver called again, I agreed to go out with him, curious what this loony boy might do next.

By our fifth date he'd calmed down a little and stopped begging me to marry him. Instead, he took me to meet his family, who welcomed me as one of their own. His grandfather Joe, who had a thick Italian accent, reminded me of dear old Pa. Bob's father, whose nickname was Butter, for Buttermilk, was a remote southerner who drank too much. His mother, Marge, was a tiny terror of a woman who ran the Rose Room single-handedly and seemed to like me.

The family would gather every Sunday for a delicious but quarrelsome dinner. Throughout the meal and poker game afterward, everyone seemed to do or say terrible things to one another and then kiss and make up. I'd never seen anything like it. This volatile Italian family couldn't have been further removed from my own, and I was beguiled. I wasn't in love with Bob, but he clearly worshipped me. He had a great sense of humor, and his lifestyle offered adventure beyond anything I'd known. My Belmont Shore crown had been handed back. I was selling clothes at a downtown store and picking up occasional modeling jobs. Life was dull, and my mother had drummed into me that I should never settle for dullness.

When Bob told me he was going to New York to find work as a band singer, I cracked. Manhattan had spelled excitement to me ever since the days when my mother's *Harper's Bazaar* arrived in Bosworth smelling of ink. We married in September 1948 at the Lakewood Community Methodist Church, Long Beach. Twenty-one years old, I wore an ornate white lace and satin gown with a seed-pearl tiara and had two page boys scatter rose petals in my path. My father gave me away. After a reception for two hundred guests at Le Club Moderne, at which Nat King Cole played piano and Bob and Marge sang, we set off on our honeymoon to Rosarito

Beach, Mexico. When we got home, Bob drove me to Bosworth in his Ford so that he could meet the rest of my family and then on to LaFayette, Georgia, to introduce me to relatives on his father's side.

I think I began to worry within a few days of our honeymoon that our relationship might not work—and not just because his mother decided to come on the second leg. She was financing the trip after all. Even though she provided some laughs from the backseat along the way, I began to suspect by Bob's attitude, drinking and flirting with other women, that my new husband wasn't all I'd hoped he might be. Knowing that my only alternative would be to return home shamefaced to my parents, I prayed with all my heart that I was wrong.

TWO

An early modeling shot.

COURTESY OF THE AUTHOR

New York, New York

Bob and I flew to New York in the winter of 1949 with the highest expectations. He was in search of fame and fortune, and I just wanted him to prove to me that I hadn't picked a dud.

The sights, sounds, and smells of the Big Apple shocked and entranced me. I'd never seen skyscrapers, steam rising from manhole covers, or beggars in the streets. Marge had put us on a tight budget, so we checked into a single room in a hotel somewhere in the West Seventies. I'd dyed my hair platinum blond like Lana Turner's and saved for a new wardrobe, but my clothes were too flimsy for an East Coast winter and we had to blow some of our precious funds on warmer ones.

After a day or two of taking in the sights, we set to work. Bob spent his days knocking on the doors of musical agents and his nights auditioning in supper clubs, while I embarked on the tedious ritual of "go-sees" at the studios of commercial photographers. Trouble was, my "book" of modeling photographs lacked polish, and with so little experience and clothes that were hardly New York chic, I was obviously a greenhorn. Through a male model friend of Bob's named Jay, I finally managed to get an audition for a sports-wear assignment for *Good Housekeeping* magazine. Apart from the promise of ten days' work, the photo shoot was to be onboard a Furness Line ocean liner, one of the "millionaire's service" ships that plied back and forth between New York and the Caribbean. When the photographer called to tell me I'd gotten the job at three hundred dollars a day, I was over the moon. Not only would I be earning great money and traveling to places I'd only ever seen pho-tographs of, but I'd be working alongside two models named Lily Carlson and Marilyn Ambrose, both of whom were at the top of their game. Waving good-bye to Bob, I boarded the *Queen of Ber-muda* and sailed down the Hudson River bound for Nassau, barely able to believe my good fortune. Almost immediately my insides began to churn.

I'd never been on a ship before and had no idea that I'd be so seasick. For probably 70 percent of that cruise I couldn't even leave my cabin. Strangely, although I was unable to keep food down for very long, I was also ferociously hungry, with a particular craving for spinach. Lily and Marilyn took pity on me and went to the restaurant to bring me food. Whenever I was not looking quite so green, I'd be up on deck sporting madras shorts, halter tops, and cork wedges with a fixed smile on my face. While I lay recover-ing in my bunk, the girls gave me the best modeling tips I'd ever learned. New York modeling was very different from that taught by Mary Kaye. The girls told me to relax more and lean into the cam-era rather than away from it. They showed me how to utilize light to my best advantage and when to pad my clothes to enhance my shape. Needless to say, Lily and Marilyn became lifelong friends.

Our ship stopped at the newly opened Paradise Island, owned by Huntington Hartford, who asked us to pose for some publicity shots. Then we went on to Nassau, where I finally felt well enough to join a party at the Fort Montagu Beach Hotel. Four men were sitting at the next table, and one came over to introduce himself. Pulling up a chair, he sat beside me and turned on the charm. His name was Jack, and he was sailing in the area. He was very attractive with his bleached blond eyebrows and wavy brown hair. Jack was such a big flirt that he told the crew of his yacht to sail on alone because he wanted to travel back to New York with us. I liked his spontaneity, but I still wasn't interested, even when Lily informed me later that he was a well-known politician. "That's John F. Kennedy. He's a member of the House of Representatives for Massachusetts," she told me. "People say he'll go far."

Far or not, Jack acted so rashly in jumping ship that he didn't give himself time to pack and boarded without a tuxedo for the liner's first-class restaurant. Obliged to eat alone in his cabin, he'd plead with us to join him, but we never did. Throughout the journey home, he continued to make passes and was always trying to separate me from the others, but it didn't work. Not only was I seasick but I was practically still a bride. When we docked in New York, Jack introduced me to his two beautiful Weimaraners, which had been brought to meet him. In truth, I liked his dogs more than I liked him. Jack also introduced himself to Bob. "You must be Barbara's husband," he said, shaking Bob's hand. Kissing me on the cheek, Jack gave Bob an enigmatic smile and walked away. It would be more than ten years before I'd see him again.

When my nausea didn't stop even after I reached terra firma, I realized I was in trouble. It wasn't seasickness after all. I didn't dare tell a soul I was pregnant, especially not Eileen Ford, who'd agreed to take me on at her Ford Modeling Agency after Lily and Marilyn recommended me.

"Fashion photography, not runway, I think," she said, examining me with the precision of a biologist. "And of course, you'll need to lose weight." I could have laughed and cried all at once. Within days, I was offered work with *Vogue* and *Life* magazines, although not quite what I'd imagined. In one shoot for Noxzema sun cream, I was plastered in bright red makeup to make me look sunburned. The caption read: "Don't Fool with Sunburn!" I was so embarrassed by the results, but Bob cut out the advertisement and proudly showed it to everybody in his favorite West Side bar.

As our baby grew inside me, so did my nausea. Work became a disaster because I kept throwing up or passing out. In the end, Eileen Ford peered at me through her enormous spectacles in her brownstone offices on Fifty-fourth Street and informed me that no one else would hire me. She offered me dry congratulations when I finally admitted my condition and bade me a brisk fare-well. Bob and I had no choice but to head home. He was so mad at me for getting pregnant and cutting short his freewheeling night-life, while I was mad at him for flirting with my modeling friends. Not only wasn't he ready to be a father, but he wanted to stay in New York even though he hadn't found any work and spent most of what I'd earned on booze and horses.

Back in Long Beach living above the Rose Room, we had no money and quarreled about everything. Bob tended bar down-stairs until 2:00 A.M. closing, and I fed myself from the restaurant kitchen. Not that I could cook anyway. His grandmother tried to teach me how to make pasta once, but I told her, "Good luck with that!" I never mastered the art. One day I came up with the idea of starting my own modeling school. Anyone interested in fashion would surely be eager to know what I'd learned about posing and lighting, makeup and trends. If I opened a school and shared my experiences, I could work until the baby was born, and besides, I liked the idea of mentoring younger girls.

So did Bob suddenly, who styled himself general manager and could hardly wait for my pupils to arrive. With a three-thousand-dollar loan from the bank (which Marge guaranteed), I found premises at Seventh and Alameda streets. After fitting it out with floor-to-ceiling mirrors and painting it in peach hues (kinder to the complexion), the Barbara Blakeley School of Modeling and Charm was up and running. On the opening day, girls and their mothers lined up around the block. Some wanted to be models; others hoped to learn etiquette and manners. I also taught elocution by recording students' speaking voices and playing them back. When I listened to my own voice for the first time, I was horrified. All I could hear was a nasal Missour-a drawl, which made me say things like "Kaaan-sas Ciddy" and "shugg-ah." Clearly, I had work to do, so for months afterward I stayed late in my office reading Joyce Kilmer's poem "Trees" aloud until I had buffed my accent into one that sounded acceptable. "I think that I shall never see a poem lovely as a tree...."

Business flourished, and I soon had ten teenagers in each class, plus some older models who asked me to find them work. I did, and even sent some to Las Vegas for the chorus line. The majority of my pupils seemed to hang on my every word. I wasn't that much older than they were, and they related to my youthfulness. I think it helped that I dressed and looked the part. I had my hair in a "poodle cut" like Kim Novak's and always wore the latest styles from my mother's store.

When Bob wasn't trying to hit on my students, he continued running the bar, singing, and gambling. If ever he had a pocket full of money, he certainly didn't give me a dime, and I learned to stash what I earned. One time he slammed into our bedroom in the middle of the night sporting a black eye and demanding the money I'd saved for our baby. He claimed men would kill him if he didn't pay them what he owed. Sobbing as I handed him the six hundred dollars I'd taped to the underside of a drawer, I felt our baby kicking inside and knew that my marriage was doomed.

On October 10, 1950, after a two-day labor that Bob walked out of because he couldn't bear my screams, I gave birth to an eight-and-a-half-pound baby boy. We named him Robert Blake Oliver—forever and always my beloved Bobby.

I was very happy with the baby but not with his father, who flew back to New York to pursue a singing career soon afterward. It was a separation, although neither of us used that word. Marge doted on her first grandson to her dying day and was a great help looking after him, but she couldn't do anything about her errant son. Resigning myself to life as a single parent, I realized that it was up to me to make enough to raise my child. Mother gave up her job to help me, and my sister, Pat, joined me at the school. As soon as one class graduated, another would be ready to start, and we had two classes running at any time.

Then Oscar Meinhardt of Catalina swimwear contacted me. He was setting up a rival to the Miss America pageant called Miss Universe, with entrants from around the world. The first contest would be in Long Beach the following year, and Oscar asked me to be its official beauty consultant. I leapt at the chance. It was hard work but so glamorous and exciting. I loved cajoling dress shops into lending the girls evening gowns, coaxing hairdressers into offering their services in return for a credit, or persuading local citizens to take in nervous young women who barely spoke English. When the contestants embraced the makeup tips I gave them, I came up with the idea of my own cosmetics line. I persuaded Buffums' department store to stock the new Barbara Blakeley Cosmetics and promoted them via the pageant.

Bob came back broke from New York and we talked about divorce, but I was too preoccupied to pursue it, so we muddled along as before. The first Miss Universe Pageant was held on June 28, 1952, at the Long Beach Municipal Auditorium in front of twenty thousand people. I had a dressmaker copy a gown worn by Lana Turner in *A Life of Her Own*, a favorite movie of mine about an aspiring model who leaves her small Midwest town to seek her fortune in New York. In that dress, I truly felt like a film star. The actress Piper Laurie, who'd just starred in a movie with Rock Hudson, crowned our winner—a teenager from Finland. Bob had somehow talked his way into becoming an executive to the pageant and an assistant to Oscar Meinhardt. It was, I soon discovered, the perfect excuse for him to flirt with the contestants.

When Bobby celebrated his second birthday a few months later, I knew that his father and I wouldn't still be married by his third. I was only in my twenties, yet everything seemed to have happened in such a rush since I'd left Bosworth. In the space of a few years, I'd married, been a model, set up my own school, and was a founding member of Miss Universe. There was even a lipstick with my name on it. Now I was heading for a divorce, yet I'd planned hardly any of it. I'd just let things happen, which is what I continued to do my whole life.

The happy by-product of all this was that I was making a name for myself professionally. Bob tried to cash in on it too and set himself up as a promoter, producing a concert starring the singer and television presenter Joe Graydon, most famous for his number one hit "Again." Like most things Bob attempted, though, the night fell apart. The evening coincided with one of the worst storms in the resort's history, so Joe and the full orchestra Bob had hired played to an empty house. Not long afterward, Joe invited me to appear on the pilot of a new one-hour afternoon show he was hosting on KABC television in Los Angeles. On what was one of the first talk shows of its kind with music, I showcased my best students under the banner "Barbara Blakeley and Her Cover Girl Models." The pilot was such a success that it was made into a yearlong series. Television was the future for modeling, and I knew the exposure would be good for my school. I was right. Before long, I was able to open a theater next door in which to host fashion shows. Strangers began to recognize me on the street.

For a while, I thought I might enjoy being successful and

famous, but in my heart I knew that had never been my burning ambition. From the day I'd failed my screen test, I'd felt only relief at being one step out of the spotlight. With the dawning realization that I was about to become a single parent working full-time and raising a son, all I really wanted was security. I longed to meet someone who'd take good care of me and Bobby. Would I ever find such a man?

My affair with Joe Graydon was, I suppose, an accident waiting to happen. After working on his TV show and developing an easy rapport, we soon became lovers. Lonely and sad while Bob was away gambling or womanizing, I fell easily and I fell hard. Joe became the great love of my life—or so I thought.

Romance and humor mean everything to me, and Joe had both in spades. He was kind and thoughtful, all those things I'd been missing in my life. By the time we hooked up, Joe was asking his wife for a divorce. We had a lot of laughs together and would spend weekends with my friend Bobby Lasley and her husband, Jack, a bartender known as Big Jigger Jack, at their place in Corona del Mar. My Bob was still hanging around and, despite his infidelities, insanely jealous. One night I went to see Joe singing at the Circle Club in Long Beach with two of my models. Standing on the stage looking dashing in his tuxedo, my new beau proved what a consummate professional he was, singing Sinatra standards such as "All or Nothing at All." By the time he performed his signature tune, the audience was his. Singing directly to me from the stage as my girlfriends giggled, he knew I was smitten. *"This is that once in a lifetime. This is the thrill divine..."* When he strolled toward me in the middle of another song called "(I Like New York in June) How About You?" and changed the words to "Barbara Blakeley's looks give me a thrill," I thought it heady stuff.

After the show, we were all enjoying a nightcap in the lounge when Bob stormed through the door. Before I could say anything, he marched to our table and slapped me across the face. "Now wait a minute!" cried Joe, jumping up. Two bouncers rushed over, our table was upturned, and Bob was manhandled to the floor.

"Okay, Bob, that's enough," I told him, my cheek burning. "Let's go home!"

Wriggling free, he bolted for the door.

I drove back to our apartment, but Bob was gone and so was his pilot's gear. It was four days before I found out what happened to him. Blind with jealousy, he'd flown to Las Vegas in his single-engine plane on a stormy night. Flying through the notorious Cajon Pass in the San Bernardino Mountains, he had to hug the cliffs. The experience must have given him the fright of his life because three days later he rented a car to drive home. After a week of stewing, he sent me a two-line telegram: HAPPY EASTER. MY ATTORNEY WILL CALL YOU.

Deciding to celebrate, I went to the bank to withdraw some money and treat myself to a mink stole, but the modeling school account was empty; Bob had cleared out every cent. Determined not to be thwarted, I persuaded the bank to lend me the cash to buy the stole, which I insisted was necessary for a woman in my position. Amazingly, they agreed. A few days later, I instigated divorce proceedings on the grounds of irreconcilable differences. I was the first Blakeley ever to seek a divorce and probably the first to have an affair with a married man. My parents were horrified. I asked the court for seventy-five dollars a month child support, although I doubted I'd ever get a dime.

The second Miss Universe pageant was a bigger success than the first and was won by a pretty French girl, who went on to have an international acting career. I became friends with the German contestant, Christel Schaack, and moved into her apartment once I'd moved out of Bob's. When Joe's TV show relocated to San Diego's KFMB-TV, he asked me to go with him. I didn't say yes immediately; this was the fifties, after all. When I told my mother, she couldn't believe that I'd even consider living in sin, as she put it. I wished she understood that after my dreadful experiences with Bob I needed to get away and follow my heart. Having been uprooted from Bosworth and forced to acclimatize to a life far from all I'd known, I'd married to escape the religious strictures she'd imposed, only to become Bob's fool. For the first time, I was doing something utterly for myself. Leaving Bobby shared between his doting grandmothers, and the modeling school in the hands of my sister, I packed my suitcase and headed south.

San Diego was a great place to be in the 1950s, especially for a carefree young couple in love. It was buzzing, lively, and fun. When I wasn't parading models on Joe's show, I was doing live commercials for everything from dog food to mattresses. We found an oceanfront high-rise in the exclusive La Jolla resort on the edge of the city, with its rugged coastline and small-town atmosphere. Despite being happy with Joe, though, I missed my son dreadfully. Talking to him on the telephone every day wasn't enough, so I commuted to Long Beach to visit him every weekend in my white Cadillac Fleetwood convertible. I tried to oversee my business, but eventually, the school became too much of a burden and I made a gift of it to my sister and two favorite graduates.

In the fickle world of television, Joe's show didn't survive, and he found himself out of work. The world of big bands was dying, and he didn't know which way to turn. When he was offered a job as a disc jockey for a new radio show in Las Vegas, he had little choice but to accept. My mother and I were barely talking by then, and the more fundamentalist she became in her religious beliefs, the tougher her influence over Bobby. She wouldn't allow him to watch movies like *King Kong* or play any games she regarded as wicked. When I told her I was moving to Vegas with Joe, she hit the roof. As Bobby played on roller skates out in the backyard, she began to yell. Having announced that Bobby and I would burn in hell, she slapped me.

"All right, Mother," I told her, as calmly as I could. "That's enough."

I opened the screen door and told Bobby to get into my car. He was still wearing his roller skates and looked confused, so I said, "Leave them on!" I drove him over to Marge's house and asked if she'd take care of him until I was settled. After that, I announced, I would look after Bobby myself. "It's time I took more responsibility for my child," I told her firmly. I could tell she was upset. My decision all but broke my mother's heart too, but she'd pushed me too far.

It was the summer of 1956 when Joe and I moved into a small furnished apartment at the back of the Sahara Hotel. Our neighbors were casino employees and wait staff, most of whom slept during the day and worked all night. The sprawling metropolis of Las Vegas was unrecognizable from the days I'd first gone there with Bob Oliver. Then it was a small western town that still held rodeos and boasted just four casinos on its Strip—Hotel Last Frontier, the Thunderbird, the Flamingo, and El Rancho Vegas. Bob had managed to lose money in them all.

I soon picked up some modeling jobs at the Sahara and Flamingo hotels. Wearing clothes sold locally, I wandered through bars and restaurants quietly informing shoppers about each of my outfits. "This is from Fanny's in the lobby arcade," I'd say. "The dress, at a hundred dollars, is pure silk from Thailand."

"But how much is the girl in it?" some wise guy would usually joke.

"You couldn't afford it," I'd reply.

A few weeks later, I spotted an advertisement in the *Las Vegas Sun* for showgirls at the Riviera. "Minimum five feet nine inches tall," the ad insisted, but I figured half an inch wouldn't matter by the time I slipped on some heels. While I was waiting for my audition, two showgirls came to look me up and down. "You're wasting your time, honey," the brunette announced, chewing gum. She must have been over six feet tall. "They're never going to hire you. What are you doing here?"

"It's a lark," I replied with a smile, feeling short for the first time in my life. "I thought I'd see what happened." The women I'd later come to know as Ida and Penny strode off as I began to have my doubts. I had little idea what the job involved and was relieved that there wasn't a dance audition, which I knew I'd fail. Instead I gave the choreographer Dorothy Dorbin and the producer Sammy Lewis my best wedding-march walk and was hired along with a blonde named Marsha.

I moved Bobby to Vegas, enrolled him in a local school, and paid a housekeeper to babysit him after hours. I bought him a scruffy little mutt of a dog named Boots to keep him company. Joe, who had a young son of his own back in L.A., wasn't thrilled to have my "kid" in tow, but he put on a brave face and even threw a ball around the yard for Bobby every now and then.

Being a Vegas showgirl was all that I'd hoped it might be and more. The shortest and blondest in our quartet, I reached six feet in my four-inch stilettos and had to master gliding across a stage wearing a towering headdress featuring anything from the Statue of Liberty to the Eiffel Tower. I was paid $150 a week for two shows a night, six nights a week. I earned almost twice as much as the twenty-six chorus girls who danced their feet off, learned complicated routines, and did quick changes in the wings. When I was through working at the Riviera in the early hours, I'd usually try to get across town to sit in on Joe's late-night radio show or watch him sing at one of the smaller hotels. Then the next day it would be the same routine of modeling at lunchtime before my evening shows. The days were long and the nights even longer, but I had the stamina of youth and never seemed to tire.

To begin with, my fellow showgirls gave me the worst seat

in the dressing room and excluded me from their conversations. They were afraid I might horn in on their relationships with the casino bosses. It was like my first day at school in Wichita. Once I assured them I was happy with Joe, they relaxed, and the more I found out about them the more I liked them. Penny, from Texas, had run away with the circus at thirteen and learned to read tarot cards in Cuba. Ida not only was six feet and an inch but had the most vibrant blue eyes and the whitest skin I'd ever seen. Marsha, the free-spirited sweetheart from Oklahoma, became my closest friend.

Best of all, these veterans of umpteen Vegas shows taught me how to be one of the flagships of the Riviera fleet. Not only did I have to balance fifteen pounds of headdress with just a tight clamp at the temples and a chin strap to hold it on but I had to keep smiling, float down polished stairs like a goddess, and avoid the chorus girls whirling all around me.

The other girls plastered on so much makeup that, close up, they looked like Egyptian mummies. As a fresh-faced country girl, I couldn't bear to slap on that much foundation, rouge, and eye shadow, and I wasn't about to start layering hot wax onto each eyelash as Penny did each night. So I used my own makeup line and the subtle techniques I'd picked up as a model. In the end, all but Penny copied me, toning down their looks to match mine. I guess she just couldn't break the wax habit.

We formed the decorative backdrop to acts such as the comedian George Gobel and Spike Jones and the Band That Plays for Fun. In one of my first shows featuring Liberace, we wore ruffled, bare-midriff costumes and our heads were topped with three-foot-high plastic champagne bottles tipped forward at a precarious angle. Liberace was charming and gave each of us a china piano. Most of his fans, including my mother (who came to see his show several times), were not aware that he was gay. Liberace came running into rehearsals one day crying, "Help me! Help me!" as three screaming middle-aged women gave chase, seemingly determined to rip his clothes off.

As part of our contractual obligations, Ida, Penny, Marsha, and I were required to slip into cocktail dresses after our final performance and "dress up the room" in the hotel's piano lounge for an hour or more to draw in passersby. The bosses often wandered through to check that we were in situ, and there was always the "eye in the sky" security camera monitoring our every move. Bouncers kept watch too and shooed away anyone making unwanted advances, especially to the girlfriends of the bosses. Celebrities were the only exceptions to the rule. People like Cary Grant and James Stewart always turned a few heads. Howard Hughes would wander in wearing a tuxedo with the scruffiest tennis shoes you could imagine. Once he homed in on a girl he liked, he'd bombard her with gifts and flowers in the hope that she'd leave with him, just as he had with my model Shirley Lewis. I met Howard a couple of times and would smile as I was obliged to, but I saw the way he harassed the other girls so I always tried to avoid eye contact after that. Apart from anything else, those who'd been with him warned me that he was dirty and that, close-up, he smelled. Elvis Presley was working in Vegas, so he was a regular too, but he was after every girl in the place, and I avoided men who drank too much or got high. Anyway, I had Joe.

Once we'd fulfilled our duties in the lounge, we were free to do as we pleased—gamble in the casino, see a show, or go home to bed. The top acts in town that year included the Minsky Girls (the first topless showgirls in Vegas), Tony Bennett, Nat King Cole, and Frank Sinatra, who opened at the Sands soon after his divorce from Ava Gardner. Frank was doing well again after a personal and career slump, and was working with the composer and arranger Gordon Jenkins, with whom Joe had worked. Nat King Cole was also working with Gordon and was a huge success by then, with his own TV show and the hit single "When I Fall in Love." He'd broken through racial prejudices to play in Vegas alongside stars such as Lena Horne and Sammy Davis, Jr.

Whatever the rest of the showgirls decided to do after work, the others almost always went gambling, so—curious—I began to tag along. "I presume you know how to stash the cash?" Marsha asked me one night. When I looked blank, she shook her head and sighed. "You really are fresh from the farm, aren't you? Okay, watch me tonight. I have a date with a high roller, so come to the craps tables and see how I do it. When I raise my right eyebrow, I'll meet you in the restroom."

Intrigued, I watched as she hooked up with a silver-haired man in a Stetson who laid hundred-dollar chip after chip onto the green baize. Soon, he began to slide some of his chips her way so that she could gamble too. Hanging on his arm, giggling with delight, she placed her bets but almost always seemed to lose. I watched her closely but saw nothing unusual other than her reaching into her purse occasionally for a handkerchief or powder for her nose. Then she arched her perfectly penciled eyebrow at me, so I drifted away from the table and met her in the restroom.

"Quick, open your purse!" she whispered once she was certain we were alone. Reaching into hers, she pulled out a fistful of chips. There were more stuffed inside her brassiere. I could hardly believe my eyes. "Now go home and hide them somewhere. I'll pick them up tomorrow." She left in a cloud of perfume and cigarette smoke.

I went back to my apartment feeling sick to my stomach. I was a nervous wreck, convinced that the police, the bosses, or both were going to burst in any minute. I didn't dare count the chips, but I could tell there were several thousand dollars' worth. Even though I knew they were legitimately hers, they felt tainted, so I threw them in a box and hid them under the bed. Kissing a sleeping Bobby on the forehead, I slid between the sheets to wait for Joe, terrified that I'd done something criminal. I barely slept a wink. When Marsha called the next day to collect her chips, she was surprised by my reaction.

"Don't ever ask me to do that again!" I told her. "I don't know how you did it and I don't want to know." Dear Marsha, she was determined to stash enough of a nest egg to pay for her return to her small town in Oklahoma to buy "the biggest house on the hill." Stashing was tolerated so long as half was gambled back or she wasn't too obvious about it. On no account could a girl and her beau move to another casino. Sadly, Marsha was caught in the end. A drunk she was with went broke at 5:00 A.M., then demanded some of his money back. She slid a couple of chips across the table, but he shook his head and said, "Come off it! You have a lot more than that." There was a fight, and plainclothes security men arrived and unceremoniously tipped Marsha's purse upside down on the table. I guess she'd had no one to pass to that night.

After that, Marsha went to work at El Rancho Vegas, the last stop for a showgirl on the Strip. That hundred-room hotel had been the first casino in town, co-owned by the Marx Brothers, but by then it was the end of the line. I hated to see that happen to her, and unfortunately we lost touch. Three years later, El Rancho Vegas burned down. I never knew if Marsha saved enough to buy her house on the hill. I sure hope so.

Marsha had also showed me another way of supplementing her income. It was common for a woman standing at a casino table to have a stranger walk up and put some chips down in front of her as a gift. No strings. Maybe he was a big spender being nice to the "little lady." Maybe he was having a good night and feeling generous. His reward? In my case, just a smile. Needless to say, the other girls got hit on a lot more than I did. One night a funny little guy with a Kewpie doll face put stacks of hundred-dollar chips in front of me at the blackjack table, where I rarely placed a bet above five dollars. "Here, Barbara, have some fun," he said.

I was shocked; I'd never been given so much before. Turning to him, I said, "I'm sorry, but I can't accept that." He looked surprised.

The girls who were with me whispered, "Are you nuts, Barbara? That's Willie Alderman! Go on, take it." The name meant nothing to me, and I shook my head. He left, taking his chips with him.

Penny couldn't understand why I'd refused, so I told her straight. "Because some night in the future I'll get a knock on my door from that weird little guy, and I don't ever want to have to deal with that."

Ida assured me that I'd never hear from him. "Oh, Willie isn't like that!" she insisted. "He's a sweetheart. He just likes to help the girls."

I wasn't convinced. It wasn't until years later, when I read a book called *The Green Felt Jungle*, that I discovered how Mr. Alderman made his money. More commonly known as Ice Pick Willie, he allegedly specialized in killing people by sitting next to them at a cocktail bar and shoving the pointed tip of an ice pick sharply into their eardrums. Once they slumped over dead, he arranged them to look drunk and calmly walked away. My encounter with him was my first of several lucky escapes.

THREE

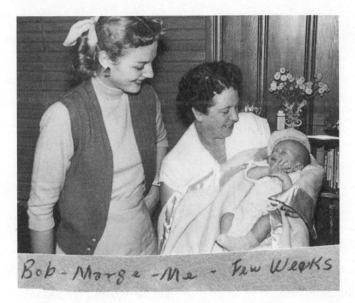

Bob - Marge - Me - Few Weeks

*I'm a proud mother with my new son, Bobby, and
my mother-in-law, Marge Oliver.*

COURTESY OF THE AUTHOR

Luck Be a Lady

"Hey, blondie—come on in here!" The greeting was casual, slurred even. The man yelling at me through the smoky half-light had his back to the bar, a tumbler of whiskey in one hand, a cigarette in the other. Standing around him was a group of equally well-dressed companions in tuxedos, their bow ties hanging limply at their collars. I recognized a couple of the faces.

"Keep walking," I said to Ida and Penny. It was four in the morning, and we were on our way home. We'd already performed two shows at the Riviera and had hurried across to the Sahara to catch the husband-and-wife singers Louis Prima and Keely Smith in their after-hours performance. I was tired. My feet hurt. My son was home in bed with his dog; the housekeeper was waiting. I wanted nothing more than to curl up and sleep too.

"Don't you know who that is?" Ida asked me with a hiss. "Aren't you even going to say hello?" She slowed her pace as the man who'd called out to me watched me keep on walking. "Talk about a high roller!" Penny chipped in. Both girls knew what they were talking about, hooked up as they were by then with Gus

Greenbaum and Sidney Weiner, two of the biggest casino bosses in town. "You should at least go and have a drink with him," Penny added.

"No way," I replied, smiling as the man with the tumbler kept staring. "I don't like dealing with drunks, and anyway, Joe's waiting."

So I kept on walking that night. I walked as fast as my aching feet could carry me past that dimly lit bar—past Dean Martin, Sammy Davis, Jr., Joey Bishop, Peter Lawford—all of them. And past the forty-two-year-old Frank Sinatra too, in spite of his calls to me, the only blonde in our trio.

Frank may once have been the idol of my Wichita teens, but his personal life (or as much as I knew about it from the newspapers) was not a pretty picture. He'd sent shivers down my spine for his Oscar-winning performance as Private Angelo Maggio in *From Here to Eternity*, but he wasn't someone I thought I'd care to know. His latest hit, "You're Sensational," from the movie *High Society* starring Grace Kelly, was being played on every radio across the nation, but that incredible voice alone wasn't enough to tempt me in. His self-styled "Summit of Cool," featuring the men alongside him who'd later become known as the Rat Pack, may have been the hippest set in town, but it was not the pack for me. Frank looked sexy that night, but I had other cards to play. It would be some time before I'd come to know just how sexy and dangerous he could be.

After I'd spent less than a year in Vegas, "Sin City" began to lose its shine, and so, sadly, did my relationship with Joe. He lost his job, and I became the main breadwinner, paying all the bills as well as half his alimony and child support. Money problems soured our once-beautiful romance. His world had changed. Rock 'n' roll was here to stay, and his smooth style and slick presentation weren't in vogue anymore. Unemployed and confused, he was short of cash, and we fought constantly.

In truth, we could never have sustained such a surreal, nocturnal existence. Each night we dressed up and plastered on makeup before going to work in places with no windows or clocks. We grabbed meals at all sorts of strange hours and snatched sleep whenever we could, scratching out a living along with so many others. Missing his own son and jealous that I was spending time with mine, Joe had never been keen to have Bobby around, and it began to show.

Even Boots the dog didn't seem happy in our first-floor apartment. Bobby wasn't having a great time either. He was taller than the other kids at school, who were mostly the children of craps dealers and waiters. As I had been, he was picked on. To make up for my long hours and his unhappiness, I spoiled him with toys, which were then stolen and sold. Increasingly, through my encounters with people such as Ice Pick Willie and Penny's and Ida's boyfriends, I began to realize how much crime and sleaze surrounded us. Vegas in those days was run by the Mob for the Mob; there was no getting away from it. They'd invested heavily in the town, and they had to spend the money they made there or be stung for taxes. That's why people like Willie Alderman could be so generous with chips. But there was a downside to all those gangsters being around, vying against one another, and when Gus Greenbaum and his wife had their throats slit, I was truly shocked. Penny was understandably upset too, but to my surprise she almost immediately started dating someone else, a man who worked for Frank Sinatra. "You win some, you lose some," she told me with a shrug. She definitely won; her new boyfriend took care of her until the day he died.

On a modeling assignment at the Flamingo Hotel (owned by Bugsy Siegel until he was murdered), I had to change in a small back room where dirty laundry was sorted. Pulling on an outfit, I glanced down at one of the wicker carts and shrieked. Lying in a heap was a sheet covered with blood—not just a drop but an entire body's worth—shiny and fresh. "Oh, my God!" I cried, pointing.

"*What is that?*" I thought the other girls would be as shocked as I was, but nobody flinched and everyone looked away.

A laundry maid fixed me with a frown and muttered, "Don't you know better than to ask questions round here?"

Shivering, I thought, Uh-oh. My days in this town are numbered.

At a time when I needed reassurance at home, Joe was far from reassuring. One night he demanded my key to our joint safety deposit box. I'd been cleaned out by Bob, and I wasn't going to let that happen again. Refusing to hand over the key, I hurried off to work. Three hours later, just as I was about to go on for the finale, Joe burst through the fire exit door backstage. He'd been drinking. I was in a black satin gown and rhinestone tiara and carrying a white ostrich-feather fan with a six-foot wingspan. "I need that key," he said, grabbing my arm. I managed to wriggle free and stepped onto the stage with the other girls as our cue—the opening bars of "Humoresque"—struck up.

In a scene reminiscent of a Marx Brothers sketch, each time I went anywhere near the wings, Joe would reach out to grab me and then rush to the other side. I, meanwhile, was teetering around with my enormous fan trying to stay in the middle and look graceful but forgetting my routine and bumping into the rest of the company. Hissing at Joe from behind my fan, I told him I'd meet him outside the fire door during the next break. As promised, I slipped there between numbers, but we had a terrible fight. Before I knew it, he'd knocked my headdress off and was pulling at my costume. The heel of my stiletto caught in the grate and bent backward. The door had slammed shut behind us, so I banged on it with my fists until one of the stagehands heard me. I fell into the building, my lipstick smeared, my tiara tilted forward, and several feathers missing from my fan. The other girls had already done the first half of the number when I came crashing onto the stage all askew with a wobbly heel and a missing earring. As I found my rightful place in the lineup, Penny hissed, "Jesus, Barbara! What the hell happened to you?"

A few days later, Joe did find my key and sweet-talked a girl at the bank into letting him open our deposit box. He took the lot—money, deeds, and legal documents. Fortunately for me, within days he decided he wanted me back, so he returned everything and I put the box in my name only.

To complicate matters further, Bob Oliver began flying into Vegas again. He'd drop in to the Riviera to see me or turn up unannounced at the apartment to visit Bobby. He never brought money. "I don't have a dime!" he'd say, pulling on empty pockets. Even though he was still tending bar, he never gave up his dream of making it as a stage singer or breaking into movies. I think he always hoped we might get back together too, but I'd just shake my head and smile if he suggested it. Bob the dreamer, the romantic fool who'd asked me to marry him on our first date.

As if I didn't have enough to worry about, a third suitor appeared out of the blue. He was a well-tailored, middle-aged man who'd sit alone at the back of the dinner theater to watch our rehearsals. He was a friend of the director Sammy Lewis, and I could tell he was important by the way the bosses reacted to him. Sammy came over to me one day and asked, "What have you done to Zeppo Marx? He's been asking questions all around the hotel about you." So that's who he was—Zeppo Marx, the former straight-man member of the wacky team of Groucho, Chico, and Harpo. I'd not only seen Marx Brothers movies as a teenager in Wichita but met Zeppo once at a Miss Universe dinner in Romanoff's restaurant in Los Angeles. I should have remembered him because I'd thought him very rude; I sat next to him, but he hardly said a word to me all night. It was only later that I realized he was deaf in one ear and I was sitting on his wrong side.

At fifty-six, with a surprisingly good singing voice and a dry sense of humor, Zeppo had taken early retirement to do the things he enjoyed, which included gambling, women, golf, management, and anything mechanical. He was successful at all five, especially the last, which made him more money than comedy ever did. He invested some of it in the El Rancho casino with his brothers and was a regular at the craps tables. Divorced with two adopted sons, he was carefree and single with lots of show business friends and plenty of girls. Now he'd set his sights on me. Eagle-eyed Penny was the first to spot him. "That Zeppo Marx can't stop staring at you," she told me. "He's a good guy to know. Lucky girl!" I wondered how lucky I'd really be. After my experiences with Bob and Joe, I wasn't looking to start afresh with anyone, least of all someone with a reputation as a womanizer, even if he was a funny, rich one.

One night just before the final show, I peeped out from behind the stage curtain to check how full the house was. To my surprise, Zeppo, Joe, and Bob were sitting together in a booth right at the front of the theater. A few nights earlier they'd sat separately, staring daggers at one another across the room, so when the show was over, I'd declined to sit with any one of them for fear of setting them off. Now, it seemed, they'd decided to join forces so that I'd sit with all three of them.

As part of our Spike Jones floor show that night, we had to do a crazy high-kick routine with the chorus girls in which only our legs showed through long slits in a heavy black curtain. The show went down well and I didn't mess up, but it was with some reluctance that I wandered out front afterward. As soon as Joe saw me approaching, he jumped up and asked, "Where were you placed in the lineup?" Flashing me a warning look, he added, "I've got twenty-five bucks riding on this."

I thought for a moment and began to count.

Bob piped up, "I said you were the twelfth."

Joe shook his head. "No," he said with conviction. "Barbara was in the middle. Twenty-second along."

Zeppo gave me a quiet, intelligent smile. "You were at the end, fifth from the left," he said. I laughed and nodded. He was right, much to Joe's dismay.

Sitting down next to Zeppo and making sure I was on his right side this time, I asked him, "How did you know?"

He gave me a wry grin. "Easy," he said. "You were the lowest high kicker."

Knowing I was the worst dancer in Vegas, Joe and Bob roared with laughter. While they made jokes at my expense, I looked across at Zeppo, seeing him in a new light.

I can't remember what it was exactly that made me realize I might end up with Mr. Marx, although marriage was truly the last thing on my mind. Maybe it was that he sent Bobby a bicycle for his birthday—a gift that infuriated Bob and Joe, neither of whom had bought Bobby anything. Perhaps it was Zeppo's ardent pursuit with dinner invitations and flowers or the new Thunderbird convertible he bought for me. Or was it the time he stood behind a group of strangers in an elevator and pulled faces until I was laughing so hard I had to get off?

Not only did Zeppo have the caustic wit of the Marx Brothers but he made fun of himself rather than of those around him. I think that may have been why he was always given the role of romantic lead while his brothers insulted him. Underpinning Zeppo's charm was his promise that he could offer a better life for me and my son. That thought was compounded for me when I took Bob to court over Bobby's nonexistent support payments only to discover that he'd skipped off to Europe.

The event that finally set me in motion toward Zeppo came when I returned to our apartment one morning and couldn't find my son anywhere. Smelling smoke, I looked into the backyard and screamed. Bobby was tied with rope and sitting on a pyre of dried wood and desert brush. The tent I'd just bought him was wrapped around his legs. Some of the rougher neighborhood boys stood in a circle laughing as they set fire to the heap with matches. As soon as they saw me running toward them, they dashed off. I unfastened the ropes and pulled Bobby free as the flames began licking at his feet. Within minutes, the tent was ablaze. My heart pounding, I hugged my child to me and thanked God I'd arrived home in time. "I was being initiated into their club," Bobby tried to explain, still coughing as I carried him inside.

"Pack up," I told him. "We're leaving!" I'd had it with Vegas. This was no place to bring up my son. There seemed little left to stay for anyway. Bob had fled, never to pay child support. Joe had cleaned out half of all I'd saved and was driving me crazy. He'd poured sugar into the gas tank of the car Zeppo had given me, ruining the engine. I was tired of our adrenaline-fueled existence in a city where reality blurred into fantasy as easily as day melted to night. As I explained to Bobby in no uncertain terms, we were leaving that afternoon. I had no idea where we'd end up, and Zeppo was the last person on my mind, but I knew we had to get out of town.

"Boots! I can't find Boots!" Bobby cried, searching all over the apartment and then the backyard. Wearily, I stopped what I was doing and went looking with him. We hunted all over for that darn dog; we even drove around in the car, but he was nowhere to be found. Maybe he'd been scared off by the other boys when they'd tied Bobby or had taken off by himself as he sometimes did. Perhaps a neighbor had taken him in. I was too exhausted and upset to look anymore, so I promised Bobby we'd alert the animal welfare agencies the minute we reached California and come back for Boots once he was found.

"But, Mother, we can't just *abandon* him!" Bobby cried, his eyes filling with tears.

"We have to!" I insisted. I wanted out of Vegas there and then. If I'd waited a day longer, I might have lost the courage to leave Joe, to walk away from my friends and the life I'd made for myself. "I'm sorry, Bobby, but we have to go—now!"

Oh, God, the tears. I broke my young son's heart that day, as well as my own. Leaving poor Boots behind is a memory that haunts us both to this day. I had friends drive around looking for the scruffy little mutt for weeks, calling out his name. I must have telephoned the city's dog pound and the Humane Society twenty times or more in the weeks and months that followed, but the answer was always the same: "We have no dog answering that description." I never found out what happened to Boots. I only hope and pray that someone kind took care of him and gave him a happy life.

Having said good-bye to Vegas, Joe, and Zeppo, I headed back to Long Beach. Living with my parents was never going to work, so I found an apartment. To pay the rent, I tried to get work locally as a model, but I'd been out of the loop for so long that I didn't know the right people anymore.

My modeling school was being closed, and my services weren't required. Before too long I was broke, all my savings gone. Neither Marge Oliver nor my parents could help, and I had no idea what to do. One day Zeppo called to see how I was. When I told him the truth, he made me an offer. "Come to Palm Springs," he pleaded. "I'll set you and Bobby up in your own place. You can commute back to L.A. to model whenever you want." With all other options running out, I had little choice but to accept.

I fell in love with Palm Springs during the winter of 1958, but not with Zeppo Marx. At least not enough to marry him then, which was what he really wanted, but I was off marriage for good. "The Springs" was a little desert town with a tremendous sense of style and glamour. Those who lived there behaved as if they were permanently on vacation, which I guess they kind of were. Zeppo rented me a two-bedroom apartment in a motel next to the famous Racquet Club, where I quickly found work modeling in the poolside fashion shows. The clothes were divine and the work not remotely as frenetic as Vegas had been.

Zeppo's house on Halper Lake Drive in the Rancho Mirage district was one of the first built just off the fairway of the Tamarisk Country Club. A dramatic, modern three-bedroom building in white tile and stucco, it stood alone overlooking the second green. Along with almost every high roller in town, Zeppo was a member of Tamarisk, which had been set up by the Jewish community for Jews. The rival club, Thunderbird, was for Gentiles, including members Bing Crosby and Bob Hope. At Tamarisk, Zeppo played golf with his friends and his brothers Chico and Gummo. Wonderfully secluded, his home nestled in citrus trees and oleander bushes with a fifty-yard lawn. Beyond a topiary garden and a high privet hedge, in what was known as the Compound, lived his neighbor Frank Sinatra.

The two men had known each other for years; Frank and Groucho even appeared in a movie together in 1951. The first time Zeppo walked me around his backyard he told me, "Frank's never around much. He's always working or on the road." I glanced across the seventeenth fairway at the hedge that separated the two properties and thought that, given Frank's reputation as a late-night-party thrower, that was probably a blessing.

Bobby and I tried to settle into our new life, but it wasn't as easy a transition as I'd hoped. Zeppo gave me such a hard time about having my son with me that, realizing I had no wriggle room, I found a good but expensive military school near the ocean in Long Beach. Zeppo agreed to pay all Bobby's tuition fees and expenses; anything to get rid of him. Although Bobby would board all week, I could still visit him every weekend and take him out. My resilient son, who'd been bounced around so much of his life already, adjusted to the Southern California Military Academy amazingly well. After a few visits, I discovered why. My lanky boy had been selling or bartering my stash of glossy eight-by-ten modeling shots, in which I was posed in anything from ball gowns to swimsuits. In return, his pubescent fellow pupils gave him sweets, polished his shoes, or made his bed. I was the school pinup! Whenever I went to visit, boys would rush up and ask me to sign photographs. I was so relieved that Bobby had found a way to make friends, even if it was cheeky. Promoted to master sergeant, he looked so dashing and handsome in his braid and brass buttons that I couldn't wait to show him off at the Racquet Club. I even commissioned an oil painting of him in his uniform, which still hangs in my bedroom today.

Alone in Palm Springs with Zeppo, I soon realized that I'd only swapped one surreal existence for another. Being a "desert rat" took some getting used to, especially after Vegas. Most "rats" played golf early in the morning, when it was cool, followed by lunch, a round of tennis, and a game of gin rummy before cocktails and dinner. I didn't play golf, tennis, or gin, so—if I wasn't modeling—I sunbathed and swam, went horseback riding in the desert, or had lunch with a girlfriend. I dined each night with Zeppo and his friends, but they were never late nights because everyone was up early the following day.

Zeppo was such an enthusiastic gambler that he placed bets on the outcome of almost every game of golf. Being such a good player, he usually won, which drove one of his opponents, the comic writer Danny Arnold, crazy. Desperate, Danny went to see a "golf psychiatrist," who told him that he'd never beat anyone wearing or using the color red. So, for their next game, Danny insisted Zeppo discard his red and white golf bag as well as the red socks he slipped over his clubs. Zeppo agreed, and Danny had the best game of his life. They were almost through to the final green when Zeppo dropped his pants to show his scarlet shorts. Needless to say, Danny lost.

One day, Zeppo took me to Harpo's house to meet his brothers. I'd heard so many stories about their mother, Minnie, and father, Sam, a hopeless tailor with one short leg and one short arm. Unable to pay the rent, the family was kicked out of every house they lived in and made money however they could. Harpo and Chico were almost identical, but Chico was a much more versatile pianist, so he would audition for jobs in houses of ill repute but send Harpo (who knew only one tune) to work. Those boys would probably still be working in brothels but for Minnie, who put them on the stage in vaudeville acts because she knew they were naturally so funny. She was right.

At Harpo's house, El Rancho Harpo, Zeppo introduced me to Gummo and his wife, Helen, as well as Groucho and Chico. Chatting with them, I learned about the nicknames they'd chosen for themselves when they were in vaudeville. Zeppo (whose real name was Herbert) was named after the zeppelin. Groucho (Julius) got his name because they were usually paid in cash and he'd put it in what was called a "grouch bag." Chico (really Leonard) was so named because he chased the "chicks" even more than the others. Gummo (Milton) got his name because he wore rubber-soled gum shoes, and Harpo, who was christened Arthur, played the harp.

Zeppo was too young for the stage when they began and joined the troupe only as a last-minute stand-in when Gummo joined the army. Zeppo was due to go out with a friend that night on a double date with some Irish girls, but instead he had to cancel and hop on a train to Texas. A few hours later, his friend was shot dead by an Irish gang who took exception to a Jewish boy dating one of their own. Show business truly saved Zeppo's life, and he stayed on as the stooge when Gummo decided to quit and go into manufacturing after the war.

When I was first presented to Groucho, he rolled his eyes at Zeppo and flapped his thick black eyebrows at me in true Groucho style. "Mmm!" he said with a leer, licking his lips. "*Quite* a dish!" He was the most outspoken of the brothers, very much in charge, and could be gruff at times, but he and I got along just fine.

After a while, I asked, "Where *is* Harpo?"

"Under the table," his wife replied. I knew the Marx Brothers were known for their off-the-wall comedy, but I didn't realize it extended to their personal lives. When Zeppo discovered where his brother was, he went over to the table, got down on his hands and knees, and began talking to him.

Looking up at me from all fours, Zeppo said, "Hey, Barbara! Come on over, I want you to meet Harpo." So I went over and stood by the table, but Zeppo insisted, "You have to get down." So I got down on my hands and knees alongside him, and there was Harpo under the table with his head pressed to it.

"Hi, Harpo," I said, feeling like an idiot. "Nice to meet you.... Tell me, why are you down here?"

He laughed. "I made a little shelf under the table for my glasses, so that I can see the television. I glued it and was holding it in place, but then my head got stuck to it, so here I am!" Harpo was so funny. I loved him. He was the sweetest of all the Marx Brothers. After we'd had our chat, we stood up and carried on as if there was nothing unusual about our host being glued to the table.

Just as Bob Oliver had before him, Zeppo took me to meet his family only because he was pressing me to be his wife. Whenever I saw he was getting up steam to propose, though, I quickly changed the subject or began an argument—anything to distract him. I didn't want to be backed into a corner and have to turn him down, so I stalled him repeatedly. He was kind and generous, but I really didn't want to marry him.

One of my chief reasons for avoiding his impending proposal, though, was that he wasn't great with Bobby. Zeppo had no paternal instincts whatsoever, despite having adopted two children in his previous marriage. Although he tried for my sake to connect with my son, he always seemed relieved when Bobby went back to the military academy or to visit his grandparents. I'd already lived with a man who hadn't taken to my son, and I didn't want to have to go through all that again. Besides, I was relatively young and missed having my own money and a career. I had too much fire in me to live a dull life of retirement. Modeling in L.A. had never lost its allure and still seemed a realistic possibility, so after five months in the idyllic date palm oasis, I scooped up Bobby, kissed Zeppo good-bye, and headed a hundred miles west.

FOUR

*My wedding day to Zeppo Marx, surrounded
by my famous brothers-in-law.*

COURTESY OF THE AUTHOR

All or Nothing at All

Hoping to make at least enough to continue to pay for Bobby's education, I presented myself at the Mary Webb Davis model agency on Sunset Boulevard. Camera-ready in my finest clothes, I sat waiting sometimes all day until they'd send me for a go-see.

Fortunately, I soon had bookings for runway shows at stores like Saks and Robinsons, modeling for some of those who made movie costumes during the Golden Age of Cinema. They liked me so much that they took me with them on the road. Traveling the globe for a fortnight at a time, we'd set up in fancy hotel suites, where I'd do a series of quick changes and show off the latest collections to prospective buyers.

The hours were long, from seven in the morning to midnight. The shoes were always the wrong size, and my feet hurt so much that I'd sit on the edge of the tub and run them under hot and cold water before easing them back in. My employers included Helen Rose and Irene Lentz (who went by their first names) as well as Howard Greer and Richard "Mr." Blackwell. Howard designed for

Joan Crawford, Katharine Hepburn, and Rita Hayworth. After hours, Howard and his significant other, Bruce, dressed me up and used me as their beard. They told one bartender in a drag club that I was really a man and had to pull him off me when he went to check me out.

Helen Rose designed the most elegant clothes and went on to become head costume designer at MGM Studios. She made the clothes for Elizabeth Taylor in *Cat on a Hot Tin Roof*, Judy Garland in *Meet Me in St. Louis*, and Grace Kelly in *High Society* and *The Swan*. When Grace married Prince Rainier of Monaco, she had Helen design her wedding dress. Irene Lentz was also a brilliant tailor. One of her biggest clients was Doris Day, and it was my frame Irene used to design the outfits Doris wore in the thriller *Midnight Lace* with Rex Harrison. I even made a small appearance in the film's trailer as Doris's double. My one and only moment on the silver screen had my face in shadow with no lines to stumble over. One night Irene fell asleep with an electric blanket covering her head and woke up with her face paralyzed. A few years later, she slashed her wrists and jumped out of a hotel window.

I never really liked Richard Blackwell, who designed for Jayne Mansfield, Dorothy Lamour, and Jane Russell, even though he used me as the fitting model on which he cut and draped many of his designs. He was mean to everyone around him, especially his boyfriend Spencer. In hotel suites, he'd have me slip in and out of up to thirty different outfits an hour with the help of my stylist Sidney while he gave a running commentary. I had to be available at any hour, so it was not unusual for Blackwell to drag me out of bed to model for prospective clients after he'd wined and dined them.

These colorful characters were gay, but it never bothered me, even coming from such a small-town background. My father always believed in the maxim live and let live, so that's what I did.

. . .

In spite of the hours, my working life was exciting, well paid, and the realization of all my teenage dreams. I knew I was a good model once I'd mastered the theatricality of it. I was able to afford the rent on a 1920s bungalow in Beverly Hills. Something was still missing, though. It wasn't that I was unhappy; how could I be when my son was such a joy to me? I had plenty of friends too but was secretly lonely inside.

Not that I was allowed to be for long, because one day Sidney, now my former stylist, turned up on my doorstep unemployed and never left. He took over my life, rearranged my furniture, and re-decorated my home. He scrawled swearwords five feet high on the living room walls, insisting they were "beat," and when two coats of paint wouldn't cover them, he draped sheets of linen over his graffiti instead. He also pretended to be my butler in the most out-rageous outfits whenever anyone came to call.

One day, it was Zeppo, who'd driven into town in his Rolls-Royce to take me out to dinner. Zep stood in the doorway as ele-gant as anything with flowers and candy in his hand when Sidney opened the door, wearing a Hawaiian muumuu. At that moment, I flushed the toilet in the lean-to part of the duplex just above Zeppo, and the leaky plumbing piddled water straight onto his head. Being a Marx brother, he loved the wackiness of the whole scene. When he returned for our next date, though, he was well prepared. I opened the front door to find him sheltering under a large umbrella.

Once Zeppo saw the sheet-draped living room, he cried, "My God, I'm in a coffin!" Zeppo could always make me laugh, and I couldn't help but love him for that. There had been so little laugh-ter when I was a child that I craved it my whole life. Whenever Zep was in town, he'd come around and take me out. He was witty and handsome, claimed to adore me, and nothing I could do or say seemed to distract him from his goal of making me his wife. Being with Zeppo reminded me that there was another life, far away from leaky cisterns and my punishing schedule, meeting the payments on my car and the house, as well as taking care of Bobby.

"I've been torching you for over a year," Zeppo finally reminded me one night in Chasen's restaurant. "Why not move back to Palm Springs and use my penthouse in Beverly Hills if you still feel the need to work?"

"But I don't play golf or tennis," I protested lamely.

"You could learn," he suggested gently.

"But there's Bobby—" I began to protest.

"Enroll him in any school you like," Zeppo interrupted. "I'll pay. During term time, you and I can fly off to Europe together or sail somewhere in my yacht. Whatever you want."

He was very convincing, and when he saw my hesitation, he added softly, "I'll take good care of you, Barbara."

I looked into his smiling eyes. Zeppo was offering me security, the likes of which I'd never known. Life would be good. Bobby's future would be secure, and he'd be educated in the finest schools. "But you haven't really proposed," I pointed out.

Just as had happened to me once before, my dinner date got down on one knee in the middle of a crowded restaurant and took my hand in his. "Will you marry me?" he asked.

I took a deep breath. "Sure," I heard myself saying. "I'll marry you, Zep."

Feeling suddenly very happy and realizing how much I'd come to care for him, I added, "I'll make you a good wife, darling. I promise." As I leaned forward and kissed him, I meant every word.

On September 18, 1959, Zeppo and I were married in the place where we met—the Riviera Hotel in Vegas. It was a quiet affair with Bobby, my parents, my sister and her husband, and a few close friends. Zeppo had already bought me a six-carat emerald-cut diamond engagement ring, and on our wedding day he presented me with a simple gold band. We'd both been married before and didn't want a fuss. Although I was a Methodist and had been married into a Catholic family, Zeppo didn't mind, and he never asked me to convert to Judaism. He said I became Jewish by injection.

After the ceremony, we went straight to the tables, where I used to help dress the room. Ida and Penny were still around, and we had a drink and caught up with all the news. Zep and I spent the rest of our weeklong honeymoon taking in shows like the one at the Copa Room of the Sands with Frank Sinatra, Dean Martin, and Sammy Davis, Jr. I sat next to Mary Benny, the wife of Jack, and the two of us laughed so hard at the impromptu way those three fed off one another. One would sit in the audience and suddenly jump up to say something; another might break into a song or pretend to be drunk. It was all unscripted, and you could tell they were having as much fun as we all were.

I moved into Zeppo's Palm Springs house, and he immediately added a room outside for Bobby, which impressed me enormously until I realized that it was to keep my son out of the way. But Zeppo could be sweet, charming, and as funny as anything when he wanted to be. One night early on in our relationship, after we'd come in from dinner at a restaurant, he watched me as I undressed. First I slipped off my dress, and then I undid the long blond hairpiece I'd worn that night and placed it in a drawer. Carefully, I peeled off my eyelashes, and then I reached into my bra and pulled out the falsies I sometimes wore to give me a little extra boost. They too went into the drawer. Laughing, Zeppo said, "I don't know whether to get into bed or the drawer!"

He bought a new yacht, which he named the *Barbara Ann*, and kept it at the Salton Sea Club or down at the Balboa Bay Club near Newport. We'd sail to Catalina Island and I'd water-ski, but I'd never been much of a sailor since the *Queen of Bermuda* days, and my namesake ended up as a party boat for Zeppo. In his sixth decade, my husband didn't have to work, even after he claimed to have lost $6 million one night alone at the craps table. Having trained as an engineer, Zeppo had made most of his money with a company named Marman, which machined parts for the war effort. He'd helped invent the Marman screw clamp, which was used to secure bombs and fitted to fuel lines in just about every airplane made during World War II. He also produced a two-cylinder motorized bicycle. He patented a wristwatch that could tell if someone was about to have a heart attack, although nothing ever came of it. When he wasn't tinkering around with bits of metal and springs, he'd run a talent agency with Gummo, representing writers and actors, including Barbara Stanwyck. He always said that the only clients he didn't like to handle were his brothers.

I continued working in Palm Springs and L.A. whenever I could, but Zeppo didn't like it. Through his showbiz friends, I was offered a couple of minor television roles and walk-on parts. In one brief appearance I made on *The Jack Benny Program*, I was in a sketch with the comedian Ernie Kovacs. Ernie was wearing a huge false mustache, which I was supposed to find ticklish when I kissed him. Just as in my screen test for Fox, I got an attack of giggles the minute I stepped in front of the camera, and when Ernie made some ad-lib wisecrack, I cracked up, only this time it was incorporated into the show.

Although Zeppo bought me a car and a mink coat, he wasn't extravagant with his gifts and only ever gave me one important piece of jewelry—a ruby and diamond bracelet. He didn't want me to have my own money. It was jealousy, I think, and fear that, if I had the means, I might escape. I should have remembered Marsha in Vegas and learned how to stash. Just like Bob and Joe before him, Zeppo also had quite a temper on him. He reminded me of a little banty hen we'd kept back in Bosworth. We'd have a fight every time a bill came in; he'd even call up my girlfriends to confirm how much I'd lost at gin rummy, and we only ever played for dimes. In the end, I made sure that all the bills came in at the end of each month so I could get his hour of yelling at me over with.

For my part, I tried to embrace his Palm Springs life as much as I could and enrolled in golf and tennis lessons. With practice and the best teacher—Zeppo—I became a good gin rummy player. My golf playing, however, infuriated him. "You're lousy," he'd tell me. "I never want to team up with you again! I've been playing this course for years, yet whenever I'm with you I see corners of it I didn't even know existed." He wanted me to concentrate on my golf, but tennis was more fun with a younger set and I wasn't about to give that up. I'd become friends with several members of the Racquet Club who were closer to my age, including Hollywood's golden couple—the actors Tony Curtis and Janet Leigh—as well as the singer Dinah Shore.

Dinah was one of the greatest ladies in the world, and we had so many laughs together. She looked like Miss Apple Pie Goody Two-shoes but had a wicked sense of humor and loved to party. Each summer in Palm Springs, when the clubhouse was closed and everyone had left, Dinah and I would don bikinis, go out onto the golf course barefoot, and play golf. It was so hot that we'd hit one ball, then run into the backyards of our friends' empty houses and jump into their pools to cool off. We'd always leave our left hands out of the water with our golfing gloves on. By the time we got back to the ball, we'd be dry.

Janet Leigh was a great gal too, a terrific lady on and off the tennis court. When I first met her, she'd just won the Golden Globe for her role in Hitchcock's *Psycho* and been nominated for an Oscar. Despite her enormous presence on-screen, she was so thin she could hardly control her two Great Danes, who'd come lumbering up and lick us all over. Her husband was a drop-dead handsome guy. Such a charmer and extremely flirtatious, Tony Curtis had a strong Bronx accent, and in one movie he had to say the line "Yonder lies the castle of my father," but instead he said, "Yonder lies the castle of *me fodder*." We'd rib him mercilessly about that. He was a great story-teller and would regale us with the tale of the time he made his first movie, in 1948, with the screen siren Yvonne De Carlo. Afterward, he had a limousine driver take him to his old neighborhood, where all his buddies still knew him as Bernie Schwartz. Hearing them call out hellos and ask him about life in Hollywood, Tony rolled down the window and shouted, "I fucked Yvonne De Carlo!"

Everyone was on diets in Palm Springs, and from the day I'd enrolled at the modeling school in Long Beach I'd wanted to lose two pounds. I drove my friends crazy. Eventually, a girlfriend named Louise Steinberg told me, "I wish you'd lose those fuck-ing two pounds—I'm fed up with hearing about it!" There were all sorts of fad diets around then, just as there are now. I lived on nothing but shrimp cocktail for a while, and that seemed to work. When Tony Curtis told me he was on a new regime, I was curious. A few days later I saw him in the clubhouse eating a huge banana split with ice cream and nuts piled on top.

"Tony!" I cried. "What happened to your diet?"

He looked down at his bowl and said, "This is it." Needless to say, it didn't work.

Marilyn Monroe, Tony's lover when they'd starred together in *Some Like It Hot*, came to the Racquet Club a couple of times when Frank Sinatra was in town. When my son, Bobby, heard that the woman of his boyhood dreams was Frank's guest somewhere just beyond the hedge, his eyes virtually came out on stalks. Tired of his talking about her, I finally said, "Well, walk on over there and say hello." To his credit, he did, and Frank introduced him to Marilyn, although I think Bobby was so tongue-tied he could hardly say a word. I heard later that the blond bombshell liked to walk around in the nude, but I never asked my son if that was the reason he came home so red-faced.

I saw Marilyn at the club a couple of times, and she was certainly very beautiful with a voluptuous figure. I could see why she'd attract the likes of Mr. Sinatra, among others. She was married to the playwright Arthur Miller at the time, but her dependence on drugs and alcohol left her vulnerable. We had a casual conversation and she seemed sweet, but we were never going to be close. A few years later she was dead. Someone told me she was playing Frank's music the night she died.

Ava Gardner, another woman who'd featured so prominently in Frank's life, came to the Springs as well. Knowing Ava was an avid tennis player, Frank built a court for her at the Compound, even though she was staying only a few days. I hardly knew him then. We'd nod a hello each time our carts passed on the golf course, but I don't think he registered who I was unless he saw me with Zeppo. Then one day, shortly before Ava was due to arrive in town, Frank called me out of the blue.

"Barbara, it's Frank Sinatra," he said. I sat up and took notice. This wasn't someone who called every day. "A friend of mine's coming into town. I'd like to set up a tennis match for her. You know everybody at the Racquet Club. Can you please organize a doubles match for her, and get someone good in?"

"I'd be happy to," I told him. I asked the club tennis pro Bill Davis and another friend, Chuck Jandreau, to make up a doubles game. We three walked across the fairway at the appropriate time to find Ava's maid mixing Moscow mules at the side of the court. I think Ava was half-looped before we started. I declined a cocktail until the end of the game, and we started playing. All of a sudden Frank appeared, and I felt nervous in his company, not least because he tried to make Ava jealous by flirting with me. At one point he even cornered me up against the chain-link fence, but by then I'd figured out his game. "You know, Frank," I told him, "I've had a wonderful day and I enjoyed my drink, but I really have to go home to Zeppo now."

Chuck, who realized what was going on, said, "I must go too," and started to head back with me. Frank walked us to the gate and told us to feel free to use his court anytime. Bill, the idiot, stayed to drink with Ava—who, I'm sure, encouraged him. My parting sight of Frank that day was his watching his ex-wife openly flirting with her handsome tennis partner. Frank had the strangest expression in those eyes of his, which swirled with every emotion. I think he held a torch for Ava his whole life.

Bill was a terrible flirt too, but he had a good heart. I was at the Racquet Club dancing with him one night when, to my surprise, Joe Graydon walked in on the arm of my old girlfriend Bobby Lasley. I hadn't seen Joe since we'd split up in Vegas, but I knew his television career had gone down the tubes and his agent had ended up giving him a job. Joe sat at the bar of the Racquet Club that night and watched me dancing with Bill. I nodded a hello, and it all seemed very civil at first. But then he made some snide remark about aging, so I answered with an equally acid comment about his losing his hair. A few minutes later, he finished his drink and left. That was the last I ever saw of him, although I understand he went on to have a successful career as a big band producer. Whatever happened between us toward the end, we'd had some good years together, for which I will always be grateful.

Palm Springs was probably at its peak during the 1960s. The place was so full of movie stars that I almost began to take them for granted. People like Gregory Peck and his wife, Veronique, became firm friends, as did Kirk and Anne Douglas.

Kirk was a great orator and told the best stories in the most eloquent way, but he was an early man. Like Zeppo, he wanted to get into a party or dinner early and then get out early. If you went to his house, he'd look at his watch after dinner, go to his bedroom, put on his pajamas, then come out and sit on the floor for a while to talk. Then he'd say, "I'm off to the disco now," and vanish.

"Disco" was his euphemism for the bedroom. He didn't care how long people stayed, he just wanted to go to sleep. Anne would stay up to bid farewell to their guests. The two of them met when she was working as his PR person in Paris. They started dating, but Kirk was seeing several girls at once. No one was safe, especially when he and Burt Lancaster were together. Undaunted, Anne planned a birthday party for him and then took off to the South of France. Kirk walked into his party to come face-to-face with all the women he'd been seeing, none of whom knew about the others. At that moment he thought, I'd better marry the one who pulled this off; she's smarter than I am!

Greg Peck was another character. I just adored him. He was a really sweet, kind guy and funny too. Not the best drinker in the world, he married the best wife in Veronique, who is still one of my closest friends. They also met in Paris, when she interviewed him for her newspaper. He asked her to lunch six months later, and they were rarely apart for the next fifty years. They had two children, and Greg had three sons from his first marriage.

With people like that as friends, nothing much fazed me, or so I thought. One day I was sunbathing in a bikini when I heard a golf cart roll up and park on the other side of the hedge. Someone stood up and peered over, but the sun was behind him so I couldn't see who it was. I thought, Go away, whoever you are. Can't you see I'm sunbathing?

A voice said, "Hi, Barbara. Zeppo told me to drop by and say hello."

There stood Clark Gable, star of *Gone With the Wind*, a movie my mother had taken me to see in Wichita when I was twelve years old. "Oh—hello," I replied, feeling suddenly self-conscious. "Would you like a drink?" Clark, who was dubbed "the King of Hollywood" in his heyday, stayed on the other side of the hedge and introduced his new wife, Kay, a former model. I had someone fetch them iced tea, and we three chatted while I stood there with virtually nothing on. Poor Clark died of a heart attack the following year, aged fifty-nine. He never saw the son Kay went on to bear him.

Whenever the weather got too hot for comfort, Zeppo and I would relocate to his penthouse in Beverly Hills. In Los Angeles he was a member of Hillcrest, the country club that had made Frank Sinatra one of its first Gentile members. A lot of Zep's friends went to Hillcrest too, including Jack Benny, Danny Kaye, Milton Berle, and George Burns. They'd all sit together at what became known as the Californian Round Table, laughing and telling jokes. Other members would sit nearby, trying to listen in. Eventually, the club managers asked the Round Table gang if they'd mind spreading themselves around the club a bit so that everyone could enjoy their humor, but of course that never worked.

George Burns was adorable, so funny and sweet. He was crazy about his wife, Gracie Allen, and would sit smoking cigars and drinking martinis and talking about her all the time. Poor Gracie was dying of heart disease by then, but even after she'd gone he never stopped speaking of her. Jack Benny was one of life's nice guys and such wonderful company. I became very close with his wife, Mary, whom Zep had introduced Jack to when she was fourteen years old. Mary had been a successful radio comedienne until stage fright put an end to her career. Remembering my disastrous screen test for Fox, I could definitely relate to that. I played golf with Jack and Mary quite often. Whenever Jack hit a ball right and she heard that telltale *ping*, she'd call out, "Doll, that sounded great!" (They always called each other "doll.") Quick as a flash, Jack would quip, "Doll, this isn't a concert!"

Danny Kaye was another good friend of Zeppo's, not least because they shared the same sort of zany humor. Danny was very successful at that time, with his own TV show. He certainly made the most of his success, and every time he came to our house he had a different girl on his arm. All these comedians were at the peak of their popularity and welcome at just about every event in town.

Frank Sinatra would sometimes ask us to parties with them, but Zeppo mostly turned down invitations to Frank's Compound. Never much of a drinker and hating late nights, Zeppo didn't relish the thought of an evening with someone who liked both. Undaunted by Zep's repeated refusals, Frank would send over a case of champagne or some fine wine every now and again. *"Because it's a new moon,"* his note might say, or *"As it's Tuesday."* He was known for being generous, and I liked that about him; his spontaneity and sense of fun weren't what I'd expected from him after all I'd heard and read. I guess even back then there was a part of me that was curious about what really made Francis Albert tick.

Restless again after two years in Palm Springs, I began asking myself how much tennis, golf, or gin I could play. Figuring it was time I paid my dues, I decided to get involved with at least one charity a year and help it organize a fund-raising event, so I volunteered my services to the City of Hope cancer hospital for children near L.A. I knew enough people in Palm Springs who would attend a fund-raising event and give generously if asked; all I needed was an attraction—perhaps a fashion show or a dinner dance maybe; a movie screening or a golf tournament.

Kirk Douglas had recently had phenomenal success in a gladiator movie called *Spartacus* with Tony Curtis, so I asked him if we could possibly show his movie in the desert. To my delight, he agreed, so I set about selling tickets and organizing a post-screening ball. Two weeks before the event, his wife, Anne, called me up. "I'm sorry to tell you this, Barbara, but you can't have *Spartacus.* Kirk didn't realize that we'd already agreed to show it in L.A. at a benefit in aid of Cedars-Sinai hospital."

I almost passed out. "But, Anne, this is so last-minute!" I told her. "We've sold tickets. I have the theater booked and everything!"

"I'm sorry, honey. This breaks my heart, but we can't do anything about it."

I had no idea how I was going to find an alternative movie or event as big as *Spartacus* on such short notice. Zeppo fled to the golf course rather than watch me fret, and I called everyone I knew. On the fairway, Zeppo ran into Frank Sinatra and told him what had happened. With hardly a moment's hesitation Frank said, "Tell Barbara not to worry, I'm just finishing up a movie with Jill St. John. She can have an early cut of that instead." When Zeppo came home and told me, I could hardly believe my ears. Not only did Frank keep his word but he flew everybody involved to Palm Springs, and we premiered the movie version of the Broadway hit musical *Come Blow Your Horn* at the theater I'd booked. It was a much lighter picture anyway, far less harrowing than *Spartacus* with all its blood and gore. There was a big party afterward, and we raised a huge amount of money. The event was more of a success than I could ever have hoped for. I was so grateful and wrote Frank a personal note of thanks.

The following day, Zeppo and I went to the Tamarisk Country Club for lunch. I spotted Frank sitting at a table and said, "I'd like to go over to thank him personally."

"Stay there!" Zeppo barked. "*I'll* go over and thank him."

I stared at my husband for a moment. I remembered when Zeppo and I had watched Andy Williams perform in Vegas; it had somehow gotten into his head that Andy was singing directly to me. "Stop flirting with him!" Zeppo had snapped as I sat innocently in my seat. I was coming to realize that my relationships with men all revolved around possession and control, which was strange because my father had been the exact opposite.

At Tamarisk, I told Zeppo, "Then please thank Frank from me," and watched as he went over to the Sinatra table. I saw Frank look up and nod politely in my direction. I smiled, and he smiled back at me. Ridiculously, I felt myself blushing. Zeppo returned to our table with an invitation for dinner that night, which he couldn't possibly refuse after the favor Frank had done for me. When we arrived at the Compound, with its guesthouses set in several acres, we found a big crowd. There was the golf pro Kenny Venturi, an assortment of comedians, and the songwriter Jimmy Van Heusen, who wasn't wearing any socks, I noticed. Other guests included the actors Robert "R. J." Wagner and his wife, Natalie Wood, as well as the rising star Warren Beatty, who was making a picture with Natalie at the time entitled *Splendor in the Grass*.

I was fascinated to see inside Frank's house for the first time. The walls of every room were covered in paintings, bold abstracts cleverly placed between softer pastels and American and old European masters, many of whose signatures I recognized. I was surprised to learn from Zeppo that Frank was a great admirer of art and that he even dabbled himself.

"He paints?" I asked.

"Apparently," Zeppo replied.

After a noisy dinner of meatballs and spaghetti (which reminded me of suppers with Bob Oliver's family), Frank, Zeppo, R. J., and I played gin rummy with a couple of people I didn't know. I had a good hand, and just as I cried, "Gin!" R. J. jumped up, threw down his cards, and stormed out. At first I thought I must have upset him, but instead he grabbed his wife, Natalie, from where she was sitting outside by the pool, pulled a chair up to our table, and made her sit with us. Everyone was stunned into silence. She stayed for a while, played a few hands, but then she was up and out again. It didn't take long to put two and two together. The handsome Mr. Beatty was waiting by the pool.

Frank was witty and charming—the perfect host, especially when he insisted that nobody was allowed to leave early, which secretly delighted me. As I was soon to discover, he liked to drink long hours and never wanted people to go because he needed company. If they drank too, they were in. Friends like Bill Holden, Robert "Mother" Mitchum, John Wayne, Glenn Ford, and Orson Welles (whom Frank called "the Big Man") were most definitely in.

People like Tony Bennett, Fred Astaire, Bing Crosby, and Henry Fonda, who didn't drink much and liked to turn in early, weren't often included. Frank still adored them though and sometimes went over to their houses for breakfast as the sun was coming up and his drinking buddies finally abandoned him.

What I found interesting about Frank in those early days was that he was rarely drunk and never suffered from a hangover. I'd watch him order a Jack Daniel's on the rocks, take a sip or two, put it down, then call the waiter to "bring another round." Each time he did, his glass went back on the tray almost full. He carried on like that all evening, staying completely in charge of his faculties while everyone around him got smashed. Meantime, he was flirting with every female at the party but always so discreetly that few but the women noticed. I watched how he worked the room and prayed it would never be my turn.

It wasn't that I couldn't handle Frank—I'd been a showgirl, after all—but I was worried about Zeppo's increasing jealousy. The previous New Year's Eve at the Racquet Club we were just leaving when I spotted some friends I wanted to say good night to. Zeppo hated that and stood by the door impatiently. As I turned to go, I was goosed from behind by Victor Rothschild, playboy and baron. Before I could say anything, Zeppo ran at Victor like a bull. He knocked two couples down before he grabbed Victor by the throat. One thing's for certain—my relationships were never dull.

I knew that Frank's reputation as a hothead superseded Zeppo's, so I didn't relish the idea of a public showdown. Both had been raised by strong mothers, so they weren't the types to compromise. In any event, I hadn't been married that long and was determined my marriage to Zeppo would work. Bobby's future was at stake as much as mine. Zeppo had even offered to adopt him so that he'd have the same surname as me—something Bobby also wanted. In the end Bob Oliver wouldn't allow it, so later Bobby simply changed his name to Marx instead.

Flirting with The Voice was the last thing on my mind that night, even though there was definitely a frisson between us. I sensed there could be more if I ever wanted it. Fortunately, though, Frank's attention was diverted elsewhere, and the full-on flirtation I feared from him didn't come my way—at least not then.

FIVE

*Danny Schwartz, Zeppo Marx, Marion Wagner, Truman Capote,
and me at the Racquet Club in Palm Springs (left to right).*
COURTESY OF THE AUTHOR

Fly Me to the Moon

In the summer of 1961, Frank invited us to the grand reopening of the Cal Neva Lodge and casino in Lake Tahoe on the California-Nevada border. Having shared in the success of Vegas, he'd applied for a gambling license of his own, bought the lodge with a group of investors, and had it completely refurbished. As almost everyone we knew was going, I persuaded Zeppo that we should too.

A gang of us flew up from Palm Springs, and when we arrived, Frank explained the routine. Cocktails (or "tini-time," as he called it) were at five o'clock, and then all the ladies would be handed three hundred dollars' worth of chips to ensure we had a good time. Boy, did we have fun in the place billed as "Heaven in the High Sierra." Even if people lost, they knew Frank would pick up their markers, just like he always did. Quite apart from the attraction of gambling, which was outlawed in California, the lodge was an elegant place to stay, with the nicest rooms in that beautiful lakeside setting. And, best of all, Frank donned his tux and stepped onto the stage later that night, giving us the kind of first-class performance only he could deliver time and again.

The Cal Neva became controversial in Frank's life later when some claimed he was too closely involved with the Mob there, but most of his show business friends knew more gangsters than he ever did. Even Zeppo consorted occasionally with those he called "the boys" when he co-owned the El Rancho casino. As Jack Benny once told me, "You have to socialize with those guys to a certain extent when they're not only your employers but your greatest fans." Frank Sinatra was the Italian idol—a Sicilian who'd made it to the top—so the wise guys treated him as their own. More important, the bosses owned the clubs where he and everyone else worked. He couldn't just ignore those he referred to jokingly as "the Harvard Boys," and with loyalty and friendship so important to Frank, he wasn't prepared to.

One of the people who'd been unable to come with us to the Cal Neva Lodge that opening weekend was Chico Marx, a fact that upset Zeppo greatly. Chico had been sick with heart problems for a while and knew his time was running out. He used to say to me, "Every morning I wake up, Barbara, I feel like I'm on velvet because I'm still alive." In October of that year, though, Chico sadly lost his fight. Zeppo was grief-stricken. Chico was his big brother, the eldest of them all, and Zeppo had worshipped him. After the funeral, we went back to Groucho's house for a wake. Crammed into the living room with scores of mourners, I noticed a strange woman staring at me. Zeppo noticed too and asked someone who she was. It was his first wife, Marion, a former Ziegfield girl he'd divorced seven years earlier, five years before he'd married me. A week later, I was playing tennis with Dinah Shore at the Racquet Club when I spotted Marion watching me in the same eerie way. I asked Dinah to introduce us. Marion was a little strange, but I think she just wanted to check me out. I felt sorry for her. She'd raised their adopted sons alone, and

Zeppo showed little or no interest in them or her, it seemed. What really bothered me though was that he hadn't even recognized the woman he'd been married to for twenty-seven years.

Life and our routines went on, with the usual rounds of games and drinks, charity events, cocktails, parties, and dinners. We might have been in a rut, but boy, what a rut. I wasn't complaining, and in those early years I was truly happy with Zeppo.

I was certainly grateful for what he did for me and for Bobby; we had a beautiful home and everything we needed for a comfortable life. I never even had to cook, which is just as well because I might have killed somebody with my food. Zeppo seemed happy enough too, and I considered our marriage a success. In many ways, we were a typical couple, each with our own interests and hobbies. One day Zeppo decided he wanted to learn how to play the electric organ so that he could serenade me. (I guess he knew I had a thing for singers.) He ordered an organ from a shop in Long Beach, but being impatient, he wanted it delivered immediately. "But it's the Easter holiday!" complained the shop owner, a man named Mr. Tonini. "I'm spending it with my family."

"Well, bring them along!" Zeppo suggested brightly. "Palm Springs is a beautiful place, and I'll buy everybody lunch." Sure enough, Mr. Tonini put the organ, his wife, and his five children in his station wagon and drove to the desert. When Zep saw all those kids, he made me take them straight to a table at Tamarisk while he went to the bar and stayed there. I sat with them, longing for some other company. Then I spotted Groucho. "Oh, look!" I cried. "There's Groucho Marx. Wouldn't you like to meet him?" The couple were big Marx Brothers fans, so I motioned over a reluctant Groucho. "This is Mr. and Mrs. Tonini," I announced happily, "and these are all the little Toninis."

Groucho scowled and asked, "Are these all yours?"

"Yes," the shop owner replied proudly.

"Been doing a lot of fucking, haven't you?" Groucho commented before walking away.

The indignant couple jumped up, grabbed their kids, and made for the door without finishing their lunch. Following them out apologetically, I spotted Harpo walking into the club. "Oh, there's Harpo!" I cried with relief. "He *adores* children. Surely you'd like to meet him?" The Tonini family fled from me as if I had an infectious disease.

O ne event in March 1962 that sent ripples around Palm Springs was the news that John F. Kennedy, the good-looking young politician who'd flirted with me on an ocean liner many years before, was coming to town.

"JFK," as he was now known, had been in Palm Springs two years earlier, immediately before his election as the thirty-fifth president of the United States. As Frank Sinatra had rallied his showbiz friends to support "the Jack Pack," the president naturally stayed at the home of his staunchest supporter. Frank had a bronze plaque screwed to his guest room door that proudly read: JOHN F. KENNEDY SLEPT HERE, NOVEMBER 6 AND 7, 1960. Everyone, especially Frank, assumed Jack would stay with him again.

Eager to make his guests feel welcome, Frank spent thousands of dollars renovating his home. Even though he'd only just finished filming *The Manchurian Candidate* with Janet Leigh and was briefly engaged to the actress Juliet Prowse (about when some comedian claimed Frank had "longer engagements in Vegas"), he somehow found the time to arrange the building of a new guesthouse, a helicopter pad, and separate accommodations for the Secret Service. He even had a red telephone installed as a direct hotline to the White House. Frank's builders were instructed to work around the clock, seven days a week, to finish in time for the presidential visit.

Jack Kennedy had become like a modern-day pop star, and everyone, especially my Palm Springs girlfriends, wanted to catch a glimpse of him. "I'm going to plaster myself into the walls of the new Sinatra guesthouse and come bursting out when JFK's in there alone!" declared one of our friends over a tennis lunch at the Racquet Club. Another proclaimed she was going to tunnel under the fairway to the Compound, while a third was going to set up a stall on the farthest green, convinced that Jack would need to buy lemonade from her in the unaccustomed heat. Never once hinting at my previous encounter with Jack in the Bahamas, I remained quietly bemused by all the fuss.

As we sat around joking about the increasingly desperate plans to get to the president, two men in dark suits suddenly marched up and flashed us their Secret Service badges. The tallest of them asked, "Which one is Mrs. Marx?" Gulping down a mouthful of my Bloody Mary, I raised my hand sheepishly. "Right," he announced, "come with us!"

"Why? Where are you taking me?" I asked, sounding braver than I felt.

"We've heard about your tunnel plan and the plastering job," one of the agents replied. "We need to interview you about the president's security."

I almost choked. Looking around at my companions, I couldn't figure out why I, of all people, had been singled out. I rose from the table with as much dignity as I could muster as everyone watched in silence. I walked out of the restaurant flanked by these gorillas as my fellow club members looked on agog. It was only when I got outside that I spotted "the Singing Cop" Phil Regan laughing at me from a bush. The whole episode was a huge gag he'd set up. I could have killed that jokester.

When Jack Kennedy eventually arrived in town, his presidential motorcade swept him straight past the Compound and on to Bing Crosby's house in Thunderbird Heights. That was a terrible loss of face for Frank. The official reason given was security—Bing's house was said to be safer because it backed onto a mountain, whereas Frank's house was open on four sides. (It had nothing to do with the Tamarisk ladies' fantasies, I promise.) Frank saw Jack's decision to stay with Republican Bing as a direct snub. He was so hurt, especially after all the trouble he'd gone to, that when his friend and JFK's brother-in-law Peter Lawford told him the news, he cut Peter off there and then and never spoke to him again. Holding a grudge, Italian-style, was yet another side of the elusive, enigmatic Mr. Sinatra.

I met up with Jack Kennedy again a couple of times during his visit. Even though he was married to Jacqueline by then with two small children, his friend Phil Regan, a kingpin in the Palm Springs social scene, was always trying to fix him up with someone. The two men came to the Racquet Club when I was playing tennis one day, and Phil formally introduced me. I acted like we'd never met before, and so did Jack. We saw each other every now and again after that and were perfectly civil. Jack was a devout Catholic and went to church to pray for his family almost every day in between hitting on all the girls, which I thought strange. He even started flirting with me all over again. Eventually I asked him if he remembered our days on the *Queen of Bermuda*. He recalled the journey to New York but apologized that he had no memory of me. I guess I was just one face among many for JFK.

It was eighteen months later, on a warm afternoon in November, when a news flash came on the car radio. "We interrupt this program to bring you a special bulletin from Dallas, Texas. Three shots were fired at President Kennedy's motorcade today," it began. "First reports say that the president has been seriously wounded..." I had to pull the car over to the side of the road to compose myself and listen to the unfolding news. The next bulletin confirmed further reports that the president had been shot as he sat next to his wife, who'd then cradled him in her lap. Then came the dreadful news: "The president, ladies and gentlemen, is dead." There was a long pause as the announcer fought to control his emotions. "This is the official word," he said finally. "The president of the United States is dead."

When I eventually reached the Racquet Club and wandered, dazed, into the lounge, the atmosphere was like a morgue. Nobody knew what to say or do. People wept openly. Many were gathered around radios and a television set, which was flashing images of the scene in downtown Dallas. I couldn't bear to look. Slumping into a chair, I could hardly believe that we'd lost the man so many saw as America's knight in shining armor. All normal life seemed to stop as the realization sank in that the Kennedy dream and its promise of a better future were over.

Frank Sinatra was devastated by the assassination of JFK, whom he described as "the brightest star in our lives." As he had when Marilyn Monroe died the previous year, he mourned by locking himself alone in a room for days at a time. He was quoted around that time as saying, "I'm for whatever gets you through the night—be it prayer, tranquilizers, or a bottle of Jack Daniel's." I'm sure he needed all three when his nineteen-year-old son Frankie, also a singer, was kidnapped in Lake Tahoe the following month. When I heard the news, I sent Frank a note of support because I couldn't imagine anything worse than my son being taken like that. Fortunately, the boy was safely returned five days later, after his father paid a ransom.

Over the next few years, Zeppo and I began to see more of Frank, especially when he was in Palm Springs. He was at the peak of his success—touring, making movies, performing in Vegas, and producing one hit record after another. After announcing, "As an overprivileged adult, I'd like to help underprivileged children," he took off on a seven-nation World Tour for Children in aid of charity. He always did at least a dozen benefits for various charities every year, for which he was never paid a penny. Extraordinarily, he'd even pay the orchestra himself. A charity that might hope for a hundred thousand dollars from an event would usually net around a million for a benefit Frank gave.

When his World Tour for Children was finally over, Frank returned to the desert for the privacy and the climate he'd fallen in love with. Having broken up with the dancer Juliet Prowse, he married the twenty-one-year-old actress Mia Farrow, announcing, "Let's say I've got a good five years left—why not enjoy them?" He divorced her almost as quickly. I read a rather sad quote from him after that in *Life* magazine that said, "If I did marry [again] it would have to be somebody out of show business, or someone who will get out of the business… All I ask is that my wife looks after me and I will see that she's looked after." There was such poignancy to that, I thought. Frank was still looking for love.

Then to add to his woes, his father, Marty, died. I met Marty once, at a party Frank threw at the Compound. It was a big event attended by stars like Angie Dickinson, Dean Martin, and Sammy Davis, Jr. Yul Brynner (whom Frank called "the Chinaman") was there too, along with the usual suspects I was coming to know, such as Frank's best friend and bodyguard, Jilly Rizzo. Marty was a great cook, as was Frank's mother, Dolly, who'd stay up all night making what she called the "gravy" for the pasta while Jilly (whom she referred to as Fuck Face) dipped bread into it. Marty made the best gnocchi I ever tasted. He'd cook at some of his son's parties when he was visiting from New Jersey and then he'd sit on his own in a corner. An illiterate boilermaker and fireman from a village near Palermo, Sicily, Marty could barely write his name and hardly spoke any English, so I sat with him and asked someone who spoke Italian to interpret for me.

We got along famously as he told me about his life. Although he'd been a boxer in New Jersey under the pseudonym of Marty O'Brien, he insisted it was Dolly who was the real fighter, a woman who'd thump anyone who made a derogatory remark about Frank. He told me of the time she hit a would-be robber over the head with a blackjack and then sat on him screaming until the police arrived. As Marty spoke of the woman he'd eloped with on St. Valentine's Day, he reminded me of my long-suffering father dealing with my willful mother. I only wished I'd picked up more Italian with Bob Oliver's family, because I could have talked to Marty all night. Frank joined us for a while and took over the translating, and it was clear the two men adored each other. They also had a similar sense of humor. Frank told me that one of the few times his father ever saw him perform—in New York about when I was sighing over his songs back in Wichita—the screams of his fans were so loud that when Frank asked Marty what he thought of the concert, his father told him, "I couldn't hear a fucking thing!"

Sadly, with heart problems and emphysema, Antonino Martino Sinatra went into a terminal decline at age seventy-four. Frank, who'd slept in his father's hospital room at the end and said Marty was one of the greatest men he ever knew, was shattered by his passing. Dolly was equally devastated, and at Marty's funeral in New Jersey, attended by thousands of Frank's fans, she tried to throw herself into the grave.

Dolly was one tough dame. She was only a little woman with deep blue eyes and a cherubic face, but her looks were deceiving. She'd been the head of a union, a midwife, and a bartender—among other things—and had a mouth on her like you wouldn't believe. She was physically abusive to Frank when he was a kid and knocked him around a lot. She even threw him down the stairs once, but she always claimed she was only toughening him up for the neighborhood. "I put the condition on him," she used to say. She also taught him how to cook, and boy, could Frank cook.

Although he had help in the kitchen, he cooked Italian food almost every day because that was all he really liked to eat. Lord help anyone who overcooked the pasta or tried to serve him ketchup. He loved good peasant fare, although strangely for an Italian, he didn't like garlic—an aversion he claimed came from when Dolly would tie an entire bulb around his neck if ever he had a chill as a child. He might sauté a little garlic for a sauce, but then he'd throw it away. During a film he made with Gina Lollobrigida in 1959 called *Never So Few*, she allegedly ate an entire bulb of raw garlic just before a kissing scene to spite him.

The dish Frank's friends enjoyed the most was one he'd get up and make for us in the early hours, when everyone was loaded. He'd place a pot of salt water on the stove, cook the pasta until it was al dente, drain it, then crack two eggs into it and grate plenty of Parmesan cheese over it before adding lots of olive oil, salt, and pepper. The hot pasta would cook the eggs. It was wonderful and the best thing to eat at three or four in the morning.

Another specialty of Frank's was pasta fagioli, which he and Dean Martin pronounced "fajool." It was Dean's favorite, and the two of them would happily finish off a whole pot together. Frank worshipped Dean, not just for his love of all things Italian but for his ability to make Frank laugh. As he always said, "Dean isn't just funny, he thinks funny."

Generally speaking, Frank was very good with the staff and never lost his temper with them, but one night when we had a full house and everyone was seated for dinner, the veal dish I'd asked for came out undercooked. I took one bite and had it sent back. Our chef sadly took offense and began throwing things around the kitchen, rattling pans and breaking dishes. Everybody heard, but nobody knew what to say. Frank smiled, asked to be excused, and got up from the table. Beyond the kitchen door, he told the chef, "I'm going to count to three, and you'd better get your fat ass out of here or else!" Even though that chef was a big guy, he couldn't run out of there fast enough.

Another night, we were in Matteo's, an Italian restaurant in Los Angeles, when the pasta was served soggy. Frank hated that more than anything else and stormed into the kitchen. Looking around, he held up his hands and cried, "Where are all the Italians?" The staff was Filipino. He came back into the dining room and, furious, picked up his plate of pasta and threw it against the wall, splattering tomato sauce all down it. Before walking out, he examined the mess he'd made and, using his finger, wrote: "Picasso." Later, the owner—his childhood friend Matty Jordan—put a frame around Frank's unorthodox work of art.

When we weren't seeing Frank socially, Zeppo and I muddled along with dinners and parties as well as keeping up with the constant rounds of gin, golf, and tennis—the last often played on Frank's court, which was the closest.

I played with the future vice president Spiro Agnew there and other guests of Frank's, but one of my most memorable doubles matches was with Bobby Kennedy, the former U.S. attorney general, who came to town not long after his brother had been assassinated. Dear Harpo had died by then, and Bobby and Ethel were staying at El Rancho Harpo, owned by mutual friends. It was they who asked me to make up a foursome, and as I recall, Bobby and I whipped them. He was a good player and nice enough, but he never had the charisma of his older brother and always lived in his shadow. Frank certainly didn't like him much and felt that Bobby had turned against him despite all he'd done to help get Jack elected. A few years later Bobby too was shot dead, at a hotel in Los Angeles. The glory days were over for the Kennedys, it seemed.

I carried on with my charity work and became head of entertainment for an organization that helped war orphans. The first year I was involved, I asked Dinah Shore to perform at the gala, and the next year I invited Lena Horne. Soon after I announced her name, a woman on the executive committee of the charity came to see me. Without flinching, she told me, "Barbara, I'm sorry, but we can't have blacks. If we have them perform for us, then they have to sit down and eat with us!" As I stared at her openmouthed, my mind flashed back to the black boy at school in Wichita and the prejudice of my youth. Had nothing changed? That's when I knew that her organization was not the one for me. I resigned immediately, telling her that bigotry and charity did not belong together. I decided to find another organization to devote my energies to; it took a while before I found the right one.

Zeppo's next-door neighbor on the other side was Hal Wallis, the producer of movies like *Casablanca*. His sister Mina, who was possibly the most unattractive woman I'd ever seen, was his head of casting and a major player. Mina had a casting couch on which she was supposed to have bedded all the greats, including Clark Gable. When she moved to Palm Springs, she called me up. "Hello, Barbara," she said, without introducing herself. "We have to know each other. I've just moved here, and you and I have a lot of the same friends."

"Well, who are you?" I asked.

"I'm Mina Wallis and I'm very important and I understand that you have a lifestyle that I like," she continued. "You go to the Racquet Club to play tennis and then you like to have lunch and then you like to play gin."

"That pretty much describes it," I replied.

"Well, could you pick me up tomorrow morning? I'd like to go with you."

I had to laugh. "Oh, is that what you'd like to do?"

"Yes," she replied. "See you at eleven." Then she hung up.

From that day on, she attached herself to me and wanted to do everything I did. It reminded me of my kid sister when we were small. Worst of all, she cheated at gin, and that's when I really lost it with her. Eventually, I had to say, "Don't call me and don't come around anymore."

A few days later she invited me to lunch, but I was on my way out. "Please drop by," she pleaded. "There's someone I'd like you to meet." So I stopped in and found a stranger standing in her living room. "Meet GG," Mina said. I recognized the profile immediately. It was Greta Garbo in slacks and a blouse, and she held out her hand and said, "*Vunderful* to meet you, Barbara," then offered nothing more. Sadly, I had to run, so I missed my chance to get to know the screen legend and find out if she truly was as aloof as she seemed.

Mina and I eventually patched things up, and I have to admit that she was an amazing powerhouse of a woman; she knew everyone, and if you asked her to do something, she would get it accomplished. When she eventually got sick and was dying, all the great stars went to see her, so maybe all her casting-couch stories were true. I guess we'll never know.

Wanting my parents near me, I made the down payment on a house for them in Palm Springs and they moved there from Long Beach. My father worked as a butcher to pay the mortgage, and my mother did whatever she could. Zeppo could have helped them out much more than he did, but he really didn't want anyone else around us—least of all my family. Although he'd been generous when we first met (and my parents adored him to the day he died), his tightness began to get to me.

Bobby didn't always get along with him either, and I think Zeppo tolerated him only because he knew my son and I were joined at the hip. One day, though, Zep flipped about something Bobby had done, and I came home to find his hands around my teenage son's throat. He looked as if he could kill him. After pulling the two of them apart, I told Bobby, "Go pack your things. We're leaving." As I threw my clothes into a suitcase, Zeppo began crying and pleading, "Please, Barbara, don't leave me," until I eventually agreed to stay. Apart from anything else, I had no place to go.

Not long after that, Bobby, who'd always been a straight-A student, lost interest in his studies and his grades started to drop. When he announced that he wanted to move to Haight-Ashbury in San Francisco, famous for the birth of psychedelic rock, I was horrified. "But, Bobby, this is your home!" I said.

Defiantly he said, "I'm going to move there and you can't stop me."

"But where would you live?"

"I'll find someplace," he declared.

This went on for days; then one morning I told him, "All right, then. I'll take you to the bus station, give you a hundred dollars, and you can buy a ticket to San Francisco." He hesitated briefly before packing a bag and getting into the car. We were three-quarters of the way to the bus station when he turned to me and said, "Mother, I don't think I want to go to Haight-Ashbury after all."

I pulled over, switched off the engine, and said, "I'm so happy you said that, Bobby, because I really want you to stay." It was the only time I ever used tough love on him. I don't know what I'd have done if he'd gone through with it. Once we returned home, things were a lot better. We found him a great new high school called Cate in Carpinteria, where he made some lifelong friends. That place really saved his life.

Bobby had gone through so much by the time he was a teenager, but he never threw it back at me, never. His real father was bumming around Europe trying to make movies, Joe Graydon was a distant memory, and Zeppo didn't much care. It's so hard to keep children grounded, but it's amazing to me how grounded Bobby still is. Open and honest, he is a very special guy. Even now, every time I look at him I know that I did something right.

Zeppo and Bobby made up their differences in later life and became friends, for which I am truly grateful. But at that point our marriage was strained, even more so after I caught Zep red-handed with some other women. It happened when I decided to make a surprise visit to the *Barbara Ann*, moored at Newport Beach. As I arrived, there was a party in full swing. The boat was full of girls drinking and having a good time. Zeppo was nowhere to be seen, but I suspected he was belowdecks. A woman in a skimpy bikini came up to me and asked, "Who are you?"

I gave her a steely stare. "Well, who are you?"

"I'm the hostess of this party!" she declared triumphantly.

"I'm Mrs. Marx," I replied. *"Barbara Ann* Marx?"

I watched as she shrank away to find Zeppo, but before she could, I left. Tellingly, his infidelity didn't hurt anything other than my pride. I guess it only confirmed what I'd suspected for some time—that Zeppo was the third man in succession to let me down. I reasoned that, although our marriage was a sham, at least now we could both be honest about it. To keep me sweet, Zeppo finally took me on a promised trip to Europe with his friend the producer Harold Mirisch, who was making a movie in France. From the minute our plane landed, though, Zeppo wanted to go home. He missed playing golf, the desert climate, and his friends; he was utterly miserable. When we bumped into the Hollywood agent and his friend Swifty Lazar in a nightclub in Paris, I wanted to dance that night but Zeppo didn't want to, nor did he want me to. The only person who had the nerve to ask me onto the dance floor was Swifty, who was so short that his famously oversize spectacles remained level with my cleavage the entire time.

We eventually cut short our grand European tour and returned home, where Zeppo reluctantly agreed to accept more invitations to events he knew I'd enjoy. Among those were the repeated requests for our company from Frank. From the late sixties, we were probably invited to the Compound or to eat out with Frank once or twice a week. We'd go to restaurants or to parties at the homes of mutual friends. We'd have them all back occasionally, but not often because Zeppo was never very agreeable to that and Frank always liked a lot of people around him so it would have to be a big production.

There were plenty of others who were happy to throw parties for him anyway, so we were usually invited along to those. At one, I was introduced to the singer Judy Garland, an old friend of Frank's and the woman who gave "the Holmby Hills Rat Pack" (as Frank and his pals were known) little rat stick pins. Frank hated the Rat Pack moniker almost as much as he ended up disliking being called "the Chairman of the Board"—a name his friend the New York radio presenter William B. Williams coined for him. "What does that mean anyway?" he'd ask, frowning. "Chairman? There's nowhere to go after that." I almost didn't recognize Judy Garland; she was so enormous and puffy-faced. It was sad to see her like that. Frank didn't seem to notice and was as protective of Judy as he had always been of Marilyn. He'd been with Judy the night her daughter Liza was born and ordered everybody pizzas during the labor. He claimed that Liza's first cries sounded to him like music from an Italian opera—"a star had been born."

The more I came to know Frank, the more I liked him. I was especially impressed by the way he treated others. Whenever we went out to a restaurant or club, I couldn't help but notice how differently people behaved around him. The excitement was tangible; from the moment Frank walked into a room in that slow, easy way of his, there'd be a buzz. Everyone from the staff to the customers would stare, and they'd never stop. Sooner or later the paparazzi would arrive, peering through the windows with their lenses. Frank disliked most of the press, but he'd happily sign autographs for fellow diners or waiting staff and pose for photographs until everyone was happy.

When we went out to eat, Frank almost always picked up the tab. He couldn't have cared less about money, and I honestly think he planned on spending every dime he ever made; he certainly spent cash like a drunken sailor. As Don Rickles once said, "Frank gets up in the morning and God throws money on him." When we arrived anywhere, Frank would hand Jilly a stack of hundred-dollar bills (which he called "C-notes") and say, "Take care of all the busboys and waitresses." His tipping was legendary, especially to the little guys. At one restaurant we went to, we were waiting for our car afterward and Frank handed the valet parker two hundred-dollar bills.

"Thank you, Mr. Sinatra!" the kid cried delightedly.

"Is that the biggest tip you ever had?" Frank asked with a smile.

The young man looked coy. "Well, no, sir."

Frank frowned. "What the? Who the hell gave you more than that?"

"Why you did, Mr. Sinatra. Last week!"

Perhaps not surprisingly because of the attention he attracted, Frank often preferred to stay home, but his dinners at the Compound were always fun affairs peppered with the most interesting guests. All the big names would be there, of course, the major stars and Hollywood producers plus numerous wives, girlfriends, and starlets. But then he'd throw industrialists like John Kluge, Laurance Rockefeller, or Kirk Kerkorian into the mix as well as Italian American friends of his and Jilly's from the early days, men who stood or sat on the periphery, eating pasta and saying little.

I soon came to appreciate that Ermenigildo "Jilly" Rizzo was the brother Frank never had. They'd first met in Miami Beach in the fifties, and Jilly soon became one of the most important people in Frank's life. Although Jilly had his own nightclub, called Jilly's Saloon, on West Fifty-second Street and Seventh Avenue in Manhattan (*the* place for Chinese food), he gave it to his brother to run so that he could move with Frank to California. They both knew it was important that Frank have someone he knew and trusted watching his back as part of what he called his "Dago Secret Service." Jilly was blind in one eye but could look at a stadium of twenty thousand people and pick out the sole troublemaker. He was a "deez, demz, and doze" guy who spoke with a monotone New York accent and said things like "Ax me anything," "When the phone don't ring, you'll know it's me," or once, when a friend died in his sleep, "He woke up dead."

The famed TV producer George Schlatter once wrote a speech for Jilly at a birthday celebration for Frank. George introduced Jilly as "the Harvard professor of elocution," and then Jilly stood up and recited a poem by someone he called "Rudolf Kipling" before ending with "... by the living God that made yous, you're a better man than I, Gunga Din," adding, "Whoever the fuck that was!" Frank collapsed laughing.

Jilly was married to Honey, a woman Frank called "the Blue Jew" because she dyed *all* her hair blue (and I mean all). The relationship didn't last, not least because she and Jilly used to have some knock-down, drag-out fights. Even after my early experience with Bob Oliver's family, it took me a long time to realize that Italians like to fight and it doesn't mean anything. At Jilly's Saloon, he employed an irreverent Chinese cook named Howie. Late at night after a show, Frank would get on the funnel down to the basement kitchen and yell, "Howie! Send up some food."

Howie would reply, "Fut you, Mr. Sinatra!" and Frank would shout back, "Fut you too, Howie!" Years later, Frank bought him a watch and sent it to be engraved. He told the jewelers that he wanted "Fut you, Howie!" written on the back, but they said they couldn't possibly. "Why ever not?" Frank countered innocently. "FUT U is the name of a university." They bought it.

Jilly would help Frank decide what food should be served at his parties and which music should be played because Jilly had a great ear. He and Frank loved all the greats, especially the old standards, but they liked a lot of modern music too. What Frank couldn't stand was to hear himself sing because he'd always find a flaw. His attitude in the studio was record it, press it, and print it, and then he never wanted to hear it again. If anyone ever played any of his songs at a party, he'd threaten to walk out. The guests he and Jilly picked would almost always include a few comedians who opened for him at his shows, such as Tom Dreesen, who cracked me up, and Don "Bullethead" Rickles, whom Frank first met when Don's mother, Etta, persuaded Frank's mother, Dolly, to give her son a break. Frank went along to see Rickles perform as Dolly and Etta had asked, but he sat hidden behind a newspaper for the entire show. He and Rickles got along famously after that. Then there were the natural comics like Dean Martin and Jimmy Van Heusen, both of whom Frank had a great bond with chiefly through their shared love of humor. Dean, the man Frank called "Drunkie," was hysterical; they were like a double act bouncing off each other. They'd find someone to pick on like Sammy Davis or James Stewart and go to work. Jimmy Stewart was adorable and would take it all in good sport as the two of them mimicked how he stammered—"Er, er, er, w-e-ell, Frank."

He'd come right back at them with "Er, er, er, w-e-ell what do you mean? Do you think I t-t-talk like that?"

Jimmy Van Heusen knew Frank from when they'd both worked with the Tommy Dorsey band in the 1930s and used to hang out at a bar in New York called Toots Shor's. Jimmy was christened Edward Chester Babcock, a name he knew he'd have to change if he wanted to be successful. Jimmy Stewart was his all-time hero, and he thought the billboard advertisement for Van Heusen shirts was elegant, so he made up his name using something from each. People were always after Frank to change his name in the early days because no one had ever heard of the Sicilian name Sinatra, but after experimenting with a couple of surnames, he rejected them. "My name is Frank Sinatra," he told them, "and it's going to stay Frank Sinatra."

Jimmy was a sweet, sweet guy. As Chester Babcock, he used to flick through the phone book and call up complete strangers.

"Hello, are you a Cock?" he'd ask. "I'm a Cock too." He stayed in touch with one woman named Elsa Cock for years. He first found her name in a phone book somewhere in Europe when he was on the road with Frank. Never bothering about international time zones, he'd call Elsa at all hours of the day and night just to say hello, often putting "my friend Frank" on the line for fun. I don't think she ever really knew who those two idiots were.

Frank and Jimmy were crazy enough individually, but together they were impossible. Loaded, they'd fly to Vegas late at night in Jimmy's single-engine plane with only a hot water bottle to pee into. Or they'd swoop low over the Salton Sea Club with Jimmy hanging on to Frank's belt as he leaned out of the plane to take photographs of a race. They didn't have lights at the Palm Springs airport in the early days, so if Frank and Jimmy came in at night, they'd have Jilly waiting on the runway flashing his car headlights on and off so they could see. I don't know how they survived.

One day, Frank and Jimmy were sitting by the pool at the Compound when they heard footsteps padding across the roof of the pool house. Frank had round-the-clock security because of all the fans who would climb fences to try to get in to see him. Vine Joubert, Frank's inimitable housekeeper (who was like a mother to him and loved him just as fiercely), would sometimes have to shoo complete strangers out of the house after they'd scaled the perimeter fence. So Frank wasn't altogether surprised to see someone he didn't know peering down at him from above. Jimmy and he took one look at each other, pulled the guy off the roof, dragged him to the swimming pool, and threw him in. Jimmy cried, "I'll drown the son of a bitch!" Every time the poor man came up for air, they'd push him down again.

Eventually, their victim pulled out a soggy sheet of paper and spluttered, "Hey, wait! I wrote a song...I have a song here...All I want is to play it for you!" Dripping wet, he pleaded, "Won't you just listen to it, Mr. Sinatra?" Frank was constantly inundated with similar requests—through the mail, left in his hotel room, his car, and his laundry—and although he listened to hundreds of tunes "just in case," the majority of them were no good, and he couldn't face listening to another dud. He called security and had the would-be songwriter thrown off the property.

Frank had so many people stay with him at the Compound. Tony Bennett, who Frank always said was "the best singer in the business," came once with his girlfriend of the time, Peggy Lee. Ella Fitzgerald was a guest. Elizabeth Taylor and Richard Burton came too, during their most tempestuous phase, in the late sixties. They drank too much and argued all the time in front of people; it was like the movie *Who's Afraid of Virginia Woolf?* in which they'd pretty much played themselves. One day I came in off the tennis court and found them sitting by the pool. As I walked past, Richard turned to Frank and said, "Wow! Those are some legs on that girl!"

Elizabeth, who was coming to the end of her Hollywood heyday, looked up and complained, "I suppose my legs are terrible?"

"They're stubby," Richard replied, taking a slug from his whiskey, "and so are your fingers."

Furious, she jumped up and rounded on him. "Then I want the biggest fucking diamond ever to go on my stubby fingers!" she cried. In due course, Richard did just as he was told and bought her the sixty-nine-carat "Taylor-Burton" diamond for over a million dollars from Cartier. Frank always said that was my fault.

Whenever it was too hot to stay in the desert, Frank would relocate to Villa Maggio in Pinyon Crest, the house he'd named after his character in *From Here to Eternity*. The property was an Alpine chalet four thousand feet above sea level and an hour's drive from anywhere. It was surrounded by a wilderness full of coyotes and snakes.

Up there playing gin, playing tennis, or lying by the pool, Frank began to quiz me about my life before Zeppo. When I told him that I'd been a showgirl at the Riviera, he asked, "How come I didn't meet you in Vegas then? Didn't you come to any of my shows?"

"I was too busy working," I replied. "Anyway, I did see you one night. You were in the bar at the Sahara with all your pallies."

"Well, what happened?" Frank asked, perplexed.

"I was walking past the door with some girlfriends and you asked me to come in, but I kept on walking."

"Why?"

"I didn't want to deal with a drunk," I told him flatly.

From the look on his face, I could tell that kind of hit him in the stomach. Frank Sinatra didn't get too many rejections.

It was at Pinyon Crest one night that our spirited game of charades ended with his hurling the clock against the door after I'd called time. I'll never forget the fire in Frank's eyes and the way he looked at me. His expression was full of anger and frustration, but there was something else—desire. I think I knew then that something would happen between us someday. I just didn't know when.

SIX

*"Sinatra in Greece with Blonde"—the photo that appeared
of me when I was secretly dating Frank.*

Angel Eyes

When Frank announced in March 1971 that he intended to retire from performing, he sent a shock wave around the world. Nobody could believe it. He was only fifty-five years old, and his voice was still as good as ever; in fact, many believed it had improved with age. What was he thinking?

But Frank was tired of entertaining people, especially when all they really wanted were the same old tunes he had long ago become bored by. He'd been singing since he was a teenager, and he felt burned out. He'd been divorced from Mia Farrow for three years, and his life was based firmly in Palm Springs. In his honor the city fathers renamed the street he lived on (Wonder Palms Road) Frank Sinatra Drive. Frank joked with Bob Hope that his road was thinner than the nearby Bob Hope Drive and that at cocktail time his was lit up while Bob's was shrouded in darkness.

Most of all, Frank was having fun. He wanted nothing more than to drink with Jimmy and his friends, play games, host dinners, and travel for pleasure, not work. He'd made more than enough money; he had his own record company, Reprise, as well as a Budweiser distributorship, shares in an airline, and numerous real estate ventures. With his own film company, he was an executive at Warner Brothers and had his own building on the Goldwyn lot. All told, he had around seventy staff. The company that made Jack Daniel's had made him a "Tennessee Squire," and his friend Angelo Lucchesi from the company gifted him a plot of land on the site of their distillery in Lynchburg to thank him for being such a devoted ambassador. Frank hoped to go see it one day. He'd set up a medical education center in Palm Springs in his father's name and planned on being even more philanthropic in retirement, so there was plenty to keep him occupied.

As he said in a statement issued to announce his retirement, the previous thirty years of touring and recording a hundred albums with over two thousand songs had given him "little room or opportunity for reflection, reading, self-examination, and that need which every thinking man has for a fallow period; a long pause in which to seek a better understanding of changes occurring in the world." Tickets to his retirement concert in Los Angeles on June 13 that year sold out within hours of being released. The event was so oversubscribed that the organizers decided to spread the evening's entertainment across three separate theaters with different acts performing in rotation and Frank moving from one to another. In typical style, he turned the night into a benefit for the Motion Picture & Television Fund, a charity close to his heart because it supported entertainers who hadn't been as lucky as he had.

Zeppo and I were offered tickets to this memorable event, which made the cover of *Life* magazine, and found ourselves in prime seats at the Los Angeles Music Center's Ahmanson Theatre. We were sat near some of Frank's closest friends, including Vice President Spiro Agnew, U.S. national security adviser Henry

Kissinger, and Ronald Reagan, governor of California. It was quite a night. There were tears in people's eyes long before the man who called himself "a saloon singer" walked onto the stage. Having just performed at the Dorothy Chandler Pavilion alongside old friends such as Tony Bennett, George Burns, and Barbra Streisand, Frank finished up at ours. Rosalind Russell, one of his closest friends, who was sitting with us, Cary Grant, and Jack Benny had to go up and introduce him just after midnight even though Roz was in pieces. "This assignment is not a happy one for me," she announced. "Our friend has made a decision... not one we particularly like... He's worked long and hard for us for thirty years with his head and his voice, and especially his heart. But it's time to put back the Kleenex and stifle the sob, for we still have the man, we still have the blue eyes; those wonderful blue eyes; that smile. For one last time we have the man, the greatest entertainer of the twentieth century." Dear Roz had cancer by then and was giving herself frequent pain shots; I don't know how she got through it.

Frank performed an amazing set that included all his greatest standards, such as "I've Got You Under My Skin," "All or Nothing at All," "Ol' Man River," and "That's Life." He sang with an intensity that I'm sure echoed the emotions in his heart and received one standing ovation after another. He'd almost always closed his shows with the song "My Way," but that night he stood in a circle of light and sang "Angel Eyes." Holding my breath as he came to the final verse, I realized why he'd picked that song. The lyrics could have been written for him:

Try to think that love's not around
Still it's uncomfortably near....
And have fun you happy people.
The drink and the laughs are on me.

While I sat wondering if this really would be the last time I'd hear Frank sing, the light shrank to a single spot on his face as he stood alone on the dark stage. Blue smoke from the cigarette he'd just lit curled around his head. "*Excuse me while I disappear. . . ,*" he sang. The light faded and then cut out as he vanished between folds of velvet in the wings. In darkness, I gasped and then allowed my tears to fall as several thousand people rose to their feet as one, calling for the encore that never came. What an exit.

Back home, I tried to focus on a son who continued to delight and infuriate me in equal measure. Increasingly rebellious and with a fighting spirit I guess he must have inherited from me, Bobby was fortunately past his Haight-Ashbury phase but still knew how to push my buttons. After leaving Cate for Berkeley, he became the only white in an all-black class of over fifty pupils.

He told me: "I want to know how it feels to be black because this is what they've endured all these years." He developed interests in the Black Panther political movement as well as yoga and the history of religions. Whenever I invited him for the holidays, I'd tell him, "You have to cut your hair and pull up your jeans, Bobby. I can't take you into Tamarisk looking like that."

One day, when he was about to go back to college, he announced, "Mother, we can never communicate again unless you read this book about racial struggle. It's called *Soul on Ice*, and it was written by one of my professors, Eldridge Cleaver."

I read a couple of chapters and thought, Ugh, but when Bobby left for Europe to spend some time with his father, I picked it up again and waded through to the end. As soon as Bobby got back, I told him triumphantly, "Guess what? We can communicate!"

"What?"

"I finished it!"

"Finished what?"

"Soul on Ice!"

Bobby shook his head and said, "Oh, Mother, that was *so* yesterday! I'll send you something much better to read." After Berkeley, he chose a college in Neuchâtel, Switzerland, to study French history, literature, and philosophy for two years. He became a linguist and embraced all things European. In that picture-postcard lakeland setting, Bobby also fell in love. The girl in question was an ivory-skinned farm girl with blond hair to her waist. She was named Sylvia, and he wrote and told me he was eager for me to meet her family, which could mean only one thing.

"Don't do anything rash," I wrote back. *"I'll fly over this summer and we'll talk."* I only hoped I wouldn't be too late.

I was still worrying about Bobby when Dinah Shore hosted her first charity golf tournament at Mission Hills in Palm Springs, an annual event that went on to become one of the highlights of the Ladies Professional Golf Association (LPGA) tour. Not surprisingly, perhaps, Zeppo refused to partner me on the course. Just as I was wondering who I could play with instead, Frank asked if I'd consider playing with "a former superstar." I was flattered, of course, but quite taken aback. I wasn't nearly good enough to partner the man who sometimes teamed up with Dean Martin, a scratch player. I also knew how impatient Frank could be—he'd infuriate Dean by suggesting they skip a couple of holes when people were already playing or head to the greens nearest the clubhouse. "Hey, Dag" (short for Dago), he'd call to Dean, "fourteen's open. Let's go!" He'd have a bar set up on a golf cart on the seventeenth fairway, at the back of his house, so they could stop and have a drink. How would he react when I was constantly hunting for my ball in the rough?

The night before the tournament Dinah threw a party at her house. I was sitting opposite Frank, and when the person next to him got up from the table, he leaned across and asked me quietly, "Would you please come over here and sit next to me, Barbara?" It was all very subtle, but we sat together for the rest of the evening.

The following day the two of us went around the course in his golf cart. We'd wave and smile at the spectators and players we passed, but mostly we were on our own. Not much was said and nothing happened, but sitting side by side in that little electric cart, our knees touching, seemed hopelessly romantic. Whenever I was about to swing my club, he'd stand close enough for me to catch his soapy, lavender scent. Our fingers might brush when he helped me choose a club or our eyes meet when we headed back to the buggy. As the tournament drew to a close, Frank smiled and asked, "Will you come and have dinner with me tonight, Sunshine Girl?" I loved that he used the nickname for me only Zeppo and a few others used around the club.

It was later that evening, as Zep played gin nearby, that Frank offered to fix me a martini in the den. When he pulled me into his arms, I was caught completely off guard, but I found myself returning his kiss with just as much ardor. There was no way to avoid that flirtation. Besides, I was as lost and lonely as he was. My marriage was all but dead. Bobby was grown and living abroad; I didn't have to protect him anymore. Whatever happened next between Frank and me—and I knew then that something would— I wouldn't try to stop it. I was happy again, for the first time in years, and it felt so good.

Eva Gabor always threw terrific poolside parties at her home in Palm Springs. The younger sister of the actresses Zsa Zsa and Magda, Eva was a four-times-divorced socialite in the Pamela Harriman mold. She was crazy about Frank; they dated for a while and she'd been hopeful of marriage. When they split up, someone recommended that she see a shrink in Pasadena, but when she got there the analyst told her he had three patients who thought Frank was going to marry them. That news alone helped her get over him.

Standing at Eva's bar during one of her parties by the pool in late May 1972, I got chatting with a friendly barman who asked me about my vacation plans. "I'm flying to Switzerland to see my son, and then I'm going to Monaco to visit my friends the Ittlesons," I told him.

A voice at my elbow startled me. "Monaco?" I knew who it was before I turned. "I'll be in Monaco too in a couple of weeks. Maybe we could meet up?" Frank's eyes, which seemed bluer than ever, dared mine to look away. Nobody else in the world could look right through you the way Frank could. "I know the Ittlesons," he added, drawing on his cigarette. "We could get together."

I shrugged my shoulders. "Sure," I replied as nonchalantly as I could, although my stomach was doing backflips.

"I stay at the Hôtel de Paris. I'll call you when I get into town." Frank smiled and walked away, moving to another guest and another conversation as if nothing at all had just happened.

I'd first met Henry Ittleson and his wife, Nancy, at the Hillcrest Club in L.A. Henry, who was one of Zeppo's favorite gin rummy partners, had founded the Credit and Investment Company in New York in the 1930s and used his and Nancy's considerable wealth to set up the Ittleson Family Foundation. Nancy, a caramel blonde addicted to tennis, had the best houses, the finest china, and the most expensive crystal, but she liked to surprise her guests by serving home-cooked American fare like fried chicken and ham. She was a hoot.

Eager to get away from the increasingly stifling atmosphere at home, I'd jumped at the chance to stay with the Ittlesons after my planned visit to Bobby in Neuchâtel. I hoped to persuade my hippie son to accompany me to Monte Carlo for what I knew would be the trip of a lifetime. Whether he would agree to or not was anybody's guess. By the time I boarded my plane for Europe, the butterflies in my tummy were doing somersaults. Quite apart from what might happen in Monaco, I could only guess what Zeppo would get up to while I was away. While my second marriage disintegrated around me, Bobby was talking about marrying a girl I'd never even met. I'd told him he was far too young and needed to finish his education, but that only seemed to make him more determined to defy me.

And then there was Frank, who was in London as I left but had promised to fly down and meet me, far from prying ears and eyes. Even within the relatively safe company of the irreproachable Ittlesons and with Bobby as a chaperone, I knew I was crossing a line. What was I letting myself in for? Was I about to be seduced by one of the world's greatest romantics? Would it be something to fold away in my memory, a story to lift out and tell my grandchildren one day? Could I, Barbara Blakeley, live with that?

Not only was my entire future at stake personally and financially, but I was in danger of losing my only son to a world far away from mine, in Switzerland. Was I also at risk of losing my heart to the one man some might say was the worst possible choice a woman could make? Only time would tell.

I am rarely superstitious and have never believed in omens that are supposed to foretell an event in the future, good or bad, which is just as well, because my journey to the South of France was beset with misfortune.

A strike by French air traffic controllers meant that after leaving Bobby I had to travel to the South of France by train from Geneva. It was twilight as I boarded the overnight Swiss Rail train alone and was shown to my four-berth second-class cabin, which, fortunately, I had to myself. Bobby wasn't with me or even really speaking to me after I'd not only forbidden him to marry Sylvia but told him that he couldn't bring her with him to the Ittlesons' as he'd asked. "Henry is absolute death on houseguests," I explained. "Besides, they run a straight house, and Nancy tells me they have only two guest cottages, so I'm sure they wouldn't be thrilled to have you in one of them with some girl. As it is, they're going to have a rough time accepting your bohemian style!"

Bobby's face fell. My visit to him in Neuchâtel hadn't been the success he'd hoped it would be. After meeting Sylvia with the big blue eyes at her parents' vineyard home, I told him, "This is not the girl or the family for you." Although I hated to dampen my son's youthful passion, I was convinced that his marrying Sylvia would be a mistake. I knew what I was talking about. I'd married impetuously young, and although doing so had given me the gift of a son, the failure of that first marriage had scarred me for life.

"Well, Mom," he told me calmly, "without Sylvia, I'm not coming to Monaco."

So I was alone in my carriage that night as the train climbed a mountain pass in the shadow of Mont Blanc. The doubts that had been worming their way into my brain since I'd set off from Los Angeles seemed to dig deeper with every *clickety-clack* of the train taking me into the Alps and then down to the Côte d'Azur. Frank probably wouldn't even show up, I told myself. His schedule was famously changeable, and with an air strike, how could he even get to France from London?

My thoughts were interrupted by a sudden, loud bang. The train gave a lurch before grinding to a halt, almost throwing me from my seat. Rolling up the shade, I could see men running around in the dark. Somewhere, a woman was screaming. After what seemed like an age, the door to my compartment flew open and several people backed in, carrying three injured men. In faltering English, a gendarme told me that the train had hit a car on the track. The survivors, bloodied and bruised, were laid on the three spare bunks. The gendarme took off his hat, gave me a shrug, and slid my door shut. The train lurched again and set off, leaving me alone with the groaning victims, none of whom spoke any English. No doctor came, so for the next hour or so I did what I could to comfort them. Mercifully, two stops later they were removed by paramedics and taken to a local hospital.

Needless to say, by the time I arrived in Nice I was exhausted and shaken. Nancy Ittleson, fresh and chipper, was waiting to greet me, but my suitcases were not. They'd been mislaid. "Don't worry," she said gaily, trying to cheer me up. "We're the same size. You can have the run of my wardrobe." She drove me the twenty miles toward Monte Carlo and then up to their French villa, named Rien ne va Plus, meaning "no more bets," on a bluff at Roquebrune-Cap-Martin overlooking the Mediterranean. Leading me down some steps in the garden, she showed me my pretty guest cottage, with the most breathtaking views I'd ever seen. I finally began to relax.

"Frank called," she said casually as I tested the bed. "The strike means he's stuck in London. They won't even let private planes take off."

"Oh, that's a shame," I replied lightly, before allowing her to lead me back up to the villa to choose an outfit for the party she was throwing that night.

My first evening in the hills above Monaco was so unbelievably glamorous that I found myself wishing Bobby was there to enjoy it with me. Among the crowd of twenty sophisticated Europeans dining under the stars was Prince Rainier of Monaco, who insisted I stop calling him Your Highness. His wife, the former actress Grace Kelly, was on a shopping trip to Paris.

At a long table laden with glassware, silver, and flickering candles, everyone sat and chatted animatedly, switching from French to English to Italian as easily as breathing. At one point during the evening, I stood back to observe the scene, with its beautiful people who seemed to take little notice of the glittering coastline below. In a borrowed designer dress and with a glass of champagne in my hand, I couldn't help but reflect that Barbara Ann Blakeley had traveled a very long way from Bosworth, Missouri. I felt bubbly with happiness.

When I eventually retired to my guest cottage, at around

three in the morning, I found three dozen white roses waiting on my bedside table. The card attached to them read, *"I'll be there. Francis Albert."*

The morning brought more good news. Bobby telephoned to say he'd changed his mind and would arrive the next day, without Sylvia. Even more surprisingly, he assured me he'd cut his hair. As I replaced the receiver, the phone rang again, so I picked it up in case Bobby had forgotten something.

"Barbara? It's Frank," the voice said down a crackly line. "I'm still in London, but I'm on my way. Tell Nancy I'll make it for dinner. You be there too."

The conversation was short but sweet, and I was only able to say, "We're looking forward to seeing you," before the line went dead.

Later that morning in the pool, Nancy asked me if I liked my flowers. "Frank's so gallant," she said wistfully. "He sent me roses too." Just as I was wondering if I'd read too much into my bouquet and Frank's subsequent phone call, Nancy's maid arrived to tell me my suitcases had been delivered from the station. At least I'd be able to wear the purple Oscar de la Renta dress I'd chosen especially for the occasion.

Frank arrived just as the cocktail party was starting. When he walked into the Ittlesons' drawing room, he brought with him his usual palpable air of excitement. He kissed all the women on both cheeks, Continental-style, and introduced us to his companions, who included Fritz Loewe, the composer who cowrote the scores for *My Fair Lady, Gigi,* and *Paint Your Wagon.* Then, whiskey in hand, Frank regaled us with the tale of how he'd defied the strike once he made it as far as Orly airport. Warned that there would be a further four-hour delay, he ordered his pilot to take off anyway. His G2 Gulfstream must have been about the only aircraft in the clouds all the way across France. "I didn't want to miss a minute more of this," he told the crowd, but his eyes were fixed firmly on me.

Rainier arrived, and he and Frank greeted each other like the old friends they were. Someone asked Rainier where they'd first met. The ruler of Monaco told us that, when he was courting Grace during the filming of *High Society*, he'd visited the film set. Everyone was terribly polite in the presence of European royalty and offered him endless cups of tea. Sensing his disappointment, Frank finally told him, "Come to my trailer for a Jack Daniel's."

"Oh, brother!" cried the prince. "Where have you been all this time?" They'd been pals ever since. The two of them launched into fond recollections of the woman Frank called Gracie (referred to as Her Serene Highness everywhere else in Monaco). Frank said he was most indignant when Grace was presented with a platinum record for a song before he received one. "It was for 'True Love,' of all things," he added.

"Worse still, she sang it with Crosby!" Rainier teased.

Just before dinner, Frank managed to get me on my own in a corner. "You look beautiful tonight, Barbara," he told me. "I've been thinking about you."

My face felt warm, and it wasn't just the champagne. "It's the same with me," was all I managed to say before Nancy arrived to announce that dinner was served. We ate ham and beans, mashed potatoes, and coleslaw on Sevres porcelain. It was delicious, but I could barely eat and pushed the food around my plate. As the evening came to a close, Frank drew me to one side and said quietly, "I'm going to take you to dinner tomorrow night with Nancy, Henry, and a few of the others. Let's see each other afterwards." Reddening, I nodded.

The following day I borrowed Henry's red Mercedes and drove to Nice to meet Bobby at the station. When my six-foot-four-inch son stepped off the train with his wavy chestnut hair and square-jawed grin, he looked the spitting image of the man who'd fallen for the Queen of Belmont Shore all those years earlier. He was equally lovelorn. "I'm *really* going to miss Sylvia," Bobby complained with a sigh as I drove him back to the Ittlesons' villa.

"She'll wait," I told him gently. Nothing could burst my bubble.

L e Beach Club of the Hôtel de Paris in Monte Carlo had several tiers of striped canvas cabanas or small beach huts that faced the sea. The Ittlesons had taken one in the second tier, and Frank had three in the tier below ours, positioned to avoid the prying lenses of the paparazzi. Fritz was in his group, along with Jilly, an older American couple, and two attractive women in swimsuits. Frank assured me that these last were beards so that the press wouldn't suspect who he was really with.

I introduced my son to Frank that afternoon with some trepidation. Even though Bobby was an adult, he'd been hurt or rejected by every man I'd brought into his life, and being overprotective, I was worried how Frank would react to my son. With three children from his first marriage, Frank had left their mother when they were very small. I needn't have been worried as far as Bobby was concerned, though. When I strolled down with him to meet everyone, Frank jumped up and gave him a welcoming hug. The two of them hit it off immediately and wandered off together to talk batting averages and touchdowns. Frank also introduced Bobby to Rainier and Grace's children, the princesses Caroline and Stephanie, and Prince Albert, known to us as Alby. The four of them also hit it off instantly, and Alby and Bobby in particular forged a close friendship that has endured to this day.

The pace Frank set once he arrived was exhausting. This was clearly someone who liked to be entertained. The man who'd almost died at birth was determined to live every minute of the second chance life had thrown him. He wouldn't let anyone slow him down. We were out every day and expected to party every night. One day I told him, "I really can't go out tonight, Frank. I'm sorry, but I just don't feel like it. I'm too tired."

His eyes took on a glint. "You're going, Barbara. You're going tonight, and you're going every night," he told me. As I was soon to learn, there was no arguing with Frank. That night he hosted dinner for twelve at Le Pirate, an outdoor restaurant renowned for its eccentricities. Our crowd included Pat Henry, the producer Sam Spiegel, and the actor Vince Edwards and his wife. Robert Viale, the crazy owner, greeted us with fireworks and gunfire while a gypsy band played frantic fiddle music and dancing girls whirled around us playing tambourines. We were shown to long benches at trestle tables while acrobats dressed as pirates swung between the branches of the trees. Mr. Viale produced a Nebuchadnezzar of champagne and sliced off the neck with a sword. The house donkey wandered between tables eating food from plates, showing a preference for lobster. There was a huge fireplace, and every now and then waiters would hurl chairs or tables into the roaring flames. When we'd finished eating, we were encouraged to do the same with our plates. Anyone who wanted to go up to the first-floor bar had to climb a large tree in the center of the courtyard to reach it, but if they did they were pelted with food by fellow guests. It was insane.

Bobby's eyes were popping right out of his head. He leaned toward me and shouted, "We're in a nuthouse!" Frank, sitting at the head of the table, loved the craziness of it all and kept ordering more champagne, more food, and more music. This man of the world, who must have seen just about everything there was to see, took childish delight in the pranks happening all around us. But then I shouldn't have been surprised. Swifty Lazar, one of the smartest-dressed people I knew, had warned me what a practical joker Frank was. He told me how he'd returned home one day to find his immaculate wardrobe bricked up and plastered over. Frank would also have the food and drink moved to his house half an hour before Swifty was to throw a party.

Frank and Dean Martin used to puncture tiny pinholes into the filters of friend's cigarettes so they wouldn't draw, or snip into their bow ties so that when they went to put them on the ties would fall apart in their hands. Cherry bombs were another favorite; those red-colored party explosives were thrown into yards, used to blow up mailboxes, tossed as ammunition against journalists, or set off at the end of someone's bed. Frank and Dean had a brown terry-cloth robe made for Sammy Davis, Jr., at the Vegas steam room where they wore white robes, the same place where they shoved a naked Don Rickles out of the steam room door into the crowded pool area. Frank, a man who never slept on planes, regularly stuffed candy into the slipped-off shoes of those foolish enough to nod off.

After dinner at Le Pirate, Frank took us to the casino and bonded further with Bobby over a blackjack game. He liked to play only blackjack and craps, and was happy to teach my son a few tricks. Then he took me to the card tables and taught me the game of chemin de fer. It was so romantic sitting next to him at the card table as he leaned over to see what hand I'd been dealt and advised me which card to play. Henry Ittleson wandered off discreetly to play his usual baccarat. The casino saved a chair for him every night, and he didn't like anyone to watch him while he played with his big square chips. When he caught me spying on him through a crowd that had gathered because he was winning so much money, he was very upset, especially when I asked, "Do you ever *lose* that kind of money too?"

"Of course I do!" he snapped. "Look, other men have women, horses, or cars. My only hobby is gambling, and I put aside a million dollars a year for it, so that's that." When Henry eventually died, the casino put his chair down on the table and didn't use it for a year.

After the casino that night in Monaco, we went to Regine's nightclub New Jimmy'z. Frank's friendship with Bobby was sealed the minute he spotted my son ogling the girls. "Okay, kid," he said, laughing. "We're going to have a good time." At around two in the morning, Frank turned to Bobby and said, "All right, buster, time to go and get some sleep. I'm going to take your mother back to the hotel to have a drink with friends. We'll take you home."

I patted Bobby's hand and asked, "Is that all right, darling?"

"Sure, Mom," Bobby replied. "It's been a long day." His expression betrayed no hint of what he might be thinking. I hoped mine didn't either.

When Regine saw that we were preparing to leave, she whispered something to Frank, who shrugged and smiled. "Paparazzi," he explained. Rising to our feet, we were led out through the kitchen past stacks of dirty pots and pans to a rear door. It was an arrival and exit route that I was coming to accept as the norm. Outside, Frank's Packard sedan waited incongruously amid the garbage cans, his Monaco driver, Bruno Viola, at the wheel. A few camera flashes popped as we drove out onto the street, but Bruno stepped on the gas and sped us away.

As I waved good night to Bobby at the Ittlesons' gate twenty minutes later, I spotted a familiar item half-hidden in the passenger well of the car. It was my canvas beach bag, which must somehow have been sneaked out of my guest cottage at Rien ne va Plus while we were out. Folded neatly inside were a swimsuit and an outfit for the beach in the morning. I looked across at Frank in astonishment, but he didn't even return my stare. So, no more bets, please . . .

Frank's two-bedroom suite at the Hôtel de Paris, with its penthouse view of the harbor on three sides, was the finest I'd ever been in. Large French doors opened out onto a terrace. Classical music drifted up from below. Exquisite silks adorned the windows;

the beds and sofas were comfortingly overstuffed. The whole place looked like a movie set. As Frank opened the bottle of champagne that was waiting on ice, I wandered out to the balcony of that big white wedding cake of a building, and the view almost stopped my heart. Car lights traced a line along the coastal highway all the way to Cap Ferrat. Stars twinkled high above. If my first night at the Ittlesons' had seemed like an earth-based dream, then surely this was heaven.

Lucky girl, Barbara Blakeley, I thought to myself. Remember this moment.

Frank handed me a champagne flute, and we toasted each other. Setting our glasses down, we moved closer, and then he enfolded me in the gentlest embrace.

A few hours later, we watched as the dawn crept through the windows and clung to each other ever tighter. The warm Mediterranean light heralded the end of our idyll; it was a new day and a return to our pretense that there was nothing between us. Only now it would be that much harder to pretend.

Rising reluctantly and dressing in the beach clothes that one of his minions had chosen for me, I blew Frank a kiss, left his suite, and headed downstairs. The grand hotel lobby was full of people, so I ducked out of the elevator and headed instead for the arcade of shops, from where I could slip away more easily. If anyone saw me, I hoped they'd think I just came up from the beach. My head down, sunglasses on, I was startled by a familiar voice.

"Barbara! It *is* you!" It was Greg Bautzer, Zeppo's attorney. "What are you doing here?"

I turned to a rack of postcards and quickly picked a couple out. "Oh, hi, Greg," I replied as casually as I could. "I'm staying at the Ittlesons'. I just stopped in to buy these on my way to the beach."

"Uh-huh," Greg said, smiling. A notorious womanizer, this

was the man who'd represented Lana Turner, Ginger Rogers, Howard Hughes, and Ingrid Bergman in everything from multimillion-dollar Vegas property deals to high-profile divorces. "Postcards, eh?" he added, and wandered off chuckling to himself.

I didn't fool Bobby either. He was sunning himself at the beach club and gave me a knowing look when I arrived. "Morning, Mom," he cried. "Glorious day!" To my relief, he was refreshingly matter-of-fact and never once made comment or passed judgment. That was his hallmark. In the years to come, Bobby would become one of my closest confidants in the unfolding drama of me and the man we sometimes called FS.

Frank appeared at lunch, and we nodded each other a courteous hello. Halfway through our meal, he waved a hand for silence, so I stopped to listen along with everyone else. "I have special plans for dinner tonight," he announced, adding enigmatically, "Bring your passports." After an uneventful afternoon at the beach and a much-needed nap to catch up on my beauty sleep, I met everyone outside Frank's hotel and stepped into one of the two cars waiting to take us on our mystery tour. Before we knew it, we were at the airport, then on board Frank's private jet, headed for Athens. "I fancied Greek food tonight," he explained, laughing. He took us to a wonderful restaurant for dinner and then on to a classical concert on the grounds of some ancient ruins. Afterward, we went to a nightclub where belly dancers jiggled all around us and we were once again encouraged to smash our plates.

Bobby was having the time of his life, and so was I. Not only did Frank make sure to include my son in everything but he seemed to really like him; it was heaven to see. I'd never experienced anything like this with my previous men, who'd always made comments like "Do you *have* to bring the kid?" This was like a miracle.

Frank had booked us in the Hilton Hotel, overlooking the Acropolis, and as we left the nightclub and headed back to our rooms, the paparazzi pressed in and took some shots of us sitting

in the back of his car. SINATRA IN GREECE WITH BLONDE the headlines ran the next day (not that I knew until later). If Zeppo spotted
them back in Palm Springs, he never said so, and as I left Frank's
hotel room in the early hours of the following morning, Zeppo
Marx was the last person on my mind.

Frank and I floated on air for the next few days that beautiful
summer. I prayed that no one would find out about our affair
and spoil everything. We had to be especially careful around the
Ittlesons because they were old friends of Zeppo's. Nancy knew,
I'm certain, but she was a good enough girlfriend not to let on.

What I thought might just be a one-time experience and
something to remember in years to come turned into night after
glorious night of romance in some of the most glamorous venues
in Europe. Frank was tender and kind, generous and funny. He'd
walk past my chair humming "I've Got a Crush on You" or brush
his fingers against my shoulder as if by accident. He was probably
the most gentlemanly person I'd ever met—opening doors, helping with my coat, jumping up to freshen my glass.

He was without fail polite, warm, gracious, and giving. Everywhere he went he'd stop to buy extravagant gifts for friends and
family, shipping parcels home or having surprise packages and
flowers delivered to our rooms. He remembered everything from
friends' favorite colors to what kinds of cologne they wore. He ad-
dressed store and hotel staff by their first names, recalling them
from previous visits. He led Nancy and me into a jewelry shop and
almost bought the place out. He chose me some beautiful earrings
and a ring and then later went back on his own to buy me something else, telling me, "You'd look *maaarvelous* in this!" (using an
intonation he'd picked up from his friend Noël Coward).

During lazy afternoons down on the beach, Frank was never
happier than with his nose buried in a book. I was surprised to
discover that the man whose mother never read and whose father

barely spoke English devoured literature voraciously, anything from bestselling fiction to history, politics, the arts, and biography. Passionate about reading and with an endless curiosity despite having quit high school, he'd recommend books to friends, buy them copies, and then swap notes. He was especially interested in the history of our country and of other nations, and could remember entire tracts of things he'd read, often quoting them verbatim. He also completed crosswords—the hard ones—quickly and in ink.

Between chapters and clues, we'd talk while others swam or sunbathed. Frank quizzed me closely about my years with Zeppo, and I admitted how sterile things had become between us. In return, he opened up in a way that surprised and pleased me. He spoke of the emptiness he felt a year after retiring and how difficult he was finding it to adjust to a life of leisure. He'd had more than thirty thousand letters from fans the world over urging him to return to the stage. He even received one from the man whose voice had first inspired him to sing and with whom he'd starred in *High Society* with Grace Kelly. Bing Crosby wrote, "*I can't believe you're going to remain supine for long. You're at the peak of your form and you still have so much to give.*" When Frank quoted me letters like that, I wondered if he was reconsidering his decision or privately dreading a future without performing.

As for my future, I didn't know what was going to happen. Often in the days leading up to the end of our time together in that hopelessly idyllic setting, I wanted to ask, "Is this it, Frank? What happens after Monaco?" but I didn't dare. I was too afraid of the answer. This was Frank Sinatra, after all. Women the world over fell at his feet. He had the pick of them all, young and old, so why would he choose the wife of an old friend living in the same small town? I had to be realistic. This was a summer romance, and when the vacation ended, it would almost certainly end too. It wasn't as if I wanted to spend the rest of my life with him anyway.

There was way too much baggage with FS—his fame, his previous women, his hell-raising reputation, not to mention his mercurial nature. There were too many strange characters around him all the time, and I didn't like that either. Zeppo may have been night to Frank's day in terms of excitement, but at least he understood the importance of time spent alone.

When Monaco ended, Frank would undoubtedly move on to the next town, the next party, the next country, the next girl. That was all he knew. He already had plans to fly to Portugal to visit Spiro Agnew and his wife. There was an American presidential campaign going on, and Frank would offer every support to his friend, even though they didn't share the same political stance. There would almost certainly be a woman or two in Agnew's party who, I was sure, would receive the same sort of flattery and attention I'd been getting. I accepted that and, strangely, didn't feel jealous. Everything would go back to just as it had always been, for Frank and for me.

By the time he squeezed my arm and kissed my cheek as he made his long round of farewells at the beach club, I'd resigned myself to the fact that our Mediterranean love affair was just that—a fleeting, wonderful thing. "Take care of yourself, Barbara," he told me with a smile, and I assured him I would, happy that I'd at least have my memories to feed on.

SEVEN

*Frank with an armful of roses he gathered from
the stage for me.*

Where the Air
Is Rarefied

Picking up the threads of my Palm Springs life after Europe was far harder than I'd imagined. Whereas previously I'd been complacent about my marriage and resolved never to divorce Zeppo however difficult things became, I now found myself beset by secret yearning. In my determination to remain Mrs. Barbara Marx, I hadn't counted on one Francis Albert.

Then Frank flew back into town and, within days, made it clear that he wanted us to pick up where we'd left off, which really set the cat among the pigeons. I was flattered but refused to meet him secretly. Palm Springs was too small, and everybody knew everybody else's business. What if Zeppo found out? And how long was my fling with Frank likely to last? I couldn't risk everything for what might turn out to be just another of his fleeting romances. If Zeppo threw me out, the only place I could go was the house I'd bought for my parents. I could have done it (and gone back to work if I'd needed to), but after years of not earning a living, it would have been that much harder. Bobby had gone to the Sorbonne as he'd hoped, and it would cost money to keep him in Paris. He'd spent some time in Monaco and a summer with his father in Rome. He'd even helped Bob make a movie called *Frankenstein's Castle of Freaks*, in which Bobby, his grandmother, and his father all had minor roles. The film bombed, of course, which meant that Bob would never be able to help with his son's education, or anything else for that matter.

The idea of living with my parents held little appeal. My father wasn't in the best of health, and my mother was still complaining about him even though they remained locked in their love-hate relationship to the exclusion of everyone else. When she found out that my marriage to Zeppo was in trouble, she was furious and warned me not to succumb to the Sinatra charm. That was until one day when Frank telephoned her house to speak to me. She picked up the phone, and Frank, mistaking her for me, said something romantic and sexy. I was standing right next to her and watched as she melted. "Oh, my God! That voice alone could send a girl!" she said as she handed me the receiver in a daze.

Frank never stopped pursuing me, and whenever we saw each other, he'd try to get me on my own. He'd walk away from me singing "If It Takes Forever I Will Wait for You" or some other tune that I knew was intended for me. He was a great actor and a great singer, so he knew exactly how to tug at the heartstrings. He was so romantic, but I still held him at arm's length and carried on my unmerry way. One night Pat DiCicco, a friend of Frank's, cornered me. "How does it feel to have three men in love with you at the same party?" he asked.

"What do you mean?"

He reeled off the names—Zeppo, someone else I can't recall, and Frank. I shook my head and laughed, but what he'd said about Frank struck a chord.

Zeppo and I were still living in the same house, although not the same bedroom. We put up a good front and went out together as husband and wife, visiting our usual haunts. In spite of the fact that Frank and I weren't seeing each other (or perhaps because we weren't), there was still a constant frisson between us. Even sitting next to him made me jittery. When Zeppo began to pick up on that sexual tension, he became irrationally jealous even though *he* was far from faithful. I suppose the fact that he thought I might be falling for Frank Sinatra was finally something to be jealous about.

Whenever Zeppo flipped out about Frank, I neither denied nor confirmed anything. After all, I hadn't done anything wrong since Monaco. Eventually, Zeppo drove himself crazy and announced abruptly, "I can't take this anymore, Barbara! I think we should separate."

"I think that's a wise decision," I replied cautiously. "How do you want to do this?"

"Damn it, I'll give you a divorce," he said as if that was what I'd been asking for all along.

Ironically, having never paid much attention to Bobby when he was a kid, Zeppo began to take him to Tamarisk for lunch whenever he was home from school. In his stepson's company, he'd get loaded and start acting out. I'd hear it from other people in the club, never from my loyal son. It was an increasingly uncomfortable situation for us all, and I knew that, as soon as our divorce was negotiated, I'd have to move out. I just didn't know where I should go.

Eden Marx, Groucho's third wife, owned a small house right near the golf course off Tamarisk that she wanted to sell. It would be perfect for me, but unsure what I'd be able to afford, I hesitated in making an offer. To my surprise, Frank stepped in and bought it. "It's a good investment," he told me with a shrug. Even though the house was his, Mr. Generous put it in my name and had his lawyer hand me the deed. By then everyone knew that Zeppo and I were divorcing, so I accepted Frank's offer, packed my bags, and moved out of my marital home. My friend Bee Korshak helped me move in, and as we sat eating baloney sandwiches, surrounded by boxes and dirt, a delivery arrived from Frank. It was a case of Château Lafite. We washed down our everyday fare with wine worth hundreds of dollars a bottle.

Although I'd loved Zeppo in the beginning and had truly wanted our marriage to work, I didn't feel sad about leaving him at that point, because I knew that it was his behavior, not mine, that was to blame. If he hadn't been so unfaithful, if he'd been the stepfather Bobby deserved, if he'd been less tight with money and more generous with his attentions, then we might have remained married until the day he died.

From the moment I left Zeppo, Frank and I officially became a couple and I his constant companion. A few weeks later he took me as his guest to *the* party of the year in Palm Springs—the prestigious New Year's Eve affair at the home of his friend Walter Annenberg, American ambassador to the United Kingdom. Walter, who was also a media magnate and philanthropist, told me I was the "best thing in the world for Frank." He added, "If that idiot ever sees sense and asks you to marry him, you must have your wedding here at Sunnylands." That was some offer—Sunnylands was *the* premiere estate in Palm Springs, a vast acreage of palm oasis and a beautiful house filled with the most incredible art. Even with the support of such high-profile friends as the Annenbergs, eyebrows were raised at first about Frank dating me, but people soon grew accustomed to seeing us together and the scandal began to settle down. There were naysayers, of course, but our real friends knew we were great for each other.

There was only one person who dared to express his disapproval publicly—Groucho Marx. He came up to us at a charity event one day and said to Frank, "Why don't you let Barbara go? You don't want her. Let her go back to Zeppo." Everyone knew Frank had a trigger temper, but Groucho was a fearless octogenarian. Fortunately, Frank chose not to respond and I didn't say a word either, so dear old Groucho repeated his statement before going off with that funny little walk of his. I was both astonished at his nerve and touched that he was still so protective of his little brother Zep. It was one of the last times I ever saw Groucho alive.

Not surprisingly, I was a little uncomfortable staying on in Palm Springs while the divorce was being finalized. People take sides when a marriage breaks up, and some of the friends I'd made through Zeppo fell away for a while out of loyalty to him. Danny Kaye was probably the one who showed his feelings most obviously. His enmity was understandable, but it still hurt me.

Since his retirement, Frank had kept himself busy with painting, golf, reading, and crosswords. He still traveled a lot, picking up awards here and there as well as visiting friends, but he needed more to occupy his mind. A model railway enthusiast, he'd had a special train room built at the Compound for his two hundred or so trains, replicating the layout of the famous Lionel showroom in New York. His museum-quality setting featured yards of tracks on two levels amid scenery of mountains, factories, houses, and bridges as well as a miniature replica of Hoboken. It also had an old Western town, a billboard announcing one of his sellout concerts, and a New Orleans riverboat. From the ceiling hung replicas of all the planes he'd ever owned. In the wood-paneled room built as an extension of an old railroad caboose, he played with his favorite locomotive—the high-speed Japanese one he'd traveled on several times. On the wall were hung all sorts of station signs and slogans, including his favorite, which said: HE WHO DIES WITH THE MOST TOYS WINS.

Once he was in that room, Frank was a child again, the same little boy who'd pressed his nose against the glass of the Lionel model train store. His mother, Dolly, had pawned her fox fur to buy him his first set, a sacrifice he never forgot. In his special room that took him back to those days, he wore a bright red engineer's hat with a visor and blew a whistle while the sounds of trains and engines played. He loved it, and so did his friends, who would happily don hats and blow whistles too. Many of them bought him new or unusual trains as gifts, happy to find something to give the man who had everything. He had a solid gold one with his initials set in diamonds and rubies, which was a present from one of the Vegas hotels; a locomotive that was a gift from the Vatican; and a crystal version of the train that inspired Glenn Miller's "Chattanooga Choo Choo." Whenever his electrician came by to help Frank fix any problems with the track, the two of them would spend hours together "testing" the entire system. I'd pop my head around the door sometimes just to watch Frank, happy to see him so playful and animated, a glass of Daniel's in his hand.

Model trains were going to hold Frank Sinatra's attention for only so long, however, and his restlessness soon kicked in again. Turning his attention to politics, and with the encouragement of his friend the California governor Ronald Reagan, he made the surprise decision after years registered as a Democrat to change his wavering allegiance. He publicly backed the Republican Richard Nixon instead of Senator George McGovern for president. As he said at the time, it was about the man, not the party anymore. No one could believe it at first; the news was that shocking. Frank Sinatra—Jack Kennedy's most famous supporter—a Republican? I couldn't believe it either; even though Spiro Agnew was such a good friend of Frank's and Frank had already endorsed Reagan for governor, this seemed such a major shift. But the Kennedys were long gone, and Frank was in the mood for change. He also had a secret ambition to become U.S. ambassador to Italy and was promised that he might be considered for the position, although it never worked out. In spite of that, his Sicilian-bred loyalty to Nixon and to his friend Spiro was to prove lifelong. Even when they both eventually fell from grace, he never deserted them like so many of their friends did. As Frank said, "Everyone makes mistakes—even presidents."

When Frank was invited to Washington in January 1973 to help organize Nixon's inaugural gala, he asked me if I'd like to accompany him. I jumped at the chance, happy to leave Palm Springs and the controversy about my private life. Zeppo had hired some top-flight lawyers (including Greg Bautzer) to fight me over our divorce settlement, and as a stalwart of the Jewish and golfing communities, he had a lot of people on his side. What I didn't know was that as I flew east from one tricky situation, I was flying straight into another.

Frank's dislike of journalists stemmed from, I think, the forties, when he and his first wife, Nancy, were having problems and he felt that the gossip columnists unduly hounded him. His mistrust was further inflamed by what some reporters said about him when he was rallying support for Kennedy, and the allegations they never stopped making about his involvement with the Mob. From the moment we arrived in Washington, Frank and I were closely followed by the press and photographed at every opportunity. Just as we were leaving a political party at the Jockey Club in the Fairfax Hotel, a female reporter stepped forward to ask me about my marital status. I tried to brush off the woman I learned later was Maxine Cheshire, the society columnist for the *Washington Post*, but she wouldn't give up. Frank politely asked her to leave us alone. Finally, she said, "You *are* still married to Zeppo, aren't you, *Mrs.* Marx?" Embarrassed, I didn't know how to respond.

I could tell from Frank's expression that the night would end badly. He grabbed the arm of my coat and said, "Let's go, baby." But being Frank, he couldn't just let it go, so he let rip, calling Ms. Cheshire a "two-dollar broad" and something worse. Then, for good measure, he added that she wasn't worth as much as two dollars and stuffed a single dollar bill into her glass. As he walked me out, I thought, Oh, my God! but I have to admit there was also something exciting about what Frank had done. I'd never felt quite so defended in my life. The incident reminded me of a similar event years earlier in Ciro's restaurant on the Strip when Frank walked in with Judy Garland. When he heard someone ask, "Who's the broad?" Frank was so indignant on Judy's behalf that he pushed the man into the restaurant phone booth, punched him, and slid the door shut. Then, as an afterthought, he opened the door and said, "The lady's name is Garland. Spelled G-A-R-L-A-N-D." That was so typical of Frank. To hit the guy was one thing, but to give the event a comic punch line turned it into a scene from a movie. As I was fast coming to appreciate, Frank's life was like a series of little movies.

In spite of his famously short fuse, Frank had such strong feelings about manners and class, punctuality and style. He dressed in only the finest footwear, made especially for him and polished so hard you could see your reflection in the leather. He had an intense dislike for brown shoes and would use the moniker Mr. Brown Shoes for anyone he didn't take to. His tailored English and Italian suits had to be hung, stored, and pressed just so. He wore the best Cartier watches and a gold pinkie ring inscribed with the Sinatra family crest. He described himself as "symmetrical, almost to a fault," and once admitted, "I live my life certain ways that I could never change for a woman."

As well as looking immaculate, he spoke impeccably well and always tried to behave in a gentlemanly way. He expected others to do the same, and when they didn't, he'd lash out in frustration and disappointment. Several journalists were resented because they showed what he considered to be a lack of fairness from the safety of their newspaper columns or in the pages of lazily written books that merely pasted together a bunch of untruths. Despite the letters of complaint Frank wrote about the lies repeated ad nauseam, he rarely felt vindicated. There were only a few reporters he liked, one of them Larry King, whom he'd met in Miami when they were both starting out. Another was the Brooklyn-born *New York Post* columnist and author Pete Hamill, a fellow boozehound who wrote the only book I ever liked about Frank (until this one) called *Why Sinatra Matters*. He also liked Jim Bacon from the *Los Angeles Herald Examiner*, a few sports columnists, and an editor in Hawaii whose heart bypass he once funded, but that was about it.

The fallout from Frank's very public confrontation with Maxine Cheshire at the Fairfax lasted for several weeks. If I'd hoped to escape the glare of publicity by getting away from Palm Springs, I was wrong. Not everyone was indignant on Ms. Cheshire's behalf, however. Far from it. Some expressed their admiration for what Frank had done after she'd been so rude to me, and his friend Henry Kissinger called him up the next day to say he'd overpaid her. Unfazed by the controversy, Frank went on to perform at a White House dinner where President Nixon asked him, "What are you retired for? You really should sing."

After giving it some thought, Frank made another surprise announcement, one that was almost as shocking as his political volte-face. His two-year retirement—or "vacation" as he called it—was over. He said that he'd had "the most wonderful time of my life" for two years but he was ready to cut a new record and go back on tour, and by that he meant the world. His fans were delighted. Apart from a few private charitable or political engagements, he'd kept his word about staying off the stage. Only I knew the real reason behind Frank's decision to go back to work again that year. Although he'd undoubtedly missed the applause and wanted to reconnect with his fans, his timing was yet another way of protecting me. If I went on tour with him for a year or so, it would keep me out of Palm Springs and away from Zeppo and his friends. Frank would almost certainly have made a comeback sooner or later, but quietly and thoughtfully, my romantic lover had come up with a plan to whisk us away even earlier.

He went back into the studio with his old friends the producer Gordon Jenkins and the arranger Don Costa and recorded his bestselling album *Ol' Blue Eyes Is Back*, featuring some interesting and new material he'd never sung before. The song he chose as the opening track was "You Will Be My Music," written by his friend Joe Raposo, which I watched him record in New York. That was such a romantic moment in a lifetime of romantic moments—Frank looking directly at me as he sang that song with all the tenderness in his heart:

> *Wanting you is everything*
> *You will be my music*
> *Yes, you will be my song.*

The words were so lovely, and he told me afterward, "This is our story, baby." It was a difficult song to sing and a little too rangy for him, but he liked the words so much he sang it time and again, always dedicating it to me as "the love of my life." Another number he'd often sing to me was called "You're So Right (for What's Wrong in My Life)," which had the lines, *"You just fill every void in my life"* and *"Through the darkness of night, you're my one shining light."* I couldn't have agreed more.

To launch *Ol' Blue Eyes Is Back*, Frank performed in a TV special of the same name, for which Gene Kelly came out of retirement. Frank and Gene performed a fun song-and-dance routine together to a song called "We Can't Do That Anymore." Frank opened and closed the show with "You Will Be My Music" and told his audience that he missed making music. He also joked that he had to come out of retirement because after two years his golf handicap was still seventeen. He said that he'd been away from the business for so long he had to spell his name to telephone operators, and spoke self-effacingly about some of the "underwhelming" movies he'd made in his career, including *The Kissing Bandit* in 1948. His was a warm and intimate performance by a man who clearly loved being back in the spotlight. Just about everyone we knew came along for the ride and to welcome him back. It was the most incredible night, and when he said the words "Good night and sleep warm," the entire audience rose as one.

Jack Benny went crazy when he heard the title of Frank's new album. "How come you're calling yourself Blue Eyes?" he asked Frank indignantly. "Don't you know that's *my* nickname?" It might have been once, but from the day Frank's album was released, no one but Frank Sinatra would ever be recognized by that nickname again. Poor Jack tried to bill himself the Original Old Blue Eyes after that, but it never really worked.

I thought Frank Sinatra was invincible in those early days and impervious to any normal anxieties and concerns. But I was surprised to discover that he was nervous about the quality of his voice and feared it might have lost something in his absence from the microphone. He told Larry King during one interview, "For the first four or five seconds onstage, I tremble. I worry, Will it be there?" Strangely, he'd never been unduly concerned about what smoking or drinking might do to his voice and admitted to his doctor in all honesty that he often drank a bottle of Jack Daniel's a day. When the doctor realized he was serious, he said to him, "My God! How do you feel in the morning?"

Frank smiled and told him, "I don't know. I never get up till the afternoon."

Partly on the advice of his friend the opera singer Robert Merrill, Frank believed that as long as he warmed up by practicing his scales for an hour or so every day, his voice could take anything. I'd hear him singing *"Come talk a waaaaalk with me"* or *"Let us wander by the bay"* as he shaved or dressed. He was never one of those singers who wore a scarf or avoided winds. "I catch colds from people, not drafts," he'd complain. Twice in his career he lost his voice completely and was instructed not to speak for several days. He had to write on a chalkboard instead. That frightened him, but not as much as the surgery he had to remove some polyps from his throat. Fortunately, there were no adverse effects.

Having had only a few music lessons in his life, he worked out his own routine, which included swimming in the pool as part of his vocal training. Using a trick he'd learned years earlier so that he could hold key phrases for twenty-five seconds or more, he'd remain underwater for several minutes at a time to maintain his remarkable breath control. Not that I ever benefited from his breath control at home, because The Voice had never been one to sing around the house and hated to perform for friends at parties. He complained that was like "singing for his supper." Now he worried that his "reed was rusty" because it was out of practice, but he needn't have. The public and critical acclaim for Frank's new album only endorsed his decision to go back on the road. One review in the New York *Daily News* summed it up when it said, "We thought we were through writing love letters to Frank Sinatra, but here we go again..."

In January 1974, Frank began what would turn into a massive comeback tour of the United States, Europe, the Far East, and Australia. His first concert was at Caesars Palace in Las Vegas, where the marquee read, HAIL SINATRA. THE NOBLEST ROMAN HAS RETURNED. As usual, Frank walked onstage without any fanfare or introduction. "If they don't know who I am by now," he'd say, "then they shouldn't be here." In what developed later that year into a series of sellout concerts that would include shows with Ella Fitzgerald and Count Basie in Vegas and then on Broadway, Frank was truly back where he belonged.

His show at Caesars Palace was another milestone event, and a lot of our friends flew in just to be in the audience. Although I'd been back to Vegas a few times with Zeppo, it still felt strange for me to be in Sin City again almost two decades after my stint at the Riviera. I realized how far I'd come from the days when I'd wandered through the lobby of the Flamingo Hotel modeling pantsuits and cocktail dresses. This time, the models homed in on me as I sat having lunch or chatting with a friend. And as Vegas came alive at night, the showgirl Barbara Blakeley found herself with the highest roller of them all, strolling through casinos and nightclubs on the arm of Frank Sinatra. I couldn't help but notice the latter-day Marshas, Idas, and Pennys ogling our every step across the pit. At the few shows I went to with Frank, I watched the chorus girls dancing their poor feet off, remembering those days so well. I applauded extra hard for the showgirls doing their balancing act with ever more elaborate headdresses.

Later that summer, we flew to Australia for the next leg of Frank's tour. Our trip coincided with the threatened impeachment of President Nixon over the Watergate scandal, and Frank was deeply concerned for his friend. We were hardly in Australia a day or two when we had a run-in with the press. Frank didn't like their constant demands for interviews or the tone of some of the things they wrote about us (although he kept anything like that from me). After getting trapped in the middle of a pack of pushy reporters all asking him questions and then hearing of a female journalist masquerading as me to try to get him alone, he was in fighting spirit. On one of his first appearances onstage, he laid into the press, calling them "bums, parasites, fags, and buck-and-a-half hookers." I sat in the audience that night and thought, Oh, boy! Not surprisingly, perhaps, the Australian Journalists Association not only objected to what he'd said but claimed Frank had "insulted the nation." One of the headlines read, OL BIG MOUTH IS BACK, and the press enlisted the support of the transportation, waiters', and stagehands' unions so that the next leg of Frank's tour had to be canceled. Unable to perform, Frank made his way to Melbourne Airport and found the city's press waiting on the tarmac for an apology. Well, good luck with that, I thought. Needless to say, we left them flapping in our exhaust fumes.

By the time we arrived in Sydney, the strike action had gone national. People protested outside the hotel with placards, although a lot of them were on Frank's side. The unions refused to refuel Frank's plane and said he would get home only if he could "walk on water." They wouldn't even provide room service at our five-star hotel unless Frank issued an apology. Jilly, of course, made sure we had everything we needed. What the press didn't realize was that Frank Sinatra never apologized to anybody. Ever. Period. Not even to me. One time years later when I was packing to leave him after a fight we'd had about something stupid, I told him I'd only stay if he said sorry. Under duress, he finally admitted, "I didn't mean to hurt you." It was a half-assed apology, but it was the only one I ever got. He always said, "There are two things I never do—yawn in front of the woman I love, and apologize." The latter was not in his psyche, for to apologize would be to admit that he might have been wrong.

Frank's lawyer Mickey Rudin spent several days trying to negotiate a way out of the deadlock. Mickey's adversary was Bob Hawke, the future Australian prime minister, who was working his way up politically in a labor union. Frank agreed to film a one-time television special as part of the deal, but the apology became the sticking point. While we stayed under siege in our hotel suite waiting for a solution, the international press picked up on the story, and news soon reached America. Henry Kissinger sent Frank a telegram asking, DO YOU NEED ME TO SEND THE NAVY?

One afternoon, Mickey came hurrying into our suite and said, "Pack up, everyone, quick! We're leaving." He and Mr. Hawke had finally come up with wording that seemed to satisfy everyone, although it was not a direct apology. Mickey told us the building was virtually surrounded and there was no way the press would let us through. So, clutching my jewelry case, I was bundled out of a fire exit with Frank and the rest of our crew, across a roof, down a fire escape, and into an alley. The media were waiting at the front of the hotel with TV cameras and lights, expecting Frank to emerge any minute to read his statement, but he never did. Poor Mickey went down in his place and took hell from them. When they demanded to speak to Frank, he told them, "I'm sorry, but Mr. Sinatra has left the building." They almost lynched him. We sped to the airport with furious reporters in hot pursuit, and when we got to the plane, Frank instructed his pilot to taxi down the runway and take off despite all the control tower's instructions to "abort! Abort!"

The story of us being "under siege" in Australia ran and ran. As in Chinese whispers, the details were enlarged upon and exaggerated until few knew the real truth. Even comedians made mileage out of it. Bob Hope said on TV that the Australians finally let Frank out of the country right after the boss of the union woke up to find a kangaroo head on the next pillow. Frank swore he'd never set foot on Australian soil again, but we did go back years later for a hugely successful tour when the dramas of 1974 had been long forgotten. Thirty years later, someone made a movie about our experience called *The Night We Called It a Day*, in which Melanie Griffith played me and Dennis Hopper played Frank. I was amazed that what had seemed to be such a minor episode in our lives was deemed worthy of the Hollywood treatment.

After a brief respite in Palm Springs to rest, Frank and I set off again. During that first year we crisscrossed America, completed a five-nation tour of Europe, and traveled to the Far East. I loved every minute of it. Each day was a new adventure, yet another experience to be logged in the memory banks.

I woke up with Frank in places like Paris, London, Vienna, Tokyo, or Munich and had to pinch myself each time I looked across to see his tousled head on the pillow next to mine. Throwing open the window of whichever suite in whichever town we happened to be in, I'd marvel at the amazing views from each new rooftop. From the moment he woke up to the minute he closed his eyes, Frank liked to be busy and surrounded by people. Depending on where we were and who was around, we'd dine with friends of Frank's like Ingrid Bergman or Cary Grant, Lauren Bacall or Sophia Loren. It wasn't all Hollywood glitz, though; I might equally find myself eating linguine with some obscure musician or comic Frank had worked with years before but never lost contact with.

We were having the time of our lives, and Frank was clearly as happy as I was, especially once he was onstage. His shows were sellouts, and I knew he was relieved to be back in the spotlight soaking up the applause. Although I'd seen him perform before, I think on that comeback tour he really came into his own, commanding the stage with a maturity and presence I'd never known anyone else to possess. It had always astounded me that when he walked into a room he'd create a kind of shock wave, like a surge of electricity around him that demanded absolute silence. He sparked the same reaction in a theater. Sitting in the front row of a concert, I could feel people's hearts pounding all around me. He'd receive a standing ovation just for walking out onstage. There was a palpable, physical sensation before Frank even sang a note. Seeing him up there was an almost religious experience for his fans. I don't think there's anybody alive who could still get a reaction like that.

Frank not only wanted me to be at every concert but insisted that I sit up front so that he could see me and sing to me. He'd almost always dedicate at least one number to me, often "My Funny Valentine," and would point me out to the audience. "Take a bow, sweetheart," he'd instruct. Then when I stood up, he'd say something like "Ladies and gentlemen, this is my roommate." With Frank, a compliment was half a put-down and half-flattering but always said with love.

He handpicked all his songs and worked closely with his musical director, arranger, and the orchestra. As an avid reader, writer, and admirer of novelists and poets, he favored tunes with the best lyrics, which he felt held the attention of both him and his fans. He especially liked a song called "Something," which George

Harrison had written a couple of years earlier for the Beatles. Frank would slow it right down and said it was the most beautiful number because it was a love song that never actually said "I love you." He liked to sing sad or romantic ballads, but he also loved jazz and working with people like Louis Armstrong, who was great fun to be with but who I thought was a little too "on" all the time. Frank especially loved anything by Cole Porter or Irving Berlin, and a favorite was "Here's That Rainy Day" by Jimmy Van Heusen. Sammy Cahn and Jimmy wrote a lot of Frank's music, and they worked really well together because they understood how he'd make each song his own. Every time he sang a number anew, Frank would change it in some small way with that perfect enunciation of his. Timing was everything, and his was strictly original. He had a gift for it, along with that unique texture to his voice, which could be a powerhouse or soft and sexy when needed. Either way, that voice was God-given; there is no question about it.

At the end of each number, Frank would almost always credit the songwriter and those responsible for the orchestration, paying tribute to people like Rodgers and Hart, Don Costa, George Gershwin, or the writers of newer tunes like Joe Raposo and Jim Croce. "Isn't that a pretty ballad?" he'd ask his audience with almost childlike delight, or "Don't you think that's the most *maaarvelous* love song?" Always happy to share the credit for a song, he'd speak glowingly of Cole Porter being "in his shining hour" or Nelson Riddle "at his peak."

Songs like "Strangers in the Night" or "My Way," which he'd been asked to sing over and over again since the 1960s, did absolutely nothing for him. He always said the words were not subtle enough, too "on the nose." Knowing that he'd still have to sing them at every concert, he'd try to lighten the experience by joking with the audience that those tunes had kept him in pizza for years. He'd play with the words or add a phrase every now and then like Dean did with his "*bourbon* (instead of *pennies*) *from heaven*" or *"when you're drinking, you get stinking"* (instead of *"when you're smil-ing"*). In "The Lady Is a Tramp," Frank would sing *"She's broke, and it's oke,"* or add things like *"She likes the cool, fine, koo-koo wind in her hair."* Anything for a laugh.

Before Frank went onstage each night he'd tell me what his finale would be (in the early days it was almost always Paul Anka's "My Way"), and as soon as he finished the penultimate number (often a torch song like "One for My Baby") and I heard the open-ing bars of "My Way," I'd reluctantly get up from my front-row seat. With the steadying arm of a security man to lead me away in the darkness as unobtrusively as possible, I'd hurry through the labyrinth of backstage passageways and into a limo waiting at the stage door, its engine running. At the end of each performance, Frank would wait for a cue from the wings that I was ready, then tell his audience something like "Sleep warm. May you live to be a hundred years old, and may the last voice you hear be mine." Sometimes he'd say it in Italian before taking his final bow. He'd select a single rose from among the many flowers thrown onto the stage, and then he'd walk off with it. He'd be out the back door and sitting next to me in the limo, glowing with heat and excitement, before his fans had even stopped applauding.

"Here, beautiful," he'd say, above the sirens of the police mo-torcycle outriders howling as we set off. Presenting the rose to me with a kiss, he'd smile and add almost shyly, "This is for you." There was rarely any sitting around after the show like some per-formers do, swathed in warm towels. If ever there was a lineup of visitors outside his dressing room door, that would be before a show, not after. Once a show was over, the night was just begin-ning, and Frank needed to be away from the theater. He wanted companionship and chatter, his drinking buddies and me.

As the limo sped us away, he'd lean back against the leather seat in his stage tuxedo and smile. He'd be in a buoyant, elec-trically charged mood, a post-show high that would take him hours to come down from as he quietly relived every note of the performance he'd just given. As he always said, when people put their hard-earned dollars down to see him, he owed it to them to be the best he could be and give nothing short of a top-notch performance every night. That's why he wore black tie. Even after all those years of performing, the roar of the audience still moved and thrilled him, as did the sight of young people in the crowd. As he slowly unwound, he'd ask me, "Did you feel that love in the house tonight? They were so warm. I can't believe I'm still getting away with it after all these years in the business. And singing to kids too—teenagers and couples in their twenties!"

Our motorcade would whisk us back to the airport to fly someplace in our twelve-seater Gulfstream, complete with bar and kitchen, fully equipped for a party. If we were staying in town, we might go back to our hotel suite. More likely than not, though, we'd head to an out-of-the-way Italian restaurant where most of the staff wouldn't even know who was coming to dinner that night. The man paying the bill (booked under a pseudonym) would surprise the busboys by sneaking in through the kitchens to meet his twenty or so guests and heading straight to a private room or a quiet corner. Frank loved those nights best of all, I think, and the anticipation of a noisy Italian supper always lifted his spirits.

Even after the party was over and we were settled into bed together, Frank and I would usually talk into the wee small hours of the morning. There was always so much to discuss about our day—the traveling, the show, the crowd, the dinner, and the company of good friends. As the sun came up and we finally succumbed to tiredness, he would never fail to say those three little words. The last thing I heard each night before I drifted off to a deep and blissful sleep was always "I love you."

EIGHT

Celebrating a new addition to our household.

The Tender Trap

Frank was, without doubt, the most romantic man I had ever met. Not only did he make a point of telling me how much he cared for me every day but he'd leave little notes and cards around the place for me to find.

They might have been secreted inside my purse, slipped under my pillow, or stuck to the refrigerator door or a bathroom mirror. He'd draw a smiley face wearing a bow tie, and then beneath it he'd write something thing like *"Good morning, pretty—I love you, F."* *"Sweetheart!! I love you so much—I may quit drinking! Nah! But I do adore you,"* or *"To my Girl, I love you. What's-his-name."* He'd often sign himself Charlie Neat because it was the perfect moniker. Charlie was a name he used whenever he wanted to be incognito on the telephone, at a hotel or venue, and he was obsessively neat. I have kept every one of the notes he wrote me, and I still have them, pasted into a scrapbook.

Even in the middle of a world tour with its punishing rehearsal and performance schedules, Frank always took time out to surprise me with dinner plans, unexpected excursions, or trips to our favorite stores. He claimed I had a "black belt" in shopping, but then who wouldn't when repeatedly told, "Get what you want, baby—the sky's the limit." Even though I could buy myself whatever I wanted, he continued to shower me with gifts. Knowing how fond I am of jewelry, he'd pick me out something like a set of "poils" from Japan and present them to me, often in the most unlikely way.

One night we were preparing to go out for a gala dinner in Monte Carlo, and I was having my hair done in our suite. Not yet dressed, I was wearing a smock while a hairdresser tended to me at my dressing table. Frank strolled in wearing his tux and asked, "What are you wearing tonight, sweetheart?"

"That oyster silk gown you like," I replied, smiling at his reflection in the glass.

"What jewelry?"

"Oh, I don't know. I might wear my ruby and diamond choker, but I haven't decided."

He reached into the pocket of his dinner jacket and pulled out the most incredible necklace I had ever seen in my life. There was no velvet box, no fancy wrapping, just a necklace dripping with diamonds and emeralds, ending in a final drop of a rock the size of a quail's egg. "Try this," he said, casually slipping it into the pocket of my smock. "It was made for Madame Cartier."

My hairdresser gasped.

Lifting it out and staring at it more closely, I held my breath. This was *the* Cartier Necklace, the talk of Monte Carlo. It had been the centerpiece of the Boutique Cartier window next door to the casino. Only the previous day I'd stopped and stared at it in awe with some of my girlfriends. Speechless, I draped it around my neck as Frank fixed the clasp. I could feel the weight of it on my skin, and the coolness of the stones. I'd always loved emeralds, and these were the finest I'd ever seen, not that I could see them very clearly because my eyes misted over with tears of gratitude and love.

"I don't know what to say!" I finally whispered.

He kissed the nape of my neck. "Then say nothing. Just turn a few heads tonight."

As I arrived at a gala on Frank's arm that night wearing the Cartier Necklace, Caroline Tose (the wife of Leonard, who owned the Philadelphia Eagles) came rushing up to me and, staring at the necklace, asked, "Is *that* what I think it is?" When I nodded, she cried, "Holy shit!" From then on, that piece of jewelry was known to us as the Holy Shit Necklace.

Frank had such a great eye for a good stone, and he really appreciated fine jewelry. I don't know where he picked up that skill, but he sure perfected it with practice. The trouble was he'd buy me so much jewelry, especially when we were traveling, that I began to worry about where to keep it. In the early days, I'd wear it all at once. I might have ten necklaces hidden under my dress because I was scared to leave them at the hotel. That became rather ridiculous after a while, so I'd put what I wasn't wearing into the hotel safe whenever we went out, but that meant going back to the safe each night just to undress and hand what I was wearing back into safekeeping. That soon irritated Frank, so I had the new pieces he bought me securely shipped home and traveled with paste copies instead.

Frank's generosity extended far beyond me and others in his inner circle. He was often kindest of all to strangers. I'd wander into a room and hear him on the phone to his accountant, Sonny Golden, asking him to check out some tragic story he'd just read in the newspaper about a mother who couldn't pay her medical bills. "Make sure she's okay and has everything she needs," he'd say. "And don't tell her who sent the check." He'd be chatting with a barman in a hotel late at night and discover that the kid longed to take up golf. The next day, a brand-new set of clubs would be delivered. If Frank received nice letters from fans, they'd be invited backstage to his dressing room before watching his show from the best seats.

He'd track down musicians he'd worked with decades earlier and throw surprise dinners in their honor. He'd have Dorothy Uhlemann, his personal assistant, arrange for a terminally ill fan to be taken to his concert in a limo because she'd written and told him that she hoped to see him perform before she died. He'd fly in Frank Garrick, the man who'd given him his first job at a newspaper, for a ringside seat. He'd anonymously replace the Christmas presents a family had lost in a fire after he'd watched their story on the TV news. Or he'd sit with the newspaper circling the names of strangers down on their luck and have Dorothy send them five hundred dollars from "a well-wisher."

When an actor friend sent him a note asking for his help to "bail him out" of a Beverly Hills hotel, Frank sent the cash for the bill—attached to a parachute. When the actor George Raft had a tax bill he couldn't pay, Frank gave him a signed check but didn't fill in the amount. "Use what you need," he said. He'd offer to do a series of concerts in some ailing nightclub he used to know just to make enough money for the owner to retire or pay a medical bill. He'd invite the kids of old friends backstage if he played a university town and give them a pep talk about working hard. He paid off the mortgages, loans, and debts of just about anyone who asked him.

My bighearted man was a real gentleman, always so proper and correct—except perhaps when he got into fights. There was definitely a Jekyll and Hyde aspect to Frank's character, and he was undoubtedly a complicated individual. He once claimed to be a manic-depressive, but I don't believe he was. A depressive is down a great deal of the time, but Frank was always up, up, up.

Restless and impatient, he wanted laughs and entertainment, all the time. He'd become an insomniac after years of working late, but I also think he just didn't want to miss anything. Nor did he like the nights, or at least the blackness of night. I asked him several times what it was about nighttime that he feared, but he'd just reply, "I don't like it," as if that explained everything. He didn't sleepwalk or suffer from nightmares; he just preferred to go to sleep after daylight. When he had finally drunk enough and was ready for bed, he'd sleep like a baby for six or seven hours straight. He'd wake up refreshed and hungry for a brunch of bacon, eggs, and toast—which he ate almost every day of his life. Different performers have different ways of getting themselves keyed up for a show. Some people play sports, others go for a run. Some sit quietly and psych themselves mentally, others have sex. Frank's way was to shout at everyone behind the scenes, which is why I rarely went backstage before a show. His behavior stemmed from a combination of nerves and the need to get up steam to perform, but it wasn't pretty to be around.

Frank would snap at anyone for the slightest misdemeanor, imagined or real. He'd yell at Hank Catanneo, his concert production manager and a dear friend, and he'd scream at his son Frank Jr., who worked as his conductor for years (boy, what he went through). Frank needed to get himself so angry, so up, that when he strutted out onstage like a boxer entering the ring, he was in total command of his audience and ready to kill. It worked every time.

Those around him soon came to understand that it was part of their job to take some heat. They knew what to expect and they prayed they wouldn't be in the firing line, but if they were they accepted it with the graciousness of devoted employees who knew Frank didn't mean anything by it and would make it up to them later. When Bobby was hired as his road manager after leaving UCLA, I was worried that he'd get yelled at too, but Frank never did turn on my son—a measure of his great fondness for him, I think, although Bobby would say that his kinship to me gave him "a pass." In any event, Bobby wouldn't have minded because he couldn't believe his luck. He learned so much on tour, including how to run a show and negotiate contracts, experiences that set him on his eventual path as an entertainment lawyer. Not only that but Frank made sure to pay him a great deal of attention. He became a terrific father to Bobby. Frank always treated Bobby as if he was his own son, and I am deeply grateful.

Bobby also got to see firsthand what Sinatra-mania was all about because the fans went wild, especially in Europe. Everywhere we went, it seemed, women screamed and fainted and tried to get as close as they could. In Paris, they stormed the stage, and musicians dove for cover under their chairs as the player of the big bass waved it around to fend off hysterical women. In Amsterdam, where Frank performed at the opera house, the concert was so oversold that they had to set up extra chairs on the balcony and at the front of the stage. Even more fans stood or sat out in the streets and balconies near the theater playing Frank Sinatra music on their record players. The entire district was filled with the sound of Frank's voice as we arrived. It was incredible.

Once the show was over, we hurried into our limo and set off with a police escort, but our vehicles were quickly swamped by fans who pressed forward until they were hammering on the roof and doors. Then they began chanting Frank's name—"Frankie! Frankie! Frankie!"—and rocking the car. At one point, we were rocked so violently that our faces were almost level with the street. I was really frightened and thought, Oh, my God! This is going to be it! Somehow, Jilly managed to get us out of there by yelling at the police to push back the people so our car could move forward. It was a close call.

Before Bobby came on the road with us, he worked for the Dinah Shore television show and for our friend the producer George Schlatter on *Laugh-In*. George, who'd known Frank since the fifties, had been behind some of the most successful comedy and musical shows ever made. Frank either called him Crazy or pronounced his name Spanish-style as "Horhay." Bobby loved working with him, especially as he nurtured the idea of being a director one day (like his father). He was even more thrilled to meet one of his heroes, the actor-director Orson Welles, who was a guest on *The Dinah Shore Show*. Orson was a fabulous character and a big drinker. Frank called him the Big Man, and they had some riotous times together.

One day, Frank called Bobby up and said, "Why don't you walk into Horhay's office tomorrow and ask him if he'd like to have me on *Laugh-In*?" That was a huge gift to Bobby, because George had been asking Frank for years and he'd always refused. So Bobby went to see George and found him sitting in a big chair behind his desk. When he asked, "How'd you like Frank to be on your show?" George was so astonished he leaned back in his chair and tipped right over onto the floor.

Frank's one condition for appearing on *Laugh-In* to do a number of routines and utter the famous catchphrase "Sock it to me!" was that George arrange for him to pour gunk onto the head of the Hollywood gossip columnist Rona Barrett, whom Frank called Rona-Rat. In the end George hired a Rona Barrett look-alike to sit there gamely while Frank poured green paint all over her hair. Frank had a ball recording that show; larking around with the young Robin Williams or pretending to be a newscaster, he was in his element. He even fixed it for Jilly to make a cameo appearance on the Joke Wall.

George Schlatter always said Frank had a cast-iron stomach and liver, and he was probably right. Ever since I'd first met him, I'd realized that Frank expected his cohorts to stay up with him all night and keep him and Mr. Daniels company. George was one of the "lucky" ones, taken along for the ride. When Frank and George were together, they were like children playing and causing mayhem. Eventually, though, Frank's late nights began to be dreaded even by George. Once, George told the barman to fill up a bottle of vodka with water so that he wouldn't get too drunk. When Frank found out, he was furious and made sure that never happened again. Another time we were in Gstaad, Switzerland, visiting Roger Moore and his wife, Luisa, and staying in an apartment above George and his wife, Jolene. No matter how late we got back from a restaurant or club, Frank wanted to party. If George folded and went to bed, Frank would pound on the floor of our apartment to wake him up or telephone his room and yell, "Get up here, Crazy!" One night George crawled out of the elevator in his pajamas wearing a hard hat and waving a flag.

Our friends often formed a private pact to stay up with him in shifts over several days, so that no one person had to carouse with him night after night in what he called the American Olympic Drinking Team. Frank was eagle-eyed at spotting anyone trying to make a subtle escape and had all sorts of tricks up his sleeve for those who slipped off to bed at what he considered a premature hour. One night in Florida in the middle of a tour, Tom Dreesen went to his hotel bedroom, hoping for an early night. Not long after he'd climbed into bed, there was a pounding on his door. It was a six-foot-two bellman who said, "Mr. Sinatra would like you to join him at the bar." Tom attempted to bribe the messenger with a twenty-dollar bill to tell Frank he couldn't be found. The bellman replied, "Mr. Sinatra gave me a hundred dollars to tell you he wants you to come down to the bar." Tom groaned and said, "Couldn't you just tell him no one answered the door?" To which the bellman replied, "Mr. Sinatra said you'd resist and that if I had to drag you down to the bar, he'd give me an extra hundred." Tom and Frank stayed up until dawn. There was no beating him.

Fortunately I had a healthy constitution and could match Frank drink for drink and still know what I was doing by the time I went to bed. I also learned from his trick of never emptying his glass. Frank always said he hated women who couldn't hold their drink, who wore too much makeup or heavy perfume. He claimed to be allergic to perfume, and the only one he could stomach was Fracas, a scent by the Parisian perfumier Robert Piguet. Frank also disliked women who smoked—he thought smoking was "unfeminine." Well, I passed on the first three counts, but I did smoke, which was something he made me give up fairly early on.

Unlike Frank, who'd have a couple of drags on a cigarette and then throw it away, I used to smoke mine to the end. When he asked me to give it up, I said, "Well then, why don't you quit too?" He not only chain-smoked cigarettes but enjoyed cigars and the occasional pipe—a throwback to his admiration for Bing Crosby, I always thought. Frank told me flatly, "I can't quit, I don't want to quit, and I'm not going to quit, but you have to." It was a challenge for me, and when I was weaning myself off the cigarettes, I'd sit at the bar next to someone who smoked and say, "You light it and put it there and when I see him looking the other way I'll take a puff." If ever Frank caught me, he was quite rough on me. Eventually, I was hypnotized, and that worked.

"I've packed in smoking as you asked," I told him. "But the deal is that you can no longer smoke when I'm around and neither can anyone else. If you want to kill yourself, go ahead, but don't kill me." To my surprise, he agreed, and although he smoked un-filtered Camels to the day he died, he almost always stepped away from me to do so. He wouldn't even smoke in the car.

A friend of Frank's once said that one of the qualities that most endeared me to him was my stamina, although I think we killed a few people along the way. My son, Bobby, sure learned how to live life to the full under Frank's tutelage, and drinking and staying up all night were just part of it. In true Sinatra style, Bobby began dating some of the most eligible women on the circuit. I thoroughly approved of them all, especially those who understood the pressures of life in the spotlight in case Bobby ended up being Frank's stepson one day.

Not that Frank was offering anything like that yet. When we first started dating, the option of marrying him someday had been mentioned, but he'd never spoken about it since. I was beginning to think he might be allergic to the word *marriage*. What he was offering instead was excitement and laughter, the chance to be his lover and companion, and the joys of being treated like a goddess. He was one of the most famous men in the world, after all. Everyone, from world presidents to the Pope, had a favorite Sinatra song. Women adored Frank because he was such a romantic. Despite my secret hopes for something more permanent eventually, I knew that just to be at his side made me the luckiest girl alive.

As a respite between legs of the tour, we'd slip back to Palm Springs for a few days to unpack and catch our breath. I think it was then that I first realized Frank's mother, Dolly, was as unhappy about our relationship as Zeppo's friends and family seemed to be. She rarely visited the Compound if I was there and barely acknowledged me if we saw her elsewhere.

I heard through the grapevine that she'd asked Frank, "Aren't there enough whores around? Why do you have to work on your best friend's wife?" Not that I should have been surprised. Dolly was a feisty little dame who had a hold over Frank like no one else. They had such a love-hate relationship, and I think she was probably the only person Frank was afraid of his whole life. Having almost died giving birth to her thirteen-and-a-half-pound son, an event that left her unable to bear any more children, Dolly had invested all her emotions in her only child and encouraged him from the start. Trouble was, she also acted like she owned him and wouldn't stop bossing him around, as well as bad-mouthing everyone from me to his children and his ex-wives. A Catholic who became more devout the older she got, she despaired of his three failed marriages and wanted Frank to find a "good, Catholic" girl and settle down. Sadly, I didn't fall into either category.

In spite of Dolly's open hostility to me, though, I liked her very much. She was fun, with a terrific sense of humor; I could certainly see where Frank got his from. Standing less than five feet tall, she swore like a trooper and had a filthy nickname for everyone, but she cooked like an angel. She liked nothing more than to have Frank and his Italian American friends, like Jilly, Joe Tomatoes, and Gerry the Crusher, around dipping bread into her "gravy." She'd always bawl them out about it, but she didn't mind. Nor did she seem to mind "Uncle Vincent" living with her until the day he died. He was a sweet man, some distant relative or old family friend who'd lived under the same roof with her and Marty forever, although no one could remember why. As bighearted as her son, Dolly took him in, fed and cared for him selflessly. The more I got to know Dolly, the more I admired her. She was a survivor, as I was. I hoped that, as time went on and she realized that Frank and I were serious about each other, she'd change her mind about me.

It wasn't just Dolly who was putting pressure on us in those early days, although her feelings toward me certainly placed Frank in a difficult position. Our bigger challenge, however, was probably overfamiliarity with each other. As the months passed and we continued with his grueling touring schedule, Frank and I were thrown together twenty-four hours a day, seven days a week, in hotel suites, limousines, theaters, trains, and planes. Most of the time I can honestly say the experience was nothing short of wonderful; it was a real thrill, and I felt privileged and honored to have such a ringside seat. But with Frank's constant need to be entertained after he'd entertained, staying up late night after night, drinking with his buddies on top of the traveling, the rehearsals, and the shows, the days were long and the nights even longer, and one or the other of us wasn't always at our best. I'd defy any couple not to fight every now and then under those circumstances.

Although Frank never stopped being the romantic, he could be difficult with those around him—especially if he'd had too much to drink or felt a show hadn't been perfect. He was never more keyed up than in the hours following a performance, when he needed to burn off some of that incredible energy he'd built up. Sometimes that need manifested itself in a tantrum, but more often than not it just required him to drink with his buddies. We were at Caesars Palace in Vegas one night when I came back to our suite after a dinner out with friends and found Frank much the worse for wear. Dean was sitting at the bar mummified. Frank was lying on the floor. Others were slumped all around. I walked in, took one look at all of them, turned around, and walked out. The next day Frank asked me, "What happened to you last night?

"I went to bed," I told him. "I didn't want to watch my drunken man rolling around on the floor with his drunken bum friends." He was visibly taken aback.

Frank never went off on me like he did with some people, and he rarely yelled at me because I was one of the few who'd yell back. Realizing that, his friends began to call on me if he was in one of his moods because they knew I was their best bet at calming him down. One night at the Waldorf in New York, I was in the old Cole Porter Suite in the Towers and Frank was down in the bar with a bunch of friends when Jilly called me at around four in the morning. "Will you please come down here, Barbara?" he whispered into the telephone. "Frank's going to tear the place up if you don't." If Jilly couldn't calm him, then I knew we were in trouble.

Recalling Jimmy Van Heusen's advice that if Frank was drunk it was best to disappear, I reluctantly threw on a robe and took the elevator. I could hear Frank being belligerent even before I entered the bar. I don't know what had set him off—maybe nothing. It was usually the booze talking anyway, and I'd learned to bounce with it. When I walked in, Frank looked up, bleary-eyed, and said, "What are *you* doing down here?"

"I came to get you."

He looked around at his buddies and said, "Well, maybe I'm not ready to be got yet."

"Well, maybe you are," I replied, staring him down.

There was an awkward silence as he reached for his glass and took another slug. I shrugged my shoulders and walked back

toward the door. Turning, I said, "Frank, I'm going to take the elevator now, and I'm going back to bed. I'd like it very much if you
came with me."

He looked right back at me and then downed the last of his
drink. "Well then, why didn't you say?" He stood up and followed
me out like the puppy that he really was.

There were times, of course, when he couldn't be calmed;
he just didn't want to be. I sometimes think he acted out when
he was like that. He liked to push people's buttons and test their
boundaries. He'd always been easily bored, and his fiery personality demanded drama and performance. There was no doubt about
it, Frank Sinatra was an event, and it wasn't always the easiest of
tasks to talk him down off the ledge, but usually beneath even his
most frightening temper there was an element of humor. Either
way, coming from a family who could barely muster a bit of sim-
mering discontent, I found his Italian passion rather stimulating,
and believe me—it had its plus sides.

Another night when he'd been sitting up late with the boys,
drinking and ranting at something, I'd locked myself in my bedroom because I didn't want to be disturbed. Sure enough, around
five in the morning Frank started beating on the door. "Who is
it?" I called warily from beneath my sheets.

"Your Italian lover," he replied. How could I not let him in
after that?

My role in those early days and for all our years together was
to keep everything running so that Frank could go onstage
and do what he had to do. He could be a challenge, all right, but
it was heaven for me to be with him even when he acted out. I was
his companion, consultant, nurse, psychiatrist, and lover. The only
thing I wasn't yet was his wife.

I won't deny that it was a test of our relationship and of my
stamina, but I felt up to it even when I had concerns closer to

home. Zeppo was making our divorce negotiations difficult, which made me increasingly anxious about my future. I had little or no earning potential anymore. I owned nothing other than the house Frank had gifted me and a few nice pieces of jewelry. I worried that I had no long-term security for me or for Bobby, something I seemed to have been fretting about my whole life.

One day I was out having lunch at the Bistro in Beverly Hills with Sidney Korshak, the husband of my friend Bee, when Zeppo's attorney Greg Bautzer leaned across from an adjacent table. "Barbara," he told me, "the only thing you're going to get from Zeppo is the clap." From the expression on Sidney's face, I thought Greg was unlikely to survive the afternoon. Sidney was a powerful attorney and a formidable ally, a close friend of Frank's. Nothing moved in the world of high finance without Sidney knowing about it, and he offered me his support from then on.

He told me, "Barbara, you have no worries. Your problems are my problems. If you need my advice about anything, you call me." So I did. I called him from wherever I was with Frank—Chicago, New York, or Paris—telling him when I'd received another letter from Zeppo's attorney threatening this or that. Each time Sidney would tell me, "Leave it to me, Barbara. This is nothing for you to worry about. This is my problem now."

When the divorce was eventually settled, Zeppo agreed to pay me a fifteen-hundred-dollar monthly allowance for ten years and let me keep the 1969 Jaguar he'd given me four years earlier. Frank, not to be outdone, immediately upgraded it to the latest model. I was very grateful to Sidney for his help in the negotiations, but as we'd spoken on the telephone several times a week for almost a year, I missed talking to him. One day soon after the settlement was completed, I tracked him down to a boardroom in New York and persuaded the secretary to put me through. "Sidney!" I said long-distance. "You have another problem!"

"What now?" he replied, hoping that the legal drama was over.

"I just tried to get an appointment at the beauty shop and they say they're fully booked. Can you help?"

There was a long pause, and then *slam*, the phone went down.

Even though my divorce was finalized and I was a woman of independent means, thanks in the end to Zeppo's unexpected generosity, I was still worried about where Frank and I were heading.

The luster had undoubtedly gone from our relationship. We would fight and break up every now and then, and it wasn't always about him not being able to commit to me or being disrespectful in some way. It was about a lot of things—usually something and nothing—as most breakups are, but it was never about other women. I didn't own him; I had no claim on him to speak of, and I didn't even go there.

We were both independent, strong-willed people, after all. I hadn't survived two marriages and my time in Vegas with Joe Graydon, been a Vegas showgirl, and run my own school by being a wallflower. In any event, Frank liked strong women. That was what first attracted him to Ava, I think. And as with Ava, whenever he and I argued, it was sudden, noisy, and temporary. He never hit me, although he did once raise his hands during a fight and told me, "God, I want to punch you!"

"Okay," I replied, defiantly offering him my right cheek, "give it your best shot."

"What would you do if I did?" he challenged.

"I'd leave and you'd never see me again."

His hands dropped to his sides.

One thing Frank couldn't stand was rejection. We were at a dinner one night in Palm Desert and he did or said something that hurt me, so I got up from our table and went to call a taxi. Our friend Kenny Venturi appeared by my side (probably sent by Frank) and said, "I'll take you home." Kindly, he drove me to the house Frank had bought me. As soon as I got in I called up Dinah at her place at Trancas Beach and asked, "Do you need a roommate for tonight?"

"Why, yes, actually!" she replied, instantly appreciating that Frank and I must have had a fight. I wasn't home more than ten minutes before I'd packed an overnight bag and left for the beach. Which was just as well, because an hour or so later a drunken Frank and Jimmy Van Heusen drove over to my house and set off dozens of cherry bombs in my backyard in the hope of waking me up. They couldn't understand why they didn't get any response. Well, not from me anyway. Frank's mother was staying in a house nearby, and she responded all right. Throwing open the window, she yelled, "If you two motherfuckers don't stop all that noise, I'm calling the police!"

Frank tracked me down at Dinah's the next morning and called me up. "Why did you take off like that?" he asked, sounding like a petulant child.

"It's simple, Frank," I replied. "I knew we couldn't be speaking for a couple of days, and if that was going to happen, I decided I'd rather be at the beach." There was no answer to that.

Life was certainly never boring with Frank, and it kept me on my toes. Not that I wasn't used to a bit of drama. Bobby was once asked what it was like to be the son of Barbara Marx, and he replied, "Wherever my mother is, that's where the action is." Throughout my childhood in Bosworth, I'd looked at my parents' relationship and that of my friends' parents and decided there'd be nothing worse than being bored to death in the way they were. With the life I was leading, I was certainly in no danger of that.

As soon as Frank and I had let off steam, we'd limp back to each other's arms and only enjoy the making up all the more. We had such rapport. That's when Frank would be his most sweet and kind and loving. He'd say things like "If you want that mountain, Barbara, I'll get it for you. All you have to do is tell me what you want. If you want the moon, darling, it's yours." I'd never had any-body talk to me like that. It was amazing to hear, particularly after Zeppo.

As part of his next American tour, I asked Frank if we could find the time to visit Bosworth, Missouri, because I wanted to show him where I grew up. It had to have been more than thirty years since I'd been in my hometown. When we got there and drove around in Frank's limousine, I was astonished at how little the place had changed. Our journey across town took just a few minutes, and although the streets weren't dirt anymore, my grandparents' house looked exactly as it always had. Sadly, I couldn't locate our house—it must have been pulled down, or maybe it blew down in a cyclone. I shivered at my memories of the storm cellar. The Methodist church, school, and drugstore were just as I remembered them. The general store was still there and trading but wasn't called Blakeley's anymore, and the rail to tie the horses to had been replaced with a parking lot. I couldn't face stepping inside because I knew the mem-bers of the Spit 'N' Argue Club would be long dead and I doubted the potbellied stove still had pride of place. Frank didn't want to hang around much anyway. I was well aware of his loathing for long car journeys, so we cruised slowly past the sights I suspected I'd be seeing for the last time, then sped back toward the life I had made for myself beyond Bosworth's humble streets.

As another favor I asked Frank if he could arrange to do a show in Wichita, Kansas, because I had so many friends and fam-ily there who were desperate to see him perform. I must admit that this time I couldn't wait to go back to the town where I'd spent my teenage years to show them what the gangly country girl with the "Missour-a" twang had done with herself. I'd never lost touch with my school friend Winnie Markley, and when she heard that we were coming to town she and her husband, Jimmy Razook, threw us a party at their house. Needless to say, when we arrived there was a long lineup of people who wanted to shake hands with Frank. Everyone I'd ever known, it seemed, came out of the woodwork. He was very patient and met them all and posed for photographs with incredible grace.

Frank's show the following night was to be held in a huge sports auditorium, and fifty of my friends and relatives were all lined up in chairs right at the front of the old basketball court as Frank stepped out onto that stage. The show was a huge success. Best of all, Barbara Blakeley was officially on the map and no longer just the skinny kid with the hunched-over back.

A few weeks later Frank and I had another one of our increasingly frequent bust-ups; I can't even remember over what. I think he said something that hurt my feelings and I refused to go on with the schedule so I started packing (I always seemed to be packing in those days). It was all part of the game of cat and mouse that we played. The story about our latest split made the gossip columns, and my aunt Myrtle wrote to me from Wichita to thank me for the tickets to his show and to send me her condolences. *"I think I know why you broke up,"* she added wryly. *"He met your family!"*

The culmination of Frank's tour was a live concert billed as the Main Event at Madison Square Garden in New York with him performing in the round on a mock boxing ring without ropes. When he realized I was serious about leaving him this time, he begged me to stay on until that gig, which he was especially nervous about.

Even though he'd proved himself more than able, he was anxious about his voice. Not only would there be twenty thousand people, including celebrities like Robert Redford and Rex Harrison, in the auditorium but the show was to be broadcast around the world. I sat a couple of rows back from the raised square stage on which world championship boxing matches usually took place. Frank turned up less than an hour before the performance, walked on with hardly any rehearsal, and gave one of his most memorable performances. He needn't have worried. Even when his voice wavered a little, he was such a great communicator that he tuned in to his audience as he always did and allowed his phenomenal stage presence to overwhelm them. They were deliriously happy just to be breathing the same air. Despite fretting about our impending separation, Frank appeared happy too. He loved performing live, and New York was where it all started for him. Before he sang "The House I Live In," he spoke of his father, "God rest his soul," and how Marty had once told Frank that America was "a land of dreams and a dream land." I knew Frank meant it from the heart when he told that Garden crowd, "I have never felt so much love in one room my whole life." After announcing, "We'll now do the national anthem, but you needn't rise," he finished with "My Way."

The following day, I flew off to Palm Beach, Florida, for a break with some friends. I was still madly, crazily in love with Frank, but I knew I had to give us both a breather. Our separation this time was the longest and the most serious. For several months at the end of 1974 and beginning of 1975, we even dated other people, although I'm sure we each did it just to make the other one jealous. Frank stepped out with Jacqueline Onassis, who'd been a longtime friend from the Kennedy days and was by then working in publishing. He took her to dinner at "21" after a show in New York, which had all the papers speculating wildly, although all she really wanted was to persuade him to write his memoirs. I went out on a few dates with a dashing businessman named Gene Klein. I'm sure word got back to Frank. I flew to Europe with Bobby and Bee Korshak, and we explored Italy, France, and Spain, meeting up with Joan Collins and other friends. Frank, who continued performing in the States and Canada for much of that time, would track me down wherever I was and call me many nights to ask me when I was coming back, and to fly back and join him. I wasn't ready, so I stayed on in Europe even though I missed him terribly.

As soon as Frank felt he had suffered enough or was booked

to go on tour again and didn't want to go alone, his ardor intensified. Increasingly unable to say no to FS, I'd pack my bags all over again and board his plane for the next stage of his tour. We flew to Switzerland to begin with and then to England before traveling on to the Middle East. He was still bringing the house down across Europe in scenes that were reminiscent of his frenzied early years in the business. In London he joked that the Royal Albert Hall should be renamed the Francis Albert Hall. Ava Gardner, who'd moved to London by then because she thought the British had "more class," came to see him perform. I met her again backstage. She was very polite, and we got along fine, but I noticed that there was even more drinking going on this time.

Frank was as attentive as ever with Ava and had never stopped sending her gifts or paying her medical and other bills. He was similarly generous with his other ex-wives, Nancy and Mia, if ever they needed anything. He had plenty of money, and it was no skin off my nose. In fact, I secretly admired the way he took care of the women in his life even if they were no longer a part of it. Someone once asked me about his relationship with Ava in front of Frank, and I said, "Oh, that could never have worked!"

Frank looked up and asked, "Why?"

"Too much hurt," I said. That hit him hard, but after thinking about what I'd said, he admitted I was right.

After London we flew to Tehran. The Shah of Iran was still in power then, and his wife, the Empress Farah, had asked Frank to sing at a charity event. As we entered Iranian airspace, a squadron of military jets came to escort us into Tehran's airport, which felt so exotic. Farah was very beautiful, sweet, and gentle, the mother of four children. She had her own team of security men, who were all dark and handsome, at least six feet, four inches tall, and dressed in crisp white uniforms with gold braid and medals. They looked as if they'd walked off a film set. I was impressed. The Iranian people were delightfully warm and friendly, and we traveled around a little, buying Persian rugs and seeing some of the incredible scenery. When we left, Frank was presented with ten pounds of the finest gray caviar we had ever tasted. He expressed such delight in the quality of the prized sturgeon eggs that every year for years the Iranian foreign minister to the United States, Mr. Zahedi, would come to visit us loaded with cans of caviar. It was heaven.

Once we left Iranian airspace, the Israeli air force escorted our plane into Jerusalem. Frank was a great supporter of Israel, although he did much for many of the Arab countries too. He'd paid for a school and clinic to be built in Bethlehem and a Hebrew university outside Jerusalem and was eager to see how they were progressing. We also visited the Frank Sinatra Youth Center for Arab and Jewish Children, which he'd set up in Nazareth, and the Simon Wiesenthal Center, which he had supported. Needless to say, everywhere we went we were treated like royalty. We were invited to so many places, including the Knesset, where Frank spoke, in what turned out to be a fascinating trip.

On one of our final days in Jerusalem, we were taken to the famous Wailing Wall in the Old City. Standing on the flat, smooth stones that once formed King Solomon's Temple, I was told to write a prayer for someone I loved on a piece of paper and slip it between the cracks in the centuries-old Wall. Some friends of mine had claimed great success with the Wall in everything from matters of the heart to the sale of houses, so I took a pen and scribbled a private plea asking for continued happiness with Frank: *"And please, have him ask me to marry him,"* I added plaintively. As I folded my little piece of paper in two and stuffed it between the ancient limestone cracks, I mouthed a silent prayer.

NINE

The happiest day of my life, our wedding day in 1976.
COURTESY OF THE AUTHOR

Love and Marriage

By the spring of 1976, Frank and I had been to-gether for four years. We'd been flirting with each other even longer than that, yet he still seemed reluctant to offer me any commitment about our future together.

Neither of us was getting any younger, and Frank had a long history of losing interest after a few years. What if he met someone else? What would I do? And how would I ever find anyone who matched up to him? I was beginning to have sympathy with his first wife, Nancy, who'd never remarried since their divorce in 1951. When asked why not, she is said to have replied simply, "After Sinatra?"

Tired of waiting for Frank to "make an honest woman of me" as my mother would say, I told him during the middle of a series of concerts in Lake Tahoe that I could no longer live this way. I knew that if I left it up to him, we'd go on dating until one of us got bored or died. Although I was afraid of what he might say, I gave him an ultimatum—marry me or lose me.

"But I'm your rock!" he replied, clearly shaken.

I told him, "You're not a rock, and I can't go on like this.

I need the feeling of belonging, and I need to have someone belong to me."

He didn't respond, so, deeply wounded, I flew home. To keep occupied over the next few weeks, I threw myself into organizing a tennis tournament in aid of the Third World charity World Mercy at the Riviera Hotel in Vegas. Several celebrity friends agreed to take part, and with Bobby by my side for moral support, I decided to make the most of our time on the Strip. I tried my best to put on a cheerful façade—gambling, drinking, and staying out late—but inside my heart was secretly breaking. Was this it? Was my time with Frank finally over? The thought made me sick to my stomach.

Frank flew to Chicago to drown his sorrows with an old friend, the property developer Jack McHugh. They spent a great deal of time drunkenly swearing that they would never remarry. He'd call me every now and then, but our conversations were usually brief. I knew that I couldn't reconsider unless he was prepared to commit. As the tennis tournament progressed and the distance between us seemed to grow, I began to think that would never happen.

One day in May 1976, I was playing blackjack in the Riviera casino immediately after a tennis match when I was paged for a telephone call. "Barbara Marx," a messenger called, "paging Mrs. Barbara Marx." Making my way to the pit in my tennis whites, shoes, and pleated skirt, I picked up the phone to hear Frank's voice asking, "What are you doing?"

"Answering your telephone call."

"Are you in the pit?"

"Yes."

"I don't want to talk to you in the pit, so will you please go to your suite? I'll call you there in five minutes."

"All right," I said, "but I'm just finishing up something here, so you'll have to give me at least thirty minutes."

I did what I had to do, and by the time I reached my suite the telephone was ringing off the hook. "This is ridiculous, Barbara!"

Frank cried when I picked it up. I said nothing and waited. There was a pause before he added, "Come to Chicago."

I realized that I'd won some sort of victory, but he still wasn't offering me anything concrete. "All right," I said cautiously, "I think I can manage that in a day or two, after the tournament."

"No!" he snapped. "Come now."

"But, Frank," I protested, "the finals are tomorrow and I'm presenting the trophy."

"Have someone else do it. I've had your things packed, and there's a station wagon waiting for you downstairs. I've paid off your marker at the casino, and my plane's waiting on the runway." Taking the telephone across the room with me, I checked my closet, and sure enough, all my clothes were gone. Just as in the South of France four years earlier, he'd had someone sneak into my room. It looked as if I didn't have a choice. No more bets, please.

Excited and a little scared about what awaited me in Chicago, I hurried to Bobby's room, where I found him taking a nap. Shaking him awake, I said, "I'm flying to Chicago tonight, and I need you to present the trophy for me tomorrow. Can you do that?"

Yawning and scratching his head, my son replied, "Sure." Bless him, he didn't ask a single question. As I went to leave the room, he called out, "Happy Mother's Day." In all the excitement, I had completely forgotten the date.

Still wearing my tennis clothes, I went down to the hotel lobby and found one of Frank's drivers waiting for me. He took me to the airport, where a private plane flew me to Chicago. I was the sole passenger, and as I sipped a cocktail and watched the sky turn Sinatra orange over the clouds, I wondered what the dawn would bring.

Frank was staying at the Ambassador East, which was the nicest hotel in Chicago at the time. Feeling chilly and self-conscious in my short pleated skirt and white shirt, I walked through the lobby while a porter followed with my luggage. Aside from being unaccustomed to arriving at a hotel via the main entrance, I felt unduly nervous. I was directed to the best suite, and when the door opened a wall of scent hit me. The huge living room was filled with every kind of flower imaginable. There must have been more than a hundred bouquets in vases and baskets. In the background, soft music was playing. How I'd missed him!

Frank grinned at me and said, "Wait till you see what's in the other room." He led me through to a bedroom filled with even more roses and lilies, orchids and his favorites—gardenias. As I stood in the middle of the room, speechless, Frank casually tossed two enormous gemstones into the middle of the king-size bed. I stared at him and he stared at me, but I still didn't move a muscle.

"Well, aren't you going to look at them?" he asked impatiently. He stood by the window smoking a cigarette and forgetting my rule. I could tell he was nervous, so I didn't complain. Walking as steadily as I could toward the bed, I focused first on an enormous pear-shaped diamond that I later learned was twenty-two carats. It dazzled me with its perfection. Blinking back tears of happiness, I recalled how I'd told Frank a long time before that, if he ever asked me to marry him, I'd like a pear-shaped diamond just like one I'd seen in a magazine. This was almost identical. With a trembling hand, I picked it up and felt the weight of it. The second stone was even larger—a perfect green emerald. I didn't know what to say.

"You can have them set any way you want," Frank said as my eyes met his.

In spite of myself, I thought, That's still not a proposal! Seeing the look of childish expectation on his face, however, I realized that it was probably the closest I was going to get. Relenting finally, I ran to his arms and let him enfold me in his loving embrace. That reunion, of all our reunions, was surely the sweetest. As we lay together for the rest of the day and night telling each other over and over how much we loved each other, I was filled with such happiness that I never wanted to break the spell.

We did eventually have to get dressed, of course, and then Frank sent me to see a friend of his in the jewelry business. Praying that I was doing the right thing, I asked the friend to set the diamond in an engagement ring setting. Once the enormous solitaire was ready, I had the jeweler return it to Frank, not me, so that he could present it to me whichever way he wanted. The French-born actress Claudette Colbert was a great friend of Frank's and was in a show in Chicago at the time. She advised him what to do. "Put the ring in Barbara's soup during dinner," she suggested.

"No way, Frenchy!" Frank told her, alarmed. "She might eat it!" So they came up with another plan.

The next night Frank invited Claudette and her beau for dinner with us in a smart Chicago restaurant. As we were sipping champagne and chatting, I suddenly spotted what I thought at first was a chunk of ice in the fluted stem of my glass. Then I got it. "What's this?" I cried, feigning surprise.

As Frank and Claudette exchanged a private smile, he shrugged and said, "I dunno."

Reaching in, I fished out my ring. "Is this for me?" I asked, giving him a knowing look.

"Yes, beautiful," Frank replied, suddenly coy. "Why don't you put it on?"

Those were still not the words I wanted to hear, so I handed the ring to him and said, "Here, Frank, you put it on. Put it anyplace you want." I held out both my hands.

Shaking his head, Frank admitted defeat and carefully placed it on my left ring finger. Claudette and her boyfriend applauded that most delicious of moments, and as Frank pulled me laughingly into his arms and kissed me, I was truly the happiest woman on the planet.

Apart from Claudette and her man, no one knew our big secret, and I wondered when Frank would announce it. I told my parents and Bobby, of course, and they were thrilled, but the rest of the world could wait.

A week or so after we got back from Chicago, Frank took me to Van Cleef & Arpels in Beverly Hills to have my emerald set into a necklace, and we bumped into a woman we both knew. Thinking that Frank wouldn't want our engagement public yet, I quickly slipped my left hand behind my back.

"Hello, what are you doing here?" the woman asked suspiciously.

"Having a stone set for Barbara," Frank told her.

"What does *that* mean?"

"It's just a gift," Frank said, showing her the emerald. "Take a look."

"Oh. That's pretty."

Frank turned to me, and grinning, he said, "Show her the other one."

Uh-oh, I thought, but I did as I was told. "Wow!" the woman exclaimed. "That's *really* pretty! Does *that* mean anything?"

Frank laughed. "Of course it does, silly!" That was the closest he'd come to saying we were engaged, and I was stupidly delighted and relieved. Now I just had to wait to see what he wanted to do next.

Two weeks later we were at the Compound, sitting out by the pool. All of a sudden Frank looked up from his crossword and said, "Sweetheart, don't you think we ought to set the date?"

I thought to myself, Well, I guess that's a proposal.

He was romantic in every other way, but for some reason he just couldn't bring himself to say the words "Will you marry me?" Maybe it was because he'd said them three times before, and each time the marriage had ended disastrously. Maybe it was because he felt he'd been coerced into it this time. I didn't care; I loved the romanticism of it all—the flowers, the size of the stones, placing my ring in a glass of champagne. A born performer, that was the only way he knew how to show what was really in his heart.

. . .

Frank's mother, Dolly, and I had resolved our differences by the time her only son told her we were getting married. Once she realized we were serious, she was great and understood that she and I shared the same agenda—to make Frank happy.

She had moved to Palm Springs from the house Frank had bought her and Marty in Fort Lee, New Jersey, so that she could be nearer her son. She loved the bungalow he gave her on the edge of the Compound and the fact that she was so close by. Several times a month, she'd invite us over for delicious Italian suppers that she'd spent the entire day preparing. Frank always teased her a lot, and one night he took along a can of pork and beans and put it on his plate. The look on her face as she was about to serve him her famous meatballs was priceless.

At around this time, I decided to convert to Catholicism. I thought, I've been Methodist, Jewish, and now Catholic. I might as well. At least I'll have all the bases covered. Frank wasn't nearly as religious as his mother and went to church only at Christmas— we'd usually go to midnight Mass after a party at our house. He never asked me to change faith for him, but I could tell he was pleased that I'd consider it, especially as my doing so would smooth our path with Dolly.

The next thing I knew I was in Catholic school learning all about my new faith. I studied for about a year. Unlikely as it sounds, Dolly, that tough old dame from Hoboken, became my catechism coach and enlisted her favorite priests, Fathers Rooney, Blewitt, and Geimer, to help us. As she trained me in the finer points of Catholicism, we finally became friends. I think she realized at last what so many people had been saying—that I was good for Frank.

Even when I was with Zeppo, she'd come to realize that I was someone she could rely on. She'd ask my help with problems and the unlikeliest of tasks. By the time I was engaged to Frank, that dependence had increased tenfold. One day Dolly called to tell me, "Barbara, I've got mice. What should I do?"

"Get some cats."

"Where from?"

"The pound."

"Will you take me?"

So I drove her to the pound, picked out a couple of cats, stopped in at a vet's for them to get their shots, and delivered them back to her house. A few weeks later she called me up again. "Barbara, these frigging cats have a skin condition called infantigo, and now I've got it! I'm itching all over. Will you come and pick these mothers up?" I went over and collected the cats, took them back to the vet, and finally took them to live in Zeppo's house, where they became best friends with his two Weimaraners, Fleet and Sandy. The only trouble was Zeppo caught infantigo from them as well, whereas I seemed to be immune.

I had never forgotten Walter Annenberg's promise to me about marrying Frank. The two men had been friends ever since Walter and his wife, Lee, met Frank in Palm Springs in the 1950s. I tracked Walter down in London and placed a telephone call. "Are you sitting down?" I asked him. "You won't believe it, but Frank and I are finally getting married."

"That's wonderful news, Barbara!"

"We'd like to take you up on your offer to be married at Sunnylands."

"Great! When?"

"We were thinking it would be nice to get married on Bobby's birthday in October."

Walter was horrified. "You can't possibly wait that long! Frank's far too mercurial. It'll have to be sooner than that. I'll be in Palm Springs July tenth through twelfth."

July was only two months away, but 7/11 had always rolled

nicely off the tongue, so that was the date we picked. We were to be married in the main house in front of two hundred guests before relocating to the Compound for a reception catered by Chasen's. Lee promised to take care of everything at the Sunnylands ceremony with the help of Harriet Deutsch, another old friend of Frank's. It was so wonderfully kind of them.

To try to keep the media from intruding, we claimed that the Annenbergs were throwing us an engagement party and that we'd be marrying sometime later, at a venue to be announced. I went to see Zeppo a few days beforehand and told him the same story. His house looked out onto Sunnylands, and I didn't want him to hear it from anyone else. He seemed to take my news quite well and wished me every happiness, but there was a new sadness about him, I thought. When the press approached him later, he told them, "Barbara is a wonderful lady. Frank Sinatra could never find a better woman." Ever the gambler, he added, "I'm sorry I lost her, but that's the way it goes. You win some and you lose some."

As the big day approached, people began to fly into Palm Springs from around the world. To welcome them all the night before the wedding, Frank threw a party at a favorite haunt of his, the Ingleside Inn. A Spanish-style resort set on twenty acres, the inn had everything, including a pool, an award-winning restaurant, and the seclusion we wanted. Halfway through the evening Frank was looking around the reception when he spotted a stranger. Fearing it might be a reporter, he said to Jilly, "See the guy at ten o'clock? As you're showing him out, find out who he is."

Jilly approached the man and said to him, "Let's go, buster. You can tell me what you're doing here while you're walking."

The man held up his hands and cried, "But I'm Judge Walsworth! I'm the one who's going to marry them!" None of us had met him yet. The entire event was like that, funny and exciting and crazy. I had the feeling that absolutely anything could happen, and why wouldn't I feel that way? The impossible had already happened. Barbara Ann Blakeley from Bosworth, Missouri, was marrying Frank Sinatra.

On the morning of our wedding, July 11, 1976, I awoke to the sound of the telephone ringing. "Good morning, sweetheart," Frank said. "I can't wait to marry you today. How long are you going to be?"

I got up, took a shower, and peered out at the world. This was it, the day I'd been waiting for with all my heart. I could hardly believe it. Opening the window to breathe in some fresh air, I was blasted by a wave of heat. It must have been 120 degrees in the shade and it was only nine in the morning. What was I thinking, getting married in July?

With the help of my matron of honor, Bee Korshak, I gathered my clothes together and prepared to go over to the Compound. Bee had become my closest girlfriend in Palm Springs. A beautiful blonde who'd once been an ice skater, she also had a terrific sense of humor with a wicked side to it even though she came from Mormon stock. "The Mormons don't drink and they don't smoke, but they sure fuck a lot!" she'd say with a wink.

Whenever I had one of my fights with Frank and needed to escape, I'd call Bee and say, "Let's go somewhere!" and she'd always reply, "Okay." She didn't care where we went or what we did. Her husband, Sidney, was usually working hard in Chicago or New York (when he wasn't negotiating my divorce from Zeppo), and she was game for anything. We traveled throughout Europe, went for a spa break in Arizona with Dinah Shore and Veronique Peck, and took shopping trips to New York. Bee and I knew that as soon as bouquets of flowers began to crowd my hotel suite, Frank was ready to make up. His message might say something like *"Come back, although if you can put up with me you're crazier than I am."* I wasn't always ready to go home immediately, so I'd stay on for a few extra days with Bee just to make him wait.

Because the world's media had suspected all along that Frank and I were not merely getting engaged, Palm Springs was choked with TV crews, press photographers, and reporters. Lee Annenberg sent out trays of water and iced tea so that no one died of the heat. To avoid prying eyes, I went to Frank's house the back way, across the golf course. My mother was waiting, and she and Bee helped get me ready. I couldn't help wondering what Irene Blakeley was thinking as she helped me slip into my wedding dress that day. Back in the thirties, she'd been brave enough to rattle the bars of her Bosworth cage and rail against its confines. "Will-is!" she'd cry. "There are much better opportunities for us elsewhere." She could never have imagined how much better those opportunities would be, especially for me. In spite of our many differences of opinion over the years, I never forgot what she did for me. Thanks to her drive and determination, I'd embraced opportunity after opportunity as it came my way and was now taking on the greatest challenge of my life. As I stared at my own reflection in the mirror, just as I had stared at hers when I was a little girl, I knew I had inherited both her looks and her courage.

My wedding gown was made by the designer Halston and was off one shoulder in beige. He'd added drifts of chiffon and a single flowing sleeve. He made me an almost identical dress in pink satin for the evening party; both of them were my "something new." My "old" was an emerald and diamond brooch belonging to Bee, my "borrowed" was a lace handkerchief from my mother, and I wore a blue garter. I asked Frank to wear a brand-new beige silk and linen suit to match my dress and he carried the baby rings he'd given his children as his something old and borrowed. He wore a blue cornflower in his lapel.

Frank and I had never talked about me signing any sort of prenuptial agreement, and I was kind of surprised at that, given his history. Then when we went to collect our marriage license a few weeks before the wedding, he asked me if I had the twenty-dollar fee. As I reached into my purse and pulled out the money, he took it from me with a grin that let me know it was a setup for the words he wanted to say. "This will be the last thing you ever have to pay for," he told me with a kiss. I had no reason to doubt him.

On the morning of our wedding, Frank's lawyer, Mickey Rudin, knocked on the door of my room and asked me to go with him and Sidney Korshak to one of Frank's guesthouses. With my hair still in curlers, I did as they asked. They invited me to sit down. Then Mickey, a cigar in his mouth, slid a document across a table and said, "You have to sign this, Barbara, before you marry Frank."

I glanced down, looked up at the two men, and asked, "What is it?"

"A prenup."

I was shocked. "Does Frank know about this?"

"Of course he does," replied Mickey.

I flicked through the pages of what looked like a complicated legal contract and tried to buy some thinking time. I had few qualms about signing a prenup, but I wasn't so happy about the timing and the fact that I hadn't been given a chance to have anyone look at it on my behalf.

"I really don't think I want to sign this right now," I said finally, pushing the document away.

"Unless you do, there'll be no wedding," Mickey replied. I could tell from the expression on his face that he was serious.

A few hundred yards from where I sat, frozen in indecision, I could hear the caterers laying out the tables in the Compound's Grand Hall. In an hour or so our guests would arrive. They'd include the future president Ronald Reagan. Looking up at the man who'd held my hand through my divorce negotiations with Zeppo, I asked, "Sidney, have you seen this?"

"No, Barbara," he replied. "But if you sign this, you'll be safe."

Taking the pen Mickey offered me, I decided to trust my best friend's husband, and so I signed. "If that's all, gentlemen," I said, rising to my feet, "I'm getting married today."

As I left the guesthouse, Sidney gave me a knowing look. I knew then that he would take care of me whatever happened. In any event, I thought the document I'd just signed would probably come into play only if Frank and I divorced, and after all the trouble I'd gone through to get Frank to the altar, I had no intention of divorcing him. Nor would I let anything spoil my day. Squeezing Sidney's arm, I went to prepare to meet my groom, happy in the knowledge that Frank and I would never discuss money again.

Once I was ready to leave for the ceremony, I walked to the bar to meet Frank. An enormous smile lit up his face. "You look stunning, sweetheart." He looked extremely dashing in his suit, so I said, "You don't look so bad yourself!" I never worried about it being bad luck for him to see me before the wedding; it was hardly the first time around for either of us, and we loved the idea of arriving together. We crossed the golf course and entered Sunnylands via the back gate, and then Frank took his place in the main drawing room. He waved cheerily at all our guests and quipped, "Good-bye, y'all!"

My father was waiting to walk me down the aisle. The retired butcher who never thought he'd leave Bosworth was more nervous than I'd ever known him be. Willis Blakeley and I were a long way from Pa Hillis's general store and the Spit 'N' Argue Club. Any apprehension we had, though, was broken by the sound of Frank's voice yelling: "Hurry up, Barbara! Everyone thought *I* was the one who wasn't going to be here!" Laughing, my father gave the signal that we were ready, and the opening chords of "True Love" were struck up by Jimmy Van Heusen, who was playing the piano without any socks. Taking my father's arm, I walked down a long corridor of white marble lined with some of the most fabulous Impressionist and Postimpressionist paintings in the world, but I barely noticed them. When we turned the corner into the vision of loveliness that was the drawing room, I felt as if I had stepped into a scene from *High Society*. Only this was for real.

Real or not, ours felt like a fairy-tale wedding. Everything was fun and sentimental rolled into one. Bobby stood smilingly waiting for me a few steps away from Frank, whose eyes filled with tears of joy. Full of emotion, we took our places in front of the huge black marble fireplace under a famous Seurat painting, flanked by a Gauguin and a Van Gogh. Giant cloisonné cranes with flowers in their beaks perched on either side of us. The fireplace was dripping in gardenias as well as white roses, white chrysanthemums, and white orchids, all grown in the Annenberg greenhouses. Even though it was sweltering outside, it was a perfumed sixty-eight degrees in that room.

Many were surprised that Jilly Rizzo wasn't Frank's best man, but in truth Jilly wouldn't have been comfortable having to stand up and speak in front of two hundred people, so he happily took a ringside seat and organized security. The man Frank chose instead was Freeman Gosden—the actor who'd played Amos in the popular radio comedy *Amos 'n Andy* and whom Frank had known for years. Freeman was a gentle man from the South, perfect for this role and for the speeches to be made later.

Judge Walsworth began the ceremony, and suddenly the whole event took on a serious note. This was it, then. We were really getting married. I looked at Frank and he looked at me and neither of us looked as if we were about to bolt. When the judge reached the part where I was asked to take Frank for richer or poorer, my husband-to-be interjected, "Richer, richer!" which made everyone crack up, even Dolly, who was there to give us her support. I'd told Frank before the wedding that he didn't have to wear a ring, but he'd insisted, telling me he'd be "proud to." During the repeating of our wedding vows, I slipped a plain Bulgari band on his ring finger, and he presented me with an eternity ring of tiny diamond baguettes, which perfectly complemented my killer engagement ring.

Declared husband and wife at last, Frank and I kissed and laughed and embraced and cried all at once. It was utterly wonderful. Champagne corks popped all around us, and we toasted each other beneath an exquisite Rodin statue of Eve. Lee had had a wedding cake made for us, similar to the one we had waiting at the Compound, and so with a knife decorated with gardenias and stephanotis, we cut into it. Someone called out, "Make a wish!" but Frank sweetly said that he couldn't wish for anything more than his "beautiful bride." Ronald Reagan, the Republican presidential contender, piped up, "If you can't think of anything to ask for, I could make a suggestion!"

A fleet of air-conditioned buses ferried our guests back across the golf course for a buffet dinner at the Compound. The Grand Hall was decorated with white and yellow chrysanthemums, yellow roses, and carnations in Frank's favorite color, orange, which always made him feel happy. After we'd formally greeted our guests, I changed into my evening dress and then wandered among the friends and family who'd traveled from afar to help us celebrate this momentous day. Our friends from Hollywood, New York, Palm Beach, Chicago, and Europe mingled with buddies from the old days. Everyone was there, from my aunts and uncles to Greg and Vero Peck, Cary Grant, Kirk and Anne Douglas, and the entire Nixon Kitchen Cabinet. Roz Russell was there, even though she would die of cancer two months later and kept having to give herself morphine shots.

My father was very happy that day, especially when I told him he wouldn't have to make a speech. Once he'd gotten over his nerves and taken me to Frank's side, he was able to enjoy the proceedings. I watched him and my mother being introduced to politicians, movie stars, and billionaires, and was quietly amazed. They chatted with our guests as if they'd always had that kind of life. During the reception, various guests stood up and spoke if they felt like it, which made everything even more fun and spontaneous. Walter Annenberg said a few words, as did Ronald Reagan. Freeman's speech had great humor in it, and Judge Walsworth offered a prayer. Then Frank got up and said a lot of lovely things about me. He was such a great speaker.

Frank's friend Pat DiCicco sought me out during the reception. "Please, Barbara," he said, "do me a favor. Stay married for at least three months."

"This is our wedding day, for Pete's sake! What are you saying?" I asked. Then I figured it out. "So who do you have a bet with?"

"Paul Mano," he replied sheepishly. "Don't say anything, but whatever happens, don't get a divorce for at least twelve weeks, okay?" I have no idea how much those two bet, but knowing them, it was a lot. Pat was once married to Gloria Vanderbilt, and Paul wasn't short of a buck or two. Of course, Pat won the bet. In fact Frank and I made it not just to our third month but into our third decade. I should have insisted on a cut.

My wedding gift to Frank was a Jaguar sports car in British racing green, the first twelve-cylinder and fastest Jaguar ever made. I'd hidden it at the Annenbergs' and had someone drive it out and present it to him halfway through the reception. He was thrilled. Then during dinner, Frank disappeared, and just as I was wondering where he'd gotten to, I looked outside and gave a delighted shriek. Coming through a gate in the hedge was a peacock blue Rolls-Royce with half a dozen yellow roses tied to the windshield. Frank, who'd changed into a silk shirt that matched my dress, drove it right up to the picture window of the room where we were all eating, a boyish grin on his face. The evening party went with a swing after that. I can't even remember what time we went to bed.

We stayed at the Compound that night, and the following morning I awoke to the vision of Frank's smiling face. He was leaning up on a pillow and staring down at me. "Good morning, Mrs. Sinatra," he said before giving me a tender kiss. "You've made me the happiest guy in the world."

Later that day we drove up to his house at Pinyon Crest with half a dozen friends: the singer Morton Downey and his wife, Ann; the novelist Judy Green and her husband, Bill; and Paul and Sheila Mano. We swam and sunbathed, played games and ate and drank what we liked when we liked. It was heaven. Out on the tennis court one day, I played a winning lob, and someone shouted, "Nice shot, Sinatra!"

Spinning round, I almost tripped over my own feet. "Oh, my God!" I cried. "That's *me*!"

After Pinyon Crest, Frank and I flew to Belle-Rive, Claudette Colbert's stunning plantation-style house on the oceanfront in Barbados. The weather was beautiful, and we had a blissful ten days, madly in love. Frank told me he was so happy that he thought flowers might grow out of his nose. I had rarely seen him so relaxed. However long it had taken us to get to that point, it had been worth it in the end—for us both.

Several people asked me how I managed to calm Frank down after he'd been such a hell-raiser. My answer was "Timing." He was sixty years old when we married; he'd been everywhere, done everything, and met everyone. He said that being married to me gave him "a kind of wonderful tranquillity." As he later explained in an interview, "There were moments when it was too quiet . . . when there's something lacking somewhere. When Barbara and I were married, I found it to be a better life. She's a wonderful woman." Then, of course, he spoiled it with "It's too bad she's so ugly!" In truth, he was ready to settle down, and lucky me, I was the one he was ready to settle down with.

TEN

Frank and me with his mother, Dolly.

COURTESY OF ALAN BERLINER/BEIMAGES

You Make Me Feel
So Young

Being Mrs. Frank Sinatra took some getting used to, but my romantic husband went out of his way to make me feel loved and cherished every day, taking the time to express his feelings. He turned every day into Christmas.

Frank was often buying me something, and he would always let me know how he felt about me. For a man who was so macho in every other way, the purity of his feelings for me and his unashamed openness about them knocked me out. I'd never known anything like it in my life—not from my father, Bob, Joe, or Zeppo. Apart from making sure to tell me he loved me every night before we went to sleep, if Frank was sitting by the pool or in the den and I was in another part of the house, I'd hear him call, "Where are you, gorgeous girl?" Or he'd suddenly yell: "I *love* that woman!" or "I'm in love with Barbara Sinatra!" He'd shout something similar from the head of the table in the middle of a dinner party, embarrassing our guests. I was never embarrassed, though, and I never tired of hearing what he had to say or appreciating that he took the time to say it.

As if telling me wasn't enough, he never stopped writing me those little notes. "*Thank you for looking after me. I love you, F.*" Another, stuck to the bedroom door, said, "*I love you so much it hurts,*" and one waiting on my desk read, "*I love you. Guess oo?*" Then for Valentine's Day, birthdays, anniversaries, or no reason at all, there'd be another note or flowers, a jewelry box, chocolates, anything. In one card he wrote:

> *Sweetheart: Millions of men in the world love their wives*
> *I'm sure, but I'm surer that my love for you is so much more*
> *overwhelming. It overwhelms me each day, constantly. Just to*
> *see you every morning makes my every day. I pray we live for*
> *at least a hundred years. Charlie Neat.*

Now that I was living with him night and day, I truly understood that Frank was not only neat, but obsessively clean, taking two or three showers daily, shaving repeatedly, and brushing his teeth or using mouthwash to make sure his breath was always fresh. He smelled of soap and toothpaste, which was incredibly sexy. After a late night, he'd lounge around the house in his tailored white pajamas with navy trim—the only time he allowed himself to be "a slob." Every day he'd wander out into the garden to pick me a flower. One winter he couldn't find anything in bloom, so he brought me a twig instead. He'd sing around the house sometimes (but never if anyone else was around), and when he did, I'd know the song was for me. "*Night and day, you are the one,*" he'd croon as he sat by the pool or wandered into a room just to sing me a line or kiss the back of my neck.

Out of the blue, he'd tell me to pack a bag and fly me to San Francisco, Los Angeles, New York, or Paris for dinner. When I asked him what we were celebrating, he'd say something like "It was four years ago today that I first knew I loved you" or "Do I need a reason to spoil my bride?" Whenever we could we'd return to our honeymoon hideaway in Claudette's lovely home. Gracious and generous, with a tremendous sense of style, Claudette had a terrific sense of humor and an exuberant laugh. That famed star of the first talking pictures gave the most wonderful cocktail parties overlooking the ocean, where delicious canapés were served by white-gloved waiters. It was like walking into an elegant but welcoming movie set and, oh, so romantic to be in that magical place again with my bridegroom.

Even at home, the surprises never stopped. Frank might have stone crab claws, flown in by the bushel from Florida, which we'd eat out by the pool in our bathing suits. Or he'd have pizzas delivered from Rocky Lee's in New York, or his favorite cheesecake jetted in from Chicago. What he enjoyed most though was to get me a great gift—usually an important piece of jewelry—then spring it on me in some subtle way, just as he had with the Holy Shit Necklace. I guess I must have reacted the way he wanted each time, because he always seemed to take such pleasure in my delight. One day we were having brunch with George Schlatter and his wife, Jolene, whom Frank called Injun because of her olive skin. Jolene had been a Vegas showgirl and she and I had modeled together, so we went back a long way. We were sitting at the table when I spotted a man in a uniform standing on the other side of the glass front door. The bell rang, but strangely, no one went to answer it. Frank was still in the white robe I'd had made for him with a big *S* embroidered on the back. Because I wasn't dressed yet either, I said, "Darling, would you please get the door?"

He barely looked up from where he was eating bacon and eggs. "You get it," he replied.

The bell rang again, and as all the staff seemed to have vanished, I went to the door in my robe. The man in uniform said,

"Barbara Sinatra?" and when I nodded, he waved forward a security guard from a Brinks truck parked in the drive.

"This is for you," his colleague said, handing me a small package.

As I wandered back inside, I found George and Jolene grinning up at me, so I knew that they were in on the surprise. I opened the package to find a velvet Van Cleef & Arpels box with an enormous emerald nestling inside. Frank loved emeralds; they were his favorite stones, and he used to sit with Mr. Arpels in the back room of his store poring over the finest gems. My husband had once again chosen exceptionally well, and I was over the moon. I had the emerald set at the end of a diamond necklace, a piece I still proudly possess.

I was able to surprise him too every now and then, although that was never easy. I presented him once with a Bulgari gold signet ring with an Italian coin set into it. He slipped it on immediately, replacing the one with the family crest that he'd worn for years and that was later stolen from him. Typical of Frank, though, he then had a smaller copy of his crest ring made for me so that we had a matching pair. I could never match his thoughtfulness.

As if there wasn't enough love in the house already, we decided to have babies—Cavalier King Charles spaniels. They were adorable, and Frank was the sweetest of all with them. Our friend Judy Green gave us our first, Miss Wiggles, but we soon acquired more, including another favorite, a ruby-colored spaniel named Caroline. At one time we had two litters of eight or nine pups. Frank liked the breed so much he sent a puppy to the financier and producer Armand Deutsch and his wife, Harriet, when they lost Beau, the yellow Labrador Frank had surprised them with fifteen years earlier. He often bought dogs for friends, but only if he was certain that they loved animals and could take good care of one.

Once we owned puppies, Frank began to draw little dogs on some of his notes to me. "*Bow wow*," he wrote on one. "*Happy Mother's Day from Miss Wiggles and Caroline.*" In another, he wrote:

"*Darling, I am so happy about our new baby. I love you, F.*" He was as soft as butter when it came to animals. He always had been. He'd stop someone treading on a bug by telling them, "Hey, don't kill the little fella. That's a pal of mine." He was upset when I had one of our houseboys kill a rattlesnake up at Pinyon Crest after I found it hissing at Miss Wiggles. When we visited a friend in Acapulco who had a pet shark, Frank persuaded him to release it into the ocean. He loved cats too, and would sit in his pajamas doing a crossword with a sleeping puss we had named Bozo purringly draped around his shoulders. When one of our King Charles spaniels named Melissa was run over by a hit-and-run driver outside our house, we were both terribly upset, but Frank placed an advertisement in the local newspaper appealing for witnesses. Luckily for that careless driver, no one ever came forward to identify him.

We had another dog, a stray Afghan hound we'd taken in. She had long eyelashes and silky hair and walked like a star, so I called her Miss Hollywood. Sadly, she ate one of our kittens. Not wanting a killer in the house, I reluctantly gave her away to a man who ran an ostrich farm. A few months later, someone called to tell me that Miss Hollywood was being kept in the same pen as the ostriches and was in terrible condition. Most of her fur had become so matted that it had been pulled away from her skin. Thinking back to poor old Boots in Las Vegas, I called the owner and told him, "I want you to sell Miss Hollywood back to me." To my surprise, he didn't want to give her up, no matter how much I offered. In desperation, I called the one person I knew could help.

"Jilly, I want you to kidnap Miss Hollywood from that awful place and bring her home," I told Frank's best friend. Which is exactly what Jilly did. The owner never came looking for her, so I guess he knew he'd be prosecuted for cruelty. We took Miss Hollywood to the vet, had what was left of her fur shaved off, and brought her home, making sure to keep her away from our cats. She lived with us for several more happy years.

. . .

Having moved in with Frank once we were married, I gave my old house to the couple he called my "producers"—Willis and Irene Blakeley. It was the perfect home for my parents, and they lived there until they died.

My new marital addresses comprised the Compound in Palm Springs, Villa Maggio at Pinyon Crest, the apartment in the Waldorf Towers in New York, and a modern open-plan property at the top of Coldwater Canyon in Los Angeles. Frank also had a villa overlooking the ocean in Las Brisas, Acapulco, where I used to escape sometimes with my girlfriends. Mostly, though, we lived at the Compound. I never had any qualms about moving into a house that had such a long and checkered history for Frank. It was the perfect place for us, not least because it slept eighteen and had a restaurant-size kitchen. Best of all, it wasn't fancy. It was the most comfortable of his homes, the sort of place you could put your feet up, eat popcorn, and watch *Jeopardy!* and *Wheel of Fortune*, Frank's favorite television programs. He needed to completely relax whenever he came back from a tour, and so, increasingly, did I.

I can't say we ever had a "normal" day, but on an average one in Palm Springs, he might get up around noon and have his brunch. Then we'd play with the dogs or walk them around the property or the tennis court together. We might play a round of golf, using the cart that had OL' BLUE EYES painted on one side and LADY BLUE EYES on the other. Frank might swim or skip some rope, and then we'd spend the rest of the day sitting by the pool, reading the newspapers, doing crosswords, or planning what we were going to do that night. Frank liked to see how he felt each day before he made up his mind about our evening plans. He'd drive our friends crazy because they'd have to wait for a call from Vine, the housekeeper, to tell them where they had to be and when if they wanted to join us for dinner. One of them, Danny Kaplan, even wrote a poem about it called "Vine's on the Line." Part of it went

> *Our dear Barbara and Frank, they come and they go*
> *When they are on the road for us it seems slow.*
> *They are home in the Springs to rest in the sun*
> *But to us it's the shot of the starter's gun.*
> *They return to Palm Springs with one heralding sign—*
> *The signal they're here is "It's Vine on the line!" . . .*
> *An evening at the Sinatras' is known for rapture*
> *So stimulating and unique, it's hard to capture.*
> *The cocktails, the wine, the food, and the pasta*
> *Are all so fantastic one never says "basta."*
> *Frank and Barbara are the ultimate hosts*
> *A fact well known by friends on both coasts.*
> *There's something so special in their invite to dine*
> *We all eagerly wait—"It's Vine on the line!"*

If we were invited out somewhere Frank didn't want to go, he wouldn't, and there was no changing his mind. I'd learned early on that when he said go, we'd go. That was the routine, and I had to be ready and on time. The only occasion I might decide not to go was if I found Frank at the bar drinking gin instead of his usual Jack Daniel's. There was something about gin that turned him mean. The minute I spotted the gin bottle, I'd turn around, go to my room, and lock myself in. No amount of cajoling could persuade me to go with him, so he'd have to go out and be mean on his own.

Some of the best times were when we'd stay in, just the two of us, and Frank would prepare me a romantic meal. He'd spend an entire afternoon in the kitchen he'd designed himself, cooking up a series of delicious Italian dishes. He'd light the candles, arrange the flowers, and woo me all over again. When he was like that, he was the best. His voice was soft and sexy, and so was his demeanor. He was in the mood for love, and I was only too happy to love him in return.

Other nights, we'd host a party at home so that we wouldn't have to go out. Then Vine and I would run around and call our friends until I had an interesting group of thirty or forty people lined up, plus all the food and booze they'd need. Sometimes for fun, I'd divide our guests up into groups so that we'd have separate tables for actors, singers, industrialists, or moguls. The guest list would depend on who was in town but would include all the usual suspects, plus friends like Tim Conway, Roger and Luisa Moore, Dick and Dolly Martin, Chuck Connors, Louis and "Quique" Jourdan, or the singer Jerry Vale and his wife, Rita. Just like his father before him, Frank would cook at least one special dish to add to the menu. After dinner, we might show a first-run movie in the projection room complete with popcorn and candy, or Frank might go to his train room to oil the engines or change the cars with some of his buddies.

The Compound was very masculine in style when I first knew it, what I called "early Italian." There were plastic flowers in vases and a great deal of orange paint on everything from the walls to the oversize refrigerators. Soon after I moved in, I asked if I could do something about the décor. Frank couldn't have cared less what I did with the place; he just didn't want to get involved. He told me, "Do it exactly the way you want and *then* show me." With the help of Bee Korshak, whose judgment as an interior designer I valued, I opened up some of the rooms and created new bathrooms and dressing rooms. I also turned one of the spare bedrooms into an art studio for Frank so that he could pursue his interest in painting. I freshened everything else up with lighter desert colors and added a few feminine touches. It remained very much Frank's home, with his art collection on the walls along with all his memorabilia, including statues, photographs, and awards, as well as the red phone once installed in the den as a hotline to the White House. By the time I'd finished, though, the Compound looked what I called "late Italian."

In my childhood I'd loved going into the backyard to pick corn, melons, tomatoes, and basil for the kitchen, so I wanted to re-create a little corner of Bosworth in Palm Springs. In an underused area of the estate, I developed a garden in which I grew most of our own vegetables and herbs. My parents loved to help me plant seedlings or pick fresh produce; I often think that was where my father was happiest whenever they came to visit. With soil beneath his fingernails again, he taught me a few tricks—like how to keep bugs away by pushing a clove of garlic into the ground and setting beer traps for slugs. Out in our garden, amid the towering sunflowers and the soldiers of corn, Willis Blakeley was in his element.

The Compound's buildings and guesthouses had been named by Frank after the friends who'd stayed there over the years. There was the Kennedy house, the Agnew house, and the Cerf house (after the Random House founder Bennett Cerf, whom Frank dubbed the Bookmaker). I thought it would be fun to name them after Frank's favorite songs, so the main building became "The House I Live In," and the guesthouses were renamed "All the Way," "The Tender Trap," "High Hopes," "Young at Heart," and "The Good Life." The projection theater was "Send in the Clowns" and Frank's office—decorated with framed photographs from his more than fifty movies—was aptly dubbed "My Way." The master bedroom was christened "True Love," and the room he'd sleep in if he wanted to stay up later than I did was called "I Sing the Songs." Situated next to the pool, it was a quiet, simple space, not at all ostentatious, as one might imagine. In one corner was a statue of St. Francis, a saint Frank identified with not only because of his name and nationality but because of his love of animals.

If we weren't home recovering from a tour, or hosting guests at Easter and just about every holiday, we were on the road so that Frank could continue to entertain his fans. As well as spending long spells in the studio recording new songs, he toured relentlessly in the first few years of our marriage, with more than ninety concert performances in one nine-month period alone. Whenever we could, we'd take Miss Wiggles and Caroline with us—they were the best-traveled dogs in show business. On one tour, we landed at an airport somewhere (probably Shannon) to refuel. When we pulled up to a piece of grass, there were dozens of press photographers waiting. I guess they'd heard Frank would be dropping in and wanted to get a shot. Well, the only shot they got was of Miss Wiggles being carried down the steps by a member of the staff to the grass, where she performed right in front of the cameras. Then she was carried back onto the plane and we took off.

The schedule was nothing short of energetic. Frank drove the pace during that period (although later it was his management team that pushed him), and everyone had to go with it. As always he wanted me ringside at every concert, so I went with him 99 percent of the time. Even in his seventh decade, his stamina was incredible. People would fall like flies from flu or exhaustion all around him and he'd just keep going, as long as he had "Dr. Daniels," which he claimed killed all known germs. Not that he drank all the time. Nor did he always drink Jack Daniel's. He loved European wine and would often drink the best red wines with pasta and meat. He rarely drank water on the grounds that "fish fuck in it," but he could go on the wagon for weeks at a time, especially if there was a big tour coming up. And he never drank before a show, only afterward.

Having been the "skinny hundred-pound Dago" from New Jersey who once joked that if he lost any more weight he couldn't be seen behind the microphone, he began to develop a little middle-aged spread. So he cut out the candy he loved—especially Tootsie Rolls and cherry Life Savers, which he ate by the packet and which would dye his tongue red. For his meals, he'd eat any-thing he liked, but in child-size portions only. It worked, but diet-ing seemed to make him even more hyper. On one interminable flight to Tokyo, he didn't sleep and couldn't settle, so he walked up and down the plane, talking to people and drinking all night. He gave his concert, then got straight back on the plane and drank and walked all the way home. I don't know how he did it. I could never have sustained that. Maybe it was the adulation he always received in Japan that kept him going. The Japanese were crazy about him—their women would try to elbow me away from him. That was one country where I was truly grateful for the body-guard Frank had provided for me at concerts from the day we'd started courting.

O n the road and off, Frank had a team of people looking after his every need, so my chief role was to get the social side of things organized. My husband still needed company after a show, so I'd arrange a dinner somewhere, order a menu of (usually) Ital-ian food, make out a guest list, and figure out the seating plan. We had several secretaries and assistants in an entourage of around ten, so I had plenty of help. Once we arrived in a city, we'd take over an entire wing of a hotel; then I'd get to work finding out who was in town and available. Close friends would be sent our sched-ule and invited to join us if they could.

Knowing Frank's love for having an eclectic mix of people around him, I'd try to find singers and sportsmen, actors and in-dustrialists. I'd research who was new and hot and who was not. When we got to the restaurant, I'd tell everyone where to sit ac-cording to my seating plan and just hope I'd gotten the mix right as the wine was being poured and the antipasti served. I'd never sit Frank next to someone he didn't know or might not like. I did that only once, by accident, in Australia, when he ended up having to make polite conversation with a country singer he didn't take to at all. That's when the Mr. Hyde in his character flared up, and boy, I never made that mistake again.

The responsibility for Frank's social life wasn't entirely on my shoulders. Quite often, people would throw dinners in his honor, and so we'd go straight to a party after a show. The one thing Frank would insist on, though, was to be shown the guest list first. We arrived in New York during one nationwide tour to find that our friend Henry Kissinger had gone to a great deal of trouble to organize a party for Frank the following night.

"How kind, Henry," I said when he told me. "Thank you so much."

But when I saw the guest list, my face fell. On it was the journalist Barbara Walters, and I knew that the minute Frank saw her name, he'd refuse to attend. He used to call her Barbara Wa-Wa because he said she had a speech impediment and she always made everyone she interviewed cry. During one of his acts, he called her "the ugliest broad on TV." Sure enough, when Frank found out she'd be at the party, he said, "Cancel me."

"Cancel you?" I repeated. "But Henry's been planning this for weeks, and you're his guest of honor!"

"I'm going to bed now," Frank told me with a shrug. "If Henry calls, tell him I'm not available."

So dear Henry Kissinger, the best negotiator in the world and a recipient of the Nobel Peace Prize, suddenly found himself negotiating with me—the dummy who knew nothing. "Barbara!" he pleaded. "You've got to talk to *Fraank*. I've been planning this party forever. He can't just cancel on me."

"Henry, Frank's not going if Barbara Walters is there. You will have to disinvite her."

"I can't disinvite Barbara Walters!" Henry cried, appalled.

"Fine," I told him. "Then have your party, enjoy yourself, and we'll get together another time."

"But, Barbara, we have to work this out! Maybe I could have

her at one end of the room and Frank at the other? He'd never even have to speak to her." There was desperation in his voice.

I sighed and told him, "You know Frank. There's no working out to be done here." They were not words Henry Kissinger heard very often, I shouldn't think. He called back at least three more times and the following day even tracked me down to a restaurant where I was having lunch with some girlfriends. "Did you get a chance to talk to *Fraank*?" he asked.

"Yes I did, but Frank's not going unless Barbara Walters isn't there, and that's that." Poor Henry. He had no choice but to disinvite Miss Walters, although God knows how he managed it. Frank and I went to the party, and we both had a most enjoyable evening. I felt so bad for Barbara.

Several months later we were in Japan, and Henry called us. *"Fraank,"* he said, excitedly. "I pulled your line! Someone I didn't want to be with was at a summit I was expected to attend, and I said I wouldn't go if he was there. Guess what? It worked!"

I had my own taste of what Henry had gone through when we had the Agnews staying with us at the Compound and the Annenbergs wouldn't invite them to come to a party they'd invited us to. I didn't know why, and I didn't want to get into the reasons, so we had no choice but to leave the Agnews at home. We were in New York on another occasion when President Nixon asked us out to a restaurant. The night before the dinner the Saudi businessman Adnan Khashoggi called to see what our plans were. We'd first met Adnan in Monaco when he invited us onto his yacht for dinner. I had been impressed that there was a gift from Bulgari for every woman at the table. He had a giant-size bed, which all the men were sniggering about, but I told him, "How nice, you can get all your family in there!" He laughed, and from then on, we hit it off. When he called to see what we were up to in New York, without thinking, I invited him along to the Nixon dinner. It was me; I would have loved for it to have been Frank who made the faux pas, but it was me. When I informed Nixon's people that Adnan was coming, they told me they couldn't have him there. Apparently, he was too controversial a figure. I'd had no idea and was mortified. I had to call Adnan and ask him to understand. Thank goodness, he did.

I liked Nixon and met him several times, usually at the White House. I always found him charming and refreshingly unshowy. I was seated next to him once during a meal, and we got chatting about food. He told me of his Quaker childhood on a ranch in Orange County and how much he loved home-cooked food, especially beans. "Why, Mr. President, I love beans too!" I told him. "I have ever since the days my grandmother used to grow them and can them back in Missouri." After that, beans became our connection. "Barbara," the president would tell me with a conspiratorial smile every time I saw him, "you and I have got to go out and get that bean dinner together." Sadly, we never did.

Frank hadn't played the famous Caesars Palace in Las Vegas for a while. In January 1977, however, he was invited for a triumphant return.

We booked one of Frank's bigger planes to fly us up there on the day of the concert, January 6. His eighty-two-year-old mother, Dolly, loved Las Vegas and especially enjoyed playing the slot machines, which she'd load with coin after coin provided by Frank. He even had a slot machine installed for "Grandma" at home so she could play whenever she wanted. Naturally, Dolly was on the passenger list, along with Mrs. Anna Carbone, a widowed friend from New Jersey who was staying with her at the time and whom Frank had known most of his life.

Our flight was due to leave at noon because he was playing two shows that night and needed plenty of time to get ready. At the last minute, Dolly—who could be as difficult as ever when she wanted to be—decided that she would prefer to come later. Frank thought nothing of it and chartered a twin-engine Learjet we used often to fly Dolly and Mrs. Carbone to Vegas at around four o'clock that afternoon.

After a bumpy plane ride on an overcast day and with the weather worsening, we arrived in Las Vegas at around one o'clock. When we got to Caesars, we couldn't help but laugh at the marquee, which said simply, HE'S BACK! Once we settled into our suite, I took a nap. I knew we were going to have a late night, so I wanted to look my best. About an hour into my snooze, Frank burst into the bedroom, and the first thing I noticed was that he had a cigarette in his hand and it was shaking. "Grandma left at five but she's not here yet," he told me, his eyes strange. "They can't find her plane on the radar . . . Barbara, she's nowhere on the damn screen!"

I looked into Frank's face. I saw his fear, and I felt my own. Taking his hands in mine, I told him, "Darling, your mother's a tough old bird, and I'm sure she's going to be all right. Please don't worry. If anyone can survive, she can." I could tell from his expression that he had already started to give up hope, so I slid off the bed, dropped to my knees, and began to pray. My husband sat on the edge of the bed and watched me, his lips mouthing his own silent prayer. Dolly and I may have had our differences in the past, but we'd overcome them and truly made our peace. We had spent so much time together that we'd become friends. I knew how important she was to Frank; he was devoted to her. I couldn't imagine how he would cope if she were to die in some unexpected and horrible way.

"Let's cancel and fly home, darling," I told him. "There'll probably be good news by the time we get there."

"No," he said abruptly. "I'll do the show."

As the time drew near for Frank's first performance, he sat in a corner of our suite in a deep, impenetrable depression. The longer he went without any news, the deeper he sank. I didn't think for one moment that he could go on that night, but to my amazement, he suddenly got up, walked down to his dressing room, pulled on his tux, and swept to the theater. There was a pall of gloom among his staff and crew backstage, but up there in front of the lights, Frank was all that his devoted fans wanted him to be.

I took my place at the front and watched in open admiration as this consummate pro refused to disappoint his audience. Dolly would have wanted him to go on. He knew that. I knew it. But I don't know how he managed it; he must have sung those songs by rote. The people sitting all around me applauding wildly would never have suspected a thing was wrong until perhaps the moment he began "My Funny Valentine"—a song he usually dedicated to me—and his emotions crowded his throat. As soon as he had taken his final bow, he strode off the stage and told his manager, "We're going home." The second show was canceled as we filed into the motorcade to the airport and flew straight back to Palm Springs. Looking down over the mountains where Dolly's plane was probably lying broken, I closed my eyes and whispered one of her favorite prayers.

Back at the Compound, Frank barely said a word for two days. He sat on a couch in a corner by the bar and stared into space. It was really eerie. He didn't want to talk to anybody, not even me. I'd walk past every hour or so, catch his eye, and give him a smile, but his eyes wouldn't even flicker. Whenever he was quiet, I knew we were in trouble, but I'd never seen him that quiet before. People—family members, those with news of the ongoing search—would come in and talk to him, but he barely responded. I'd let them say their piece, and then I'd shoo them away. Nobody was going to break that ice, not even Dolly's favorite priest, Father Geimer, who came to perform a Mass. I'd never seen Frank grieving before, but I knew from Jilly that this was exactly how he'd behaved when his father, Marty, died, and after he lost Marilyn Monroe and Jack Kennedy was killed. I also knew that, once he'd spent enough time alone to figure it all out in his head, he'd get up and get on. I was right.

After two days of grieving, I walked past him once more, gave him my smile, and made a stupid face, expecting the same response as before. This time was different. "Are you crazy?" he asked, grimacing. Then he suddenly stood up and asked me to get hold of his chief pilot, Johnny Spots, who'd flown us to Vegas on the night Dolly disappeared. "Bring a helicopter," he told Johnny. "We're going to search for Grandma." In one of the Civil Air Patrol helicopters that had already been searching for Dolly for days, Frank, Johnny, and a pilot named Don Landells flew up over the San Bernardino Mountains, scouring a huge area. There was deep snow on the highest peaks, confirming that the weather had closed in that night. They flew back and forth over the bleak, wintry terrain, but all they spotted was the branch of a tree that had been broken halfway up the 11,500-feet-high Mount San Gorgonio. That's where Johnny Spots showed tremendous wisdom. He had the pilot fly Frank home, and then they went back to where he'd seen the broken branch. Instead of going down the mountain, they flew higher up, because Johnny knew that any pilot would try to get over the peak. That's when they found the wreckage, slammed into the side of the mountain at 9,500 feet. I will always be grateful to Johnny for going back alone. I couldn't imagine how it would have affected Frank if he'd found his mother's body.

The news came in late that night. The plane had broken up on impact and everybody was dead. One of the rescue teams in the area was diverted to retrieve the remains of Dolly, Mrs. Carbone, the pilot, and the copilot. They brought the bodies back down to a morgue in Palm Springs. The authorities called the house to ask someone to come and identify them. Mickey Rudin said he would go, but then he said he couldn't. Frank didn't want to go, and neither did any of his kids. Jilly couldn't face it either—he'd known

Dolly for most of his life; she was like a mother to him. When I realized that nobody else was prepared to go, I volunteered. That was not an easy task. It was horrible for me, but even more horrible for poor Frank.

At the Rosary recited for Dolly at the St. Louis Catholic Church in Cathedral City on January 12, attended by more than five hundred mourners, the Church of the Desert Choir sang her favorite song, "Hello, Dolly!" as well as "Ave Maria." Dolly was buried a week later in the Desert Memorial Park in Cathedral City next to Marty, whose coffin Frank had moved from New Jersey when his mother came to Palm Springs. Frank clung to my hand and couldn't take his eyes off his mother's flower-decked casket as it was carried in by Jilly, Dean Martin, and Jimmy Van Heusen, among others. It was an intensely moving service attended by some of Frank's oldest friends, including Barbara Stanwyck, Jimmy Stewart, and Loretta Young, but it finally drew a curtain over what had been such a traumatic episode.

As we ate Italian food in Dolly's honor after the funeral, I was just so grateful that her body had been found. Frank may have been sixty-one years old, but he was still an orphan who needed to know that his mother was at rest, next to Marty, close enough for him to visit. As Frank himself said, Dolly could finally "sleep warm."

Life went on after Dolly's death, just as it always had. Frank canceled two weeks of performances and we flew to Barbados to spend some time at the place we loved, but performing was Frank's therapy and he needed to get back on the stage. It was also what his mother would have expected, for there had surely never been a woman more proud of her son.

Driven by that thought, Frank arranged it so that our next few years were spent almost exclusively on the road. He also performed at numerous benefits, did fund-raisers for Ronald Reagan, recorded several new songs, and fulfilled commitments at Caesars in Vegas and Harrah's in Lake Tahoe. He gave a lauded performance in the TV movie *Contract on Cherry Street*. Never once forgetting his bride, he took me on vacations to Barbados and Monaco between legs of the tour. Some of his finest performances that year were in the smaller clubs, like the Latin Casino in Cherry Hill, New Jersey, places he chose deliberately to give people a chance to see and hear him on a more intimate level. He'd make a point of ensuring that tickets to any concert of his be scaled in price so that ordinary people could afford them. Not that there weren't some incredible venues as well. Flying around the world in a plane he named *Barbara Ann*, I watched my husband perform in front of the Acropolis in Athens, the Colosseum in Rome, and the Sphinx in Egypt.

It was on that trip to Egypt, with Bobby along with us, that we probably had the best time (although sadly I did catch hepatitis B from the water and thought I was going to die). President Anwar Sadat was married to a beautiful lady called Jehan. She had a birthday coming up, and Anwar asked her what she wanted. "I'm not going to say, because you'll never give it to me," she told him with a sigh. This went on for several weeks until finally he said, "Tell me what you want!"

Frank and I had gone through something similar at around the same time. He'd badgered me to tell him what I wanted for my birthday, but I couldn't think of a thing. Then on a day out with a girlfriend I drove past the Rolls-Royce showroom in Beverly Hills and spotted the most divine white Corniche with camel leather seats in the window. "I think I know what I'd like for my birthday," I told him from the car.

"Shoot," he said. To my delight and surprise, the Corniche was waiting for me in the driveway when I arrived home from my lunch. A note on it read, *"For my True Love."*

President Sadat must have wondered what he'd gotten himself

into by offering his wife anything she wanted, because Jehan asked for money to build an extraordinary city of hospitals and rehabilitation centers for the veterans of the 1967 Six-Day War, in which fifteen thousand Egyptians were killed or wounded. To be named the Faith and Hope Rehabilitation Center, it would offer vocational training for the amputees and wounded, employing other veterans to support those being treated. It was a remarkable and innovative scheme that had never been tried before. Knowing how much funding the project would require, Jehan asked Frank if he could include a visit to Cairo on his next tour for a benefit. As always, Frank's reply was "Tell me where I have to be and when." Furthermore, he flew in all his own musicians, paying their wages, airfares, and hotels. It didn't cost the charity a dime.

I think of all the men I've met in my life (and I've met quite a few), the one who impressed me the most was President Sadat. He was a man of great intelligence but also gentle and kind. When I was with him, I felt that I was in the presence of a true statesman, and I know Frank did too. The concert Sadat organized for his wife was one hell of a birthday present. Everyone who was anyone in Europe and the Middle East flew to Cairo to see what they knew would be quite a show—Sinatra performing in front of the Sphinx with the Great Pyramid of Giza in the background, all cleverly lit. Those who had paid $2,500 a head for tickets to the dinner, concert, and fashion show sat at tables set out on a carpet of rugs laid on the sand, dining on lobster and veal. Frank clearly enjoyed every minute too and said afterward it was "the biggest room I ever played." It was an unbelievable event and certainly, for me, one of the most memorable.

Our hospitality suite was a huge Bedouin tent set up in the middle of the desert near where camel trains had been passing for centuries. Poor things, they had to be rerouted temporarily. Seeing them tramping past in the dunes day after day was fascinating and primitive. It was a long way from my first sight of a camel in a textbook in Bosworth, when I'd wondered if such a strange creature really existed. Watching the camels made me want to ride one, so I asked if it could be arranged. Frank wasn't going anywhere near one, but he hung around to watch me and take photographs. After climbing up onto the back of the beast, I was led along a dirt track by a dark-skinned Arab in a long robe as Frank snapped away. It was surprisingly high up there and felt rather precarious, even more so when my camel suddenly broke free from his handler and galloped off into the desert.

As I clung on for dear life, I could hear Frank going crazy behind me, screaming at the handler in unadulterated New Jersey. "You f****** mother f*****! How could you let this happen, you son of a bitch! Get my wife back here! Go get her." He called that guy every name in the book. Fortunately, the camel finally stopped to nibble at a desert bush, leaving me shaken and breathless but unharmed. Frank, meanwhile, was still jumping around in the dust blasting the poor man responsible.

Suddenly, the hapless Arab pulled off his headdress and threw it into the dirt. He told Frank, "Look, Mr. Sinatra, I'm not Egyptian. I'm from New Jersey." Pointing to his skin, he added, "This is makeup, and you really shouldn't talk to people like that!"

Once Frank realized I was safe, he had no choice but to see the funny side.

Ever since Dolly's death, Frank seemed to find solace in the religion his mother had taught him and then me. He began to attend Mass with me more often, and he loved it when I took over a fund-raising project of Dolly's to rebuild a church in Cathedral City. With the help of a golf tournament, we managed to raise more than her target amount. One thing that kept haunting him, though, was the fact that we had never been officially married in the eyes of our church.

The more Frank thought about that, the more the omission bugged him. Still grieving for his dead mother, he told me morosely, "She'd have wanted that." As someone who'd been married three times before and who'd chosen a wife who'd tied the knot twice, he didn't believe it would ever be possible. That was until he sought the counsel of Father Tom Rooney, a family friend. To Frank's surprise, he learned that according to the laws of our faith the only marriage that counted was his twelve-year partnership with his first wife, Nancy—the only one that had been sanctified in a Catholic church. If Frank could have that marriage annulled, we would be free to repeat our wedding vows in a way that he believed would appease his mother's spirit. I loved the idea of being properly married in the eyes of the church I'd embraced as my own, but I knew the suggestion of an annulment would be controversial and I had no intention of getting involved. I hadn't been with Frank all those years and learned nothing about keeping my nose out of his private affairs. In the end, he went ahead and organized it himself. I think it was something he needed to do for Dolly.

When everything had been officially sanctioned by the authorities, Frank and I went off quietly to stay with our friend the "Irish Nightingale" Morton Downey at his home in Palm Beach, Florida. We repeated our wedding vows in a Catholic ceremony overlooking the ocean, officiated by a priest friend of Morton's. It was romantic and fun and felt like yet another new beginning. From the day we were married, Frank had always referred to me as his "bride," and I suddenly felt like one again, in another lovely gown and with tropical flowers threaded through my hair. It was on that trip that Ann Downey and I were invited to the beautiful Kennedy house right on the ocean in Palm Beach to play tennis with Teddy and some others. Rose Kennedy, the indomitable matriarch of the clan, was in residence, so after our game we were invited to her room for Mass. She was a strict Catholic and had a priest come every day. The octogenarian mother of nine had lost an eye by then and wore a patch. When we walked into the room, her one good eye homed in on me and didn't avert its gaze. There were several of us sitting there, but that tiny woman just stared and stared at me until Teddy Kennedy was so uncomfortable that he said, "Here, Barbara, come and sit over here." I moved to another seat, but the eye followed me. It was most disconcerting. I have no idea why she took such an interest or who she thought I might be. She never said.

After our romantic sojourn in Florida, Frank decided that the simple service in the Everglades wasn't good enough, so he asked me to arrange for us to be married once more in a full Catholic service in St. Patrick's Cathedral, New York. Both of us loved "St. Paddy's" and had mused about how nice it would have been to have married there the first time around, so when we were finally able to face each other, hold hands, and take our vows in the exquisite Lady Chapel, it meant a great deal to us both.

As part of the healing process after Dolly's death, Frank made another decision that came as a complete surprise. We were sitting across the aisle from each other on his plane coming home from somewhere when he scribbled a note and handed it to me. *"I want to adopt Bobby,"* he'd written. *"I love him and I want him to be my son. He deserves to be part of a bigger family."*

Startled, I cried, "But, Frank! He's a fully grown man, not a boy. I'm not sure he wants to be adopted."

"I've made up my mind," Frank replied. "I'm going to do this, for you and for him." He wouldn't listen to my protests and sent another message back to his lawyer, Mickey Rudin, sitting in another part of the plane. Mickey came forward to try to talk him out of it, but Frank was most insistent. "Just do it!" he snapped finally.

When we got home, I called Bobby to gingerly explain Frank's proposal. His reaction was as I expected. "But, Mother, I don't want to be adopted," Bobby said. "I have a father, and anyway, I already took Zeppo's name. It's very kind of Frank, but please tell him this isn't what I want at all."

Poor Bobby. I truly felt for him. The men in my life had not always been very sensitive to his needs, and at that time he was trying to reconnect with his real father, Bob, who was still in Europe. Bobby knew Bob had prevented Zeppo from adopting him all those years before, and I think my son sometimes regretted changing his name to Marx, so I completely understood his position. I pleaded his case to Frank, but my pigheaded Italian husband was determined to go ahead. In the end, his family vetoed the idea anyway, so nothing ever came of it. I tried to tell Frank it didn't matter. I said, "Look, darling, it doesn't make any difference. Why upset yourself like this? Bobby's our son in all but name anyway. I wouldn't pursue this; it's way too controversial." He finally capitulated but I knew he was wounded.

Bobby had other father-figure issues to work out anyway because in 1979 the man who'd been his first stepfather got sick. Zeppo had sold the house I'd shared with him by then and moved to a place on the golf course just off Frank Sinatra Drive (which I always thought was kind of ironic). He called me from there one day and asked me to drive him to his doctor in Los Angeles, who informed me for the first time that my ex-husband was in remission from cancer. Before too long, though, it came back. Zeppo was old and alone with all his brothers dead and no one left to love, which made me sad. In return for the kindness he'd shown them, my family took care of him in his final days.

A few days before he died, I went to visit Zeppo in the hospital. He had an awful rattle in his throat, which told me the end was near. I'd loved him once, so it was horrible to see the dashing gambler who'd wooed me in Vegas looking old and frail. In his will, Zeppo left my son a handful of possessions and some money to finish his legal education, which was thoughtful. I sent flowers and went to his funeral with Frank, and Bobby stepped up and said a few words about the stepfather who'd become a friend. It was the closing of a door for us both.

ELEVEN

With Prince Rainier and Princess Grace of Monaco at the anniversary party we threw for them at our Palm Springs home.

COURTESY OF BERLINER STUDIO/BEIMAGES

Come Rain or Come Shine

It is no secret that New York held a special place in Frank's heart. He loved having an apartment in Manhattan and always relished performing in the city and in nearby New Jersey, his home state.

One year he took me on a rare visit back to Hoboken on the west bank of the Hudson River. He showed me the site of the cold-water flat at 415 Monroe Street where he'd been born. Walking hand in hand in that square mile not far from what is said to be the birthplace of baseball, Frank showed me the streets where he grew up among gangs of Irish, Italians, and Germans. Within sight of the Lower Manhattan skyline, the Sinatra connection was recorded everywhere, from a bronze star on the sidewalk to a small museum next to the house he bought for his parents on Hudson Street. He took me to see the homes on Park Avenue and Garden Street where he'd lived as a teenager, and he drove me past the A. J. Demarest High School, from which he'd dropped out. At the local library, he told me, there was a collection of his books, paintings, and memorabilia he'd gifted in honor of his mother.

At the Hoboken jail, he told me a story that made me laugh out loud. The singing heroes of Frank's childhood had been Bing Crosby and Billie Holliday, so when Bing was arrested for being drunk in his neighborhood, Frank couldn't believe his luck. He hurried over to the jailhouse, which had its cells in the basement, their windows at street level. Getting down on all fours, Frank peered in at his incarcerated idol desperate to talk to him, sing for him, or get any professional advice he could. Sadly, poor Bing was so loaded he could barely respond and yelled at "the kid" to go away. Frank ribbed Bing about that years later when they became buddies in Palm Springs.

Frank showed me the saloons that he knew as a scrappy kid. He drove me to the site of the Rustic Cabin in nearby Englewood, where he'd been "discovered" singing songs and telling jokes in between waiting tables. Everywhere we went there were signs claiming that Frank Sinatra was here or Frank Sinatra worked there. There was a Sinatra Drive and plans for a Sinatra Park. The local diner sold a "Frank Sinatra Steak," and almost every Italian restaurant offered "Pasta Sinatra." It was his town, but just as I'd escaped Bosworth and made a better life for myself, Frank had gotten out of Hoboken. His legacy was the hope for those he left behind that they might escape too if that was what they wanted. "When I was there I just wanted to get the hell out," he once said. "It took me a long time to realize how much of it I took with me." With his strong sense of community, loyalty, and devotion to things Catholic and Italian, Frank was a Hobokenite through and through, and the place rightly claimed him as its own.

Despite his great love of New Jersey and New York, Frank didn't have a song that summed up his feelings about the place. I'd long thought that he should. When Martin Scorsese directed the 1977 musical *New York, New York*, starring Liza Minnelli and Robert De Niro (who Frank always hoped might play him in a movie one day), I had an idea. The title song written by John Kander and

Fred Ebb and belted out by Liza was such an incredibly powerful number that I suddenly realized it was perfect for Frank. It would be great for him because of his connection with New York, but I was convinced it would be a huge hit internationally too. When I first suggested that he record it, though, he dismissed my idea out of hand. "Naw, that's Liza's song," he said. "She does it great. I'd never take that away from her." Frank had been close to Liza's mother, Judy Garland, since the 1940s, and he treated Liza like a sassy daughter. His loyalty was touching.

"But, Frank," I countered, "you wouldn't be taking anything away from Liza—just doing it your way. 'New York, New York' is much more of a man's song. I mean, those lyrics—'king of the hill'? That's the story of your life!"

He wouldn't have it at first, but I'd keep trying to work my idea into the conversation whenever I could. I'd managed to influence his musical choices several times in the past simply by telling him, "Oh, I love that song, darling. It's one of my favorites," if I heard him practicing a number I particularly liked. He'd sort his music into three piles—"yes," "no," and "maybe"—and one word from me was usually enough to get something added to the "yes" pile. Our friend Steve Wynn, owner of the Golden Nugget hotels at that time, had a running joke with Frank about the song "Luck Be a Lady," which Steve understandably wanted Frank to sing whenever he performed in his casinos. Sitting opposite him on a plane en route to Atlantic City or Vegas, Steve (whom Frank called "the Kid") would wait anxiously to see which pile "Luck" would go into. Once, he made the mistake of picking up the music from the "no" pile and telling Frank, "But you have to sing this at the Nugget!" at which Frank slapped his hand and seized it back. Seeing Steve's doleful expression, he upgraded "Luck" to a maybe and then, eventually, to a yes. Frank, with mischief in his eyes, went through that routine every time he saw Steve after that.

I fell foul of Frank's obstinacy a few times too. When a

would-be songwriter cornered me backstage once and begged me to play Frank a tape of a song he'd written, I listened to the number and thought it was great. The trouble was, Frank refused to hear it, so one morning I put the tape on very loud in my bathroom next to his as we were getting ready to go out. Frank came bursting in and yelled, "What are you listening to that rubbish for? Don't you know you've got the original right here?" I had to laugh.

Getting him to sing "New York, New York" was almost as tricky; I knew I was going to have to think of some other way to persuade him. Fortunately, I had several people on my side, including friends, fellow musicians, and executives at his record company, who were all for it. After a while, Liza's show closed and her single dropped off the charts, so Frank wouldn't be treading on her toes in any way. Then in 1978, when the New York governor Hugh Carey was running for reelection, I spotted my chance. I told Frank, "Okay, then, don't record 'New York, New York,' but at least work up an arrangement to sing at Carey's inauguration gala. Try it out there and see what happens." He finally agreed and asked Don Costa to arrange a brassy version for his voice accompanied by his usual big orchestra. He performed it at Radio City Music Hall in October of that year. Brought to life with his unique phrasing and impeccable timing, the number he almost didn't sing brought the house down.

A year later Frank relented and recorded what was to become a Sinatra anthem. He incorporated it into his Trilogy set of albums—*Past*, *Present*, and *Future*—his first new recordings in six years, chiefly because he'd been so busy touring. Those albums went straight to number one and garnered six Grammy nominations. Although he never admitted I was right to have suggested "New York, New York" for him, I know he always felt a great personal connection to the song because he chose it thereafter as his closing number, replacing "My Way." Not that he gave me any credit for that; he said only that it was too strong an opener and needed to be moved to the back. The irony was that the number's biggest fan (yours truly) rarely got to hear it all the way through because, by the time he was on his finale, I'd be slipping out the side door on his cue of *"These little town blues are melting away..."* But at least I heard it whenever we went to the big sporting events, because Frank's version of "New York, New York" was adopted by the Yankees and played after every victory, a fact that made us both very proud.

Barry Manilow performed a wonderful song for Frank called "Here's to the Man," which was a fine tribute. The lyrics to the song he co-wrote with Bruce Sussman were

> *Here's to you who wrote the book from your biggest fan*
> *Here's to old blue eyes, no need for goodbyes*
> *This one's for you*
> *Here's to the man*

It was another song entitled "Here's to the Band," written by Sharman Howe, Alfred Nittoli, and Arthur Schroeck, that I also persuaded Frank to record. Because of his love of music and lyrics and his great respect for the members of his orchestra, I thought it would be the perfect song for him. It was autobiographical as well as a tribute to the band members, who did such a great job in his shows. One memorable stanza goes

> *To start at the ground and reach for the top*
> *To have such a wonderful career, I just gotta stop*
> *Stop and turn around to thank everyone that sits on the stand*
> *'Cause I wouldn't have made it without them, here's to the band!*

As the century approached its ninth decade, Frank celebrated a remarkable forty years in show business. To mark the event, and his sixty-fourth birthday, he was invited to take center stage in a glittering televised tribute.

Recorded at Caesars Palace in Las Vegas for a two-hour special on NBC, the thousand-ticket show entitled *Sinatra: The First Forty Years* was sold out months in advance. Frank and I sat at a horseshoe-shaped table decked with white flowers as the actor Glenn Ford opened the proceedings and one great entertainer after another stepped onto the stage and said nice things about Frank. Telegrams of congratulations were read out from around the world, including those from Menachem Begin and Anwar Sadat, the Israeli and Egyptian leaders we'd met on our trips to the Middle East.

With Bobby on my right, I sat next to my husband of three years and laughed with him at comics like Red Skelton, Lucille Ball, Rich Little, Milton Berle, Pat Henry, and Charlie Callas. Gene Kelly, Dean Martin, Harry James, and Cary Grant all spoke warmly and humorously about their friend. Tony Bennett sang "(Frank's) Kind of Town," and Sammy Davis, Jr., announced, "I love you, Barb," before singing two numbers. Paul Anka did a funny take on "My Way," and the tenor Robert Merrill sang the entire list of Frank's fifty movie titles before thanking him for raising $1 million for the Memorial Sloan-Kettering Cancer Center at a benefit at the Metropolitan Opera House. Frank then performed five terrific numbers, including "New York, New York," and ended with "I've Got the World on a String," which he said summed up how he felt about his life.

The songwriter Jule Styne presented Frank with the prestigious Pied Piper Award from the American Society of Composers, Authors, and Publishers; Caesars Palace donated $100,000 in his name to the cancer foundation set up in memory of his friend John Wayne, who'd recently passed away. Dean presented Frank with an honorary diploma from his Hoboken high school before leading him in his first prom dance, because he'd missed the original. It was a hilarious end to a great night. As I sat at the top table, wearing an exquisite pearl choker Frank had bought me, dressed in a strapless fuchsia gown by Arnold Scaasi, I felt like a million dollars. My delight and pride as Frank's wife must have been evident to every green-eyed female in the place.

Wherever Frank went, women threw themselves at him. Young and old, they'd scream his name and lay flowers at his feet. I only had to gaze at the sea of upturned faces during one of his performances and feel the adoration coming from the audience like a heat wave. It was unbelievable. No wonder he never wanted to quit that business.

I'd had several years of on-the-road training, so I fully accepted that women would always be part of the deal with Frank. Not only was he sexy, powerful, and charismatic but much of his charm was his flirtatiousness, and his female fans expected nothing less. From the day we took our wedding vows, though, Frank went out of his way to make me feel incredibly secure. Not only did he invite me to accompany him almost everywhere, which meant that he was rarely alone, but he never stopped showing his love for me. "Don't take any notice," he'd tell me when a woman homed in on him at a party or dinner and tried to seduce him. Even when strangers turned up at the gates of the Compound claiming to be the mother or grandmother of his child, I learned to ignore them as he did. This was old hat to him, after all. If Frank had sired as many children as people claimed he had, there would have been an entire subrace of blue-eyed singers with an aversion to garlic and an unusual obsession for neatness. In Frank's words, if he were the womanizer everyone made him out to be, he'd have been a wonder of nature preserved in a specimen jar at Harvard.

There was one female fan of his that I came to recognize because she followed him so devotedly for years. I suppose these days people would call her a stalker. Her name was Betty Brink, and she'd been left some sort of inheritance that allowed her to purchase a front-row seat for virtually every concert Frank gave. We'd spot her ringside in auditoriums across the United States, and then we'd jet off to London, Paris, or Tokyo, and sure enough, Betty would be sitting there too. It was spooky. Even more so when we'd turn up at a restaurant and find Betty sitting in the next booth, her head tilted to listen to our conversations, to which she would occasionally chip in. She had an attractive face and blond hair, and once I came on the scene, she tried to make herself over to look more like me. She even researched which hairdressers I used and asked them to fix her hair just the same. She did everything she could to imitate me, wearing the same kinds of clothes and even adopting my way of walking and talking.

One day she went into the beauty shop at the Waldorf-Astoria in New York, having made an appointment under my name. The girls there didn't know it wasn't me until she began to cause trouble, throwing cans of hair spray all over the place and making unreasonable demands. When they dialed my room and I picked up the telephone, they realized she was an impostor and threw her out. On another occasion, I received a call from one of the chicest restaurants in New York asking, "Are you coming, Mrs. Sinatra? It is two o'clock and we've been holding your table for sixteen for over an hour."

I had made no such booking, and someone, probably Betty, had called up and made the reservation to make me look bad. Not long afterward, when Donald Trump was building his fifty-eight-story Trump Tower in New York, he called and left a message with Frank's secretary, Dorothy. "Could you please ask Barbara to confirm if she wants three or four apartments in the Tower, because she only talked about three last time." I had no idea what he was talking about, but Betty Brink did. She'd gone to the building site claiming to be me, and one of Donald's staff had believed her. She'd not only viewed the prospective apartments but told them how she was going to knock down walls and decorate them just so to make a perfect place for "Frank and me" to live. I wouldn't have minded because Betty was really rather pretty, but she had an ass the size of a house.

When Frank found out about her latest trick, though, that was the end for him. He told Mickey Rudin, "You have to get rid of that crazy dame. She's not to come to the shows anymore; she's not to be sold a seat at any venue where I'm performing. In fact, she's barred from being anywhere near us." He must have made it pretty clear, because Mickey went to see Ms. Brink in person and laid it on thick.

Not long afterward, we were at Caesars Palace for a series of shows and I came down in the elevator one night to take my seat. Walking past a small bar, I looked in and spotted a woman sitting by a mirror with a heavy black veil over her face. I stopped in my tracks, wandered in, and tapped her on the shoulder. "Hello, Betty," I said. She was panic-stricken that I'd recognized her and begged, "Don't tell Mr. Rudin that I'm here, Barbara! Please don't tell him." Poor Betty, I think she was truly sick. She died a few years ago, and I heard afterward that she'd spent her entire fortune seeing Frank perform around the world and ended up in debt to loan sharks. It was so sad that the love of a man she'd never even met could have turned to that kind of obsession and ruined her life.

We had a lot of crazies after Frank over the years, and we handed most of their details to the police or the FBI. Frank was always more concerned about my safety than his own; after all, as far as women were concerned, I was the enemy. He sent me to a shooting range in Cathedral City to learn how to use a gun and had Jilly give me a tiny pistol to carry in my purse. I was also told to carry a rifle on my saddle whenever I was out riding in the desert. Fortunately, I never had to use either weapon, although I did wish I had something on me when I found a strange woman in my bedroom at the Waldorf one day. "Who are you?" I asked, taken aback.

"Are you Barbara?" she replied, frowning. An image of her

pulling out a gun and shooting me dead flashed before my eyes. I didn't respond, so she smiled and pleaded, "Barbara, I've got to talk to Frank. Please, you have to help me!"

I managed a smile and told her, "Just a minute. I'll get someone who can." I went and found Jilly, who rushed in and escorted her out of there. I have no idea what she had in mind for me or for Frank, but it could have been the end.

Another strange woman gate-crashed a party we threw at a hotel, and when I asked who she was, she told me, "I'm a close friend of the family."

"But I *am* the family!" I informed her. She turned tail and fled.

One woman tried to get in to see Frank at our home in Los Angeles because she claimed that he kept buzzing over her house in a plane. Later she followed me to a restaurant and burst in to announce she'd had a child by Frank. She carried the fantasy on and on, bombarding us with mail that said things like "I know Frank's trying to reach me, Barbara, so would you please just give him this number and tell him he can call." She was completely loco. After a while we stopped hearing from her and hoped she'd given up. One day Frank opened a newspaper in Palm Springs and saw her photograph accompanying a story that she'd been run over and killed on Date Palm Drive, just a few miles down the road from our home. God only knows what she was doing there.

Frank attracted women. He couldn't help it. Just to look at him—the way he moved, and how he behaved—was to know that he was a great lover and a true gentleman. He adored the company of women, and he knew how to treat them. I had friends whose husbands were "players," and every time the husbands had affairs my friends were showered with gifts. Well, I was constantly showered with gifts, but no matter what temptations Frank may have faced when I wasn't around, he made me feel so safe and loved that I never became paranoid about losing him.

Privately, I sometimes discussed the possibility with my two

French girlfriends (who seemed to know about these things), and one of them warned me against complacency. "No matter how much he loves you now, you don't know what could happen in the future," she said. "You must have a Plan B." Thinking of Lee Annenberg's advice when I married Frank, to "be nice, be sweet, be adorable, but look the other way," my Plan B was to look the other way, if ever I had to. I had a great life, traveling the world with the man I loved, who went out of his way, every day, to please me. From the day he'd married me, I felt cherished from dawn till dusk. He'd named a plane and a boat after me. He bought me the most exquisite things and took me to the finest places. If ever I was unwell, he'd sit with me and take care of me in the sweetest and most attentive way. I was confident that he truly loved me and that we'd both finally found contentment and tranquillity in each other's arms. And he never gave me cause to think otherwise.

With my own unhappy past and for a man like Frank, that was no mean feat. He could have had anyone he wanted. He could have left me at any point, but he never did; he never even came close. There were some who did their utmost to split us up, but that only made us more determined to stay together and prove them wrong. Ours was a deep love that would stand the test of time. I knew from the moment he kissed me on the terrace of his hotel suite in Monaco that I was the luckiest girl alive, and my luck—thank goodness—never ran out.

No matter how crazy our lives were and how much traveling we did, Frank made sure we spent a month in Monaco each summer reliving the first blissful days of our romance. It was his one guaranteed vacation a year, although he usually performed at Princess Grace's Red Cross Gala, so it wasn't entirely work-free.

He'd check us into the Churchill Suite of the Hôtel de Paris, where it all began, and we'd enjoy long days in the cabanas down on the beach just as we had when Bobby joined us from Switzerland.

The hotel staff loved having Frank to stay and would do anything for him. When he complained about the low quality of the sound system in the bar, for example, they let him replace it—to his slight regret. The speakers that once played gently muted background piano morphed into some high-tech high-fidelity system that could really hurt your ears in the wrong hands.

We'd revisit our favorite clubs and restaurants, like New Jimmy'z and Le Pirate, with the Ittlesons and any other friends who were in town. Our most frequent companions were probably Greg and Vero Peck and Cary Grant. Frank flew us to Biarritz; he treated us to the finest dinners; he borrowed a yacht for a cruise to St.-Tropez.

One memorable summer Kirk Kerkorian leased Robert Maxwell's fifty-five-meter superyacht *Lady Ghislaine* and sailed a group of us including Michael Caine, Roger Moore, and their wives to St.-Tropez for lunch and some retail therapy. We girls not only had the greatest fun shopping but then had the chance to dress up every night in clothes by our favorite designers, like Pucci and Armani, as well as our finest jewelry, including a few knuckle benders and the Holy Shit Necklace.

There were always a lot of laughs, especially when George Schlatter or "Bullethead" Rickles was around. One night Rickles and Frank and Jilly were in the bar at the Hôtel de Paris sheltering from the pouring rain. All of a sudden, there were some flashing lights and Frank scowled. "Get out there and tell those f***ers to stop taking photographs of me!" he said. "I've had enough paparazzi today. No more pictures." Jilly and Rickles went outside, took a look around, saw nothing, and came back in, soaking wet. They ordered another drink, but a few minutes later there were more flashing lights, so they hurried outside again to try to find the photographers who were irritating Frank. This went on for some time until finally they realized what the problem was. They were in the middle of a thunderstorm, and it was only lightning.

Realizing the storm had passed, they came back in and told Frank, "It's okay, we took care of it. They're gone."

Rickles usually stayed in the Hôtel Hermitage, across the street from the Hôtel de Paris, so he and Jilly worked out a special arrangement. When the time came for him to come over and start a day's carousing with Frank, Rickles would stand out on his balcony. If everything was going according to schedule and Frank was in a good mood, Jilly would stand on his balcony and wave a white napkin. If Jilly waved a red napkin, that meant Rickles should lock himself in his room and stay away until the coast was clear.

On one of his first visits to Monaco, Rickles came down to the Beach Club to meet us, but when he got to the gate, the guards wouldn't let him in. He went to another gate, but it was the same story. He wasn't a guest of the hotel and had no authorization to be there. "Hey, wait a minute!" he told the guards. "I'm friends with Frank Sinatra!" The French gorillas looked at him blankly, so he broke into "My Way." They might never have let him in but for Jilly, who heard what he described later as the worst rendition of Frank's famous song and went outside to shut him up.

Another memorable night was the Fourth of July just after Frank had won an important victory testifying to Congress about his supposed ties to shady characters and horseracing. We went to New Jimmy'z to celebrate and were sitting at one of the long banquettes near the indoor water feature that led to the pier on the shore. A photographer politely asked Frank if she could take his picture, and he told her, "Sure, baby, take as many as you want." Just as she was about to click the shutter, someone on the opposite banquette shoved her so that she fell onto the table, scattering drinks. Words were exchanged, but nothing more happened until later, when Frank, Jilly, and a few others went out onto the pier to set off cherry bombs and firecrackers to show their American patriotism.

Some of those sitting on the opposite banquette complained

that our group was too rowdy (which I'm sure they were). Among them was Hélène Rochas of the perfume house, who almost jumped out of her skin when a firecracker exploded near her. She was with a socialite named Kim d'Estainville, who picked up a half-empty bottle of vodka and threw it at us. It landed on our table, bounced off, and hit me full on the side of my head.

Bobby was the first on his feet, even though I didn't want him to get involved. He rushed over to d'Estainville, who was sandwiched between others with no easy way to get out. "Did you just throw a bottle at my mother?" Bobby demanded.

"What are you going to do about it?" d'Estainville replied.

"Get out of there and apologize!" Bobby insisted.

"Why, kid? Are you going to make me?" he said.

Before Bobby could respond, the lumpen shape of Jilly Rizzo flew with surprising grace toward the banquette. Monsieur d'Estainville didn't know what had hit him as he was grabbed by the scruff of the neck and yanked to his feet.

This can't be good, I thought, and I was right; a huge fight erupted. Everyone was throwing punches, even Frank. Tables, chairs, and lamps were flying all around me. To calm my nerves, I sat perfectly still drinking my martini and praying that nothing else would hit me. When people started taking pictures, Frank grabbed one of the cameras, pulled the film out, and threw it into the water. He then peeled off a hundred-dollar bill and handed it to the photographer as compensation. Needless to say, Monsieur d'Estainville ended up getting wet too.

Almost as soon as the trouble had begun, though, it was over. I finished my martini, Frank straightened his jacket, Jilly cracked his knuckles, and we grabbed our coats and went back to the hotel. The following morning there was a knock on the door, and four armed officers walked in asking for Jilly, who—they'd been informed—was the instigator of the fracas. Like in a scene from a Marx Brothers movie, Jilly hid, his feet sticking out beneath the heavy silk drapes, while the police conducted a quick search and left without finding him. Sitting on the couch with a bag of ice pressed to my head, watching the whole drama unfold, I suddenly knew what it must have felt like to be a gangster's moll.

Prince Rainier heard about the fight the following morning and came to ask us about it. "What in the hell happened?"

We tried to explain and I showed him my bruise, but he just shook his head. "You were in Monte Carlo, Frank, and not some backstreet joint in New York!" he chided.

Frank, Bobby, and I would spend time at the Grimaldi Palace with Grace and Rainier, swimming or playing games, or we might go with them to their summer home in the hills above Monaco at a place called Roc Agel. Grace adored Frank, and the feeling was mutual. They had a wonderful friendship, and not just because he often performed in her gala. That was always such a highlight, though, held at the Sporting Club right on the water and ending in the most spectacular fireworks display.

Cary Grant made sure he was in one of the best seats for that because he was not only a great friend of Grace's and Frank's but probably one of Frank's most devoted fans. He once said of my husband that he was the most honest person he'd ever met and had a "simple truth, without artifice" that scared people. I never forgot that. Tears would roll down Cary's face when Frank sang some of his most moving songs; Cary felt the words so deeply. Cary was such a sweetheart, and I think Grace felt closer to him than to almost anyone. They'd first met in 1955, when they were filming Hitchcock's *To Catch a Thief* in the South of France, just before she met and married her handsome prince.

Grace was a fabulous woman who liked to surround herself with her children and her friends and make everything fun. Rainier was funny too and surprisingly down-to-earth, but it was Grace who was the playful one with a gleam in her eye. She reminded me of Dinah Shore because of her wicked sense of humor and great storytelling ability. She liked to have a drink and some laughs, yet she looked like the most elegant creature alive.

She also had great compassion and was very kind to Bobby, for which I will always be grateful. Bobby worked on the one movie his father ever made—*Frankenstein's Castle of Freaks*. When Rainier discovered that the film was finished and that Bobby had even played a minor role, he insisted that he bring it to the palace for a special screening during a party he and Grace were hosting. Poor Bobby knew that was a bad idea and so did I, but Rainier could be most insistent, so my son did as he was asked. Grace assembled about thirty influential people she knew to watch the movie, whose premise was that Count Frankenstein brings a dead caveman back to life in his castle laboratory. It was described by one critic as "like a deranged Italian soap opera." As the movie started rolling, featuring its characters Igor, Goliath, and Ook, silence descended on the room like a shroud. Bobby appeared on screen, followed by his grandmother Marge, who was so short that the sleeves of her dress scraped the ground, and finally his father, Bob, hopping in front of the camera in between duties as director.

Rainier, who'd insisted that this was a good idea in the first place, clammed up. Prince Albert fled the room, leaving Bobby to face the music. Bobby sat there sweating and wanting to run away too when Grace saved the day. Having picked up on everyone's discomfort, she suddenly forced a laugh and cried, "Ha ha ha! Oh, Bobby, this is *so* funny. You never told us it was a comedy!" The ice was broken, and everyone else felt free to laugh too. What a darling she was.

In 1978, she and Rainier invited us to the wedding of their daughter Caroline to her first husband, Philippe Junot. Everybody imaginable was there, including royalty from across Europe mingling with movie stars and celebrities. The Pecks had a villa not far from Monaco and hosted several parties for us and the other wedding guests. When the paparazzi tried to climb over the fences to see in, Greg took great delight in turning the garden hose on them.

One night when Frank was cooking us all pasta, he and Greg began to nag Cary about not having a date, because he was the only one of us who was on his own. Frank asked Cary, "Isn't there a girl in London you like?"

"Well, yes, there is one," Cary admitted, "but every time I take her out all she talks about are her previous boyfriends."

Frank looked at Greg and Greg looked at Frank, and the two of them nodded. "That's it!" Frank said. "She's the one. Call her and tell her to come." So Frank sent his plane to collect this woman to be Cary's date for the week. Her name was Barbara, and within a couple of years they were married. Barbara was his fifth and final wife, and was with dear Cary until the day he died.

We had a fabulous time at Princess Caroline's wedding, but not everyone was as relaxed and happy as we were. Enjoying the setting of yet another party, this time at the villa of David Niven, I happened across Rainier standing by a tree on his own. I could tell by his face that something was wrong, so I asked him if he was all right. He complained miserably, "My daughter's marrying a playboy." Then he pointed out various members of the groom's family. "You see them? They've been married four times. And that couple there? They've been married three times." As a devout Catholic, he thoroughly disapproved. I was wondering how to slip away when I spotted Greg talking to a statuesque woman. Lamely, I made my excuses and joined them. No one introduced us, and she went on talking about her son doing this and having that until finally Greg asked, "Well, who *is* your son?"

She smiled and paused a moment before explaining, "King Juan Carlos of Spain."

Dear Greg, he made a similar faux pas on the day of the wedding. I was standing in line between him and Frank to meet the bride and groom when a man in a crisp white uniform plastered in medals approached us. When Greg shook his hand, he asked, "Don't I know you? Weren't you in *The Guns of Navarone*?" The man shook his head. "*How the West Was Won* then?" Greg pressed, frowning. No was the reply. "Well, who are you?" Greg finally inquired. To his eternal embarrassment, it was Prince Michael of Greece.

Leaving for the reception later on, we saw a famous beauty who was married to a Middle Eastern prince. She was wearing the most unbelievable diamonds, and as I passed by I leaned forward and said into her hair, "Nice ice!" She spun round and asked, "*Qu'est-ce que?* Ice?" but there was no time to explain and we moved on. A few hours later she came up to me, pointed to my jewelry with a smile, and said, "Nice rocks!"

Ava Gardner was at the reception, and Frank spoke to her briefly while I was chatting with the actor Ricardo Montalban. Then I noticed Frank speaking privately to Cary a few minutes later. Shortly afterward, Cary took Ava gently by the arm and walked her out. When he came back half an hour later, I asked him what had happened, and he smiled sadly and said, "Ava needed to go and lie down. Frank asked me to make sure someone drove her back to her hotel." I nodded my understanding and thanked him for his kindness.

Frank was still so protective of Ava, not least because she'd frequently call him up and tell him what was going wrong in her life. Once, she was badly bitten breaking up a fight between her dogs, so Frank offered to pay her medical bills. Another time she called to tell him she had pneumonia and needed to go to Barbados to recuperate, so he arranged it. He was always sending her money; that was the type of heart he had. He took care of people he loved. I never minded a bit; I knew Ava Gardner wasn't a threat anymore.

I was having a manicure at the Compound one day when Frank's housekeeper, Vine, came in to tell me I was wanted on the telephone. "Who is it?" I asked.

"Miss Gardner," she replied, giving me a look.

Ava wasn't in the habit of calling me up, so I was quite taken aback, but I took the call. After the opening niceties, Ava said suddenly in that wonderfully deep voice of hers, "Tell me, Barbara. Are you and Frank *really* happy?"

"I can only tell you this," I replied, "I'm very happy. You'll have to ask Frank if he is as happy as I am. He's in Las Vegas right now, and you can call him there if you like. I'll give you his number." I have no idea if she ever called and asked him the same question; if she did, Frank never mentioned it. All I knew was that Jilly said to me later, "So, Ava called you, huh?" I nodded, but nothing more was said.

When Grace and Rainier were about to celebrate their twenty-fifth wedding anniversary, we invited them to spend it with us in Palm Springs and were delighted when they accepted.

They came with their children, and we threw them a series of parties and dinners, inviting old friends Grace had known in the business. Frank bought the happy couple a Fabergé box as an anniversary gift, and we made sure the weeklong celebrations were as wonderful and warm as the events Grace hosted in our honor each year. We had a cake made for them, and they cut it and made speeches before Grace insisted that everyone smear icing all over one another's faces. "It's an old tradition in Monaco!" she cried, licking frosting from her chin, but to this day I think she made that part up.

In spite of her fun side, Grace was very religious and went to church almost every day. As they were staying with us over Easter, she got up at six o'clock on Easter Sunday morning and drove to a little church she liked in the mountains outside Palm Springs for Mass. The rest of us late risers chose to go to the St. Francis of Assisi Church in nearby La Quinta, for which Frank, Cubby Broccoli, Frank Capra, and Franco Zeffirelli had been the chief fund-raisers. We piled into a convoy of cars and arrived as the service was starting, virtually doubling the congregation. Father Blewitt, the celebrant, welcomed us in before inviting some of our guests to take part in the Mass. He announced to the congregation that the day's readings would be by Roger Moore, Gregory Peck, Frank Sinatra, and Tom Dreesen.

One by one, the everyday churchgoers of La Quinta began to take notice. "Isn't that Cary Grant passing the plate?" one whispered to another in astonishment. "And who's that over there?" Prince Albert walked up to the altar with the gifts while Rainier looked on. Frank stood up first, and then Roger did his bit, followed by Greg Peck, one of the greatest actors in the world, who gave a biblical reading worthy of Moses. As Frank always said, when Greg spoke, the earth stood still. Tom Dreesen read his passage, and then, just after he'd sat back down, Father Blewitt asked Tom if he wouldn't mind also telling a joke. Tom was horrified, but Frank elbowed him and said, "Tommy, get up there and tell them a joke." I worried for him, because although he always made me giggle, I wasn't sure that was his crowd. Tom's mind was clearly working overtime as he made his way to the lectern, but then he sang the lines as in a psalm, "I'm the priest of this church and I make two hundred dollars, but that's not enough." Then he sang, "I'm the bishop of this church and I make four hundred dollars, and that's not enough." Finally, he sang, "I'm the organist of this church and I make two thousand dollars, and there's no business like show business." The whole event was a scream and, without doubt, the best Easter Mass I ever attended. Father Blewitt certainly talked about it for years.

Our summers in Monaco provided us with some of the best times of our lives for many years. Having raised a great deal of money in Vegas hosting the Sinatra Magic Carpet Weekend, we decided to hold one in Monte Carlo for the Princess Grace Foundation–USA, which supports young performing artists. We charged $25,000 a head and raised well over a million dollars.

Those who bought tickets were flown into Nice and invited to parties as well as Frank's performance at the gala and all sorts of glitzy events they couldn't normally get into. Our friend the entrepreneur John Kluge let us use his yacht for some of the parties, and the advertising mogul Mary Wells Lawrence and her husband, Harding (CEO of Braniff Airways), hosted a lunch for our guests at which Prince Albert turned up in a speedboat. The venue was their eighteenth-century villa, Villa Fiorentina, at St.-Jean-Cap-Ferrat.

Dear Mary, she threw another party in Frank's honor at Villa Fiorentina one summer to which she'd invited Henry Ford and King Juan Carlos, among others. The villa was a forty-five-minute drive from Monte Carlo, and Frank hated being in cars longer than about fifteen minutes. He felt trapped in the small space, no matter how fascinating the company or interesting the scenery. It wasn't until years later that I found out he suffered from car sickness but never admitted it. Everyone (including me) just assumed he was grumpy, and no one wanted to travel with him. Needless to say, Bobby and I got stuck with him that night, and Jilly rode separately with Don Rickles. Frank never stopped complaining the whole way along that winding coastal road. "How much farther?" he'd ask. "Can't you go any faster?" Then, the closer we got, "I'm not going to this damn party."

We finally arrived at the villa with its steps leading to an enormous veranda. As we pulled in the gravel driveway, we could see everyone waiting for us in the setting sun. Musicians were playing, and the alfresco dinner was prepared. Frank stepped out of our car, took one look at those strangers on the terrace, and said to Jilly, "We're going back." I'm sure there were a lot of complicated reasons—chiefly that he didn't want to be the center of attention yet again, especially surrounded by people he didn't know and might not like. It wasn't logical for him to complain about being in the car and then choose to sit in it for another forty-five minutes, but there was little logical about Frank.

As everyone stood waiting eagerly to catch their first sight of him, he sat back in the car. I tried to persuade him to stay, but he wouldn't budge. I knew how far to push it, so I finally leaned in and asked him, "Are you sure this is what you want to do?"

"Yes," he replied. "You go have fun." And off he went, back to the Hôtel de Paris bar. Taking a deep breath and fixing a smile on my face, I turned to explain why the guest of honor wouldn't be attending the dinner thrown for him. Mary came hurrying down the steps as I began walking up them. "Where's Frank going?" she asked, with something akin to panic in her eyes.

"I'm so sorry," I replied, "but he had a terrible migraine and he simply had to go to bed."

A few feet away I heard Don Rickles tell Mary's husband, "Frank has an earache. He had to go back and see a doctor." Bobby claimed Frank had twisted his ankle. My darling husband hadn't given us enough time to get our stories straight. We could almost hear the buzz sweep across the party as our absurdly conflicting alibis were repeated and contradicted. Our little gang, regrouping later by the bar, could only shrug off the confusion we'd caused. Mary laughed it off and was extremely gracious about it. It was pretty obvious that Frank was going to do exactly what he wanted to do, and that was that. I didn't care; I had a great time, dancing the night away in that most fabulous of settings.

When I finally got back to our hotel, I knew Frank would be waiting in the little lobby bar we loved. He was sitting grinning like the cat with the cream at our corner table. "Was that worth spending half a lifetime on the road for?" he asked, proffering me a drink.

"It was a beautiful party, darling," I told him, "and I slept like a baby all the way home."

Having always had such happy days and nights in Monaco and the South of France, we had every reason to believe our delightful annual routine would continue for years to come. One terrible summer, however, more than a decade into our glorious ritual, that all changed.

After our usual month in the company of Grace and Rainier, we were due to fly to New York for Frank to keep a ten-day engagement with Buddy Rich at Carnegie Hall. On our last day, Grace invited us to Roc Agel for tennis and a picnic in the verdant hills surrounding the family farm. We had a perfect day, and then we prepared to leave. I hugged Grace good-bye and thanked her once again. "See you next year, if not before!" I cried as she waved us off. The road back down the hill to Monte Carlo was steep, full of twists and turns overlooking a sheer cliff. I had traveled down it with Grace before, when she drove me to the hospital in her old Rover to say good-bye to Henry Ittleson before he died. Grace was a fast driver but a good one. She knew the road well, and I felt completely safe. On this occasion, though, we had Frank's driver Bruno take us. When we got to our hotel, we packed, and then we flew to New York as planned.

The next day we received a telephone call from Rainier. "There's been a terrible accident," he told us, his voice breaking. "Grace and Stephanie were driving down from Roc Agel, and they went off the road. They're in the hospital. Stephanie will be all right, thank God, but they're not sure about Grace." We were badly shaken, and Frank offered to cancel his concerts and fly straight back. Rainier insisted there was no need, intimating that Grace might survive. Leaving Frank to face his waiting fans, Bobby and I flew back to Monaco but learned almost as soon as we landed that dear Gracie had died. When Frank heard the news, he said it felt as if his heart had been pierced.

Monaco went into national mourning, and the public displays of grief lasted weeks. Bobby and I attended the private family vigil and dinner before Grace's funeral, which was a huge affair. We were shepherded into a cordoned-off area away from the thousands of subjects who lined the narrow streets in searing heat. Rainier, ash gray, walked down from the palace with Albert and Caroline. It was surely the saddest of days. We walked back up to the palace afterward, and when we got there Bobby passed out from the heat. Someone grabbed him and fetched him a chair, and dear Albert looked after him; he was unbelievably thoughtful like that—even on the day of his mother's funeral.

We knew exactly where the accident had happened, on a steep hairpin bend with rocks alongside the cliff. I asked Bobby to drive me there so I could see where Grace had somehow driven her Rover down a ravine. We got out and saw the marks on the road and knew we were in the right spot, so we left flowers and said a prayer. It was all we could think to do.

Rainier was never the same after Grace died. I don't think he ever got over it.

We stayed in contact with him because he was so dear to us, but it just wasn't the same for us either. We went back to Monaco for a few more summers, but it didn't feel the same in the palace without Grace. She was a woman's woman as much as she was a man's woman, a truly special lady. She was so gorgeous and so good, and she handled all her charity work so elegantly, yet she had that fun side to her too. After a few years, we decided not to return to Monaco, and we never did, although Bobby still visits and he and I are now on the board of trustees of the Princess Grace Foundation–USA.

To remind us of happier times in Monte Carlo, Frank created what is still one of my favorite paintings. It is a vivid starburst of oranges and reds and yellows, exactly like one of the chrysanthe-mum fireworks that ended Grace's galas. He called it *Monaco Boom*. For us both, that picture represented some of the best days of our lives. Each time I see it, I think of Frank and I think of Grace and I cannot help but smile.

TWELVE

Out with Henry and Nancy Kissinger, as well as
Greg and Veronique Peck.

I Get a Kick
Out of You

Probably one of the bravest things I ever did in my life was to organize a surprise sixty-fifth birthday party for Frank. The man who so enjoyed springing surprises on those he loved did not enjoy being surprised in return.

In the months leading up to his birthday, I'd asked him, "If you could have anything you wanted in the world, darling, what would it be?"

He thought about it for a while before replying, "I'd have a fantastic jazz orchestra and I'd be the only one sitting there while they blow at me."

I thought long and hard about how I could possibly arrange that and came up with a plan to make a jazz orchestra the finale to a party thrown in his honor. It might not be exactly what he'd asked for, but it would be close. The trouble with Frank was that there was always a risk he'd turn around and walk away. I figured that if our closest friends were there, at least we could go ahead without him. With a guest list of 250, Frank's party would be impossible to keep secret if I held it at home. It would work only if I held it at the fifteen-acre desert ranch where I kept my horses—the last place on earth Frank would go. Taking my courage in both hands, I decided on a Western-style cookout with barbecue ribs, chicken, chili, and hot dogs. It took me months to get everything ready: the food, the tent off the side of our barn, the decoration of the stables with hay bales and gingham. Sworn to secrecy, Jilly helped me with the entertainment, which was to include the country singer Mel Tillis and the full jazz orchestra Frank had asked for. I never thought I'd be able to pull it off.

I invited almost everyone we knew, including the entire kitchen cabinet—President-Elect Reagan, Walter Annenberg, and Spiro Agnew. The rest of the guest list included Paul Anka, Fred Astaire, Tony Bennett, Peggy Lee, Alfred Bloomingdale, Frank Capra, Mary Benny, Don Drysdale, Morton Downey, Armand Deutsch, Sammy Davis, Jr., Johnny Carson, Henry Fonda, Peter Falk, Cary Grant, the Firestones, the Gosdens, Harry James, the Kluges, Dean Martin, Mort Viner, Jack Lemmon, Burt Lancaster, the Korshaks, Robert Mitchum, Roger Moore, Tony Orlando, Wayne Newton, Steve Ross, Don Rickles, the Pecks, the Schlatters, the Wagners, Jimmy Stewart, Orson Welles, and Dinah Shore. Most were invited along with their wives, husbands, or significant others.

Their invitations read:

Please keep this under your Stetson but I'm tossing a surprise
birthday party for my blue-eyed cowboy on December 12
at 7:15 p.m. at Dominick's restaurant, Rancho Mirage,
Highway 111. Keep it under your Stetson but wear it. The
party will be Western attire. You can be a good guy or a bad
guy, a homesteader or a dance hall queen. We want to see
you there and don't breathe a word. I've got an itchy trigger-
fingered posse ready for anyone who blabs. Please RSVP,
ya hear! Love, BAS. P.S. No gifts please.

On the night of the party, I asked our friends to meet at Dominick's restaurant before being transported to the ranch in a convoy of yellow school buses. When Milton Berle's wife, Ruth, arrived and saw the stables, she quipped, "Oh, so that's where Frank was born!"

To make sure that Frank was also dressed up, I told him that we'd been invited to a Western-style party for the birthday of his friend the cardiologist Danny Kaplan. I hired cowgirl and cowboy costumes for us and managed to get him into his blue suede jacket, red neckerchief, and tan cowboy hat without too much complaint. Then we got into his car. Mr. Punctual was driving, but as we approached the street near the stables, I suddenly said, "Oh, Frank, I have a sick horse and I just have to stop by and check on it before we go to dinner." It was all part of my master plan.

But master plans need the master to be compliant. "No," he replied flatly, his hands gripping the steering wheel. "We'll be late. You can see it tomorrow."

My heart almost stopped. "But I *have* to," I protested. "I promised the vet."

"No way, baby," he said, shaking his head. "I'm not going to the stables tonight, least of all dressed like this!" We were almost at the intersection where he'd have to turn so as not to be late for his own party, something he'd never forgive me for.

In desperation and thinking of our waiting guests, I panicked and cried, "Frank, if you love me, if you've *ever* loved me, then make this turn here—right now!" He looked across at me as if I had gone raving mad, but he knew how much I cared for my horses, and by playing on his own love for animals, I finally broke him.

"Oh, for Pete's sake!" he cried as he made the turn. Driving too fast, he bumped us up the track. The moment he pulled into the yard and saw all the party lights he got the message. "So this is what it's about," he said, eyeing me suspiciously. He knew then that I'd truly surprised him, although I don't think he was too thrilled about it. His friends were waiting, and thank goodness, everything went according to plan. I could tell Frank was nervous all night, though, because he wasn't completely in control and he didn't like that at all. Toward the end of the evening, he told me, "I want to go home," and Frank had never said that.

"Wait a minute!" I cried. "You've got to hear the jazz orchestra. That's the part you said you really wanted." He did stay for that, sitting up front by himself just as he'd wished while they played him a terrific set. But then he really did want to go home, so that was the end of that. He never thanked me for organizing his surprise party, but he didn't tell me, "Never do that again!" either. Not that I had any plans to.

I think part of the reason Frank didn't enjoy being surprised was his masculine vanity. He'd always been a little vain in an old-fashioned Italian way. Extraordinarily for someone who'd chosen a career as an entertainer, he hated to be the center of attention, especially as he got older. One of the sexiest men in the world was in his seventh decade, and he didn't like the way that made him look and feel.

The natural side effects of the aging process began to bother Frank, and it was his thinning hair that troubled him the most. After combing it across the top of his head for a while, he decided to do something about it. "I don't care what I look like at home," he said, "but if I'm going to continue working, then I think maybe I should get a toupee." He found a great wig maker in New York named Joe Paris, who matched Frank's own hair pretty well. He didn't bother wearing Joe's toupee at home or with people he knew, and he didn't mind personal photographs being taken of him without it; he'd just put it on for the benefit of his public. The fact that Frank's hair was thinning never bothered me one little bit. I even toyed with the idea of planting a big red kiss on his bald spot like I used to do with old Pa Hillis in Bosworth, but of course Frank would never have held still long enough.

Frank also suffered intermittent hearing problems, not helped by his eardrum having been punctured at birth. The medical condition that kept him from serving in the war flared up repeatedly all his life. During one European tour, he managed to go onstage in London and Dublin despite a raging ear infection. By the time I got him home, he had to have his eardrum completely rebuilt in what was pioneering surgery for the time. The deafness this caused worsened as Frank aged, and that really bothered him too—especially onstage, where he'd stand near the drummer to ensure he could follow the beat or ask for strong bass notes in his orchestral arrangements. "Give me a little extra support on the horns, fellas," he'd tell the band.

He'd always been critical of his voice, and that only intensified the older he got. He never liked to discuss a performance afterward because he knew when his voice wasn't as good as it used to be. If someone told him he'd been great, he'd reply, "It was a nice crowd, but my reed was off" or "I wasn't so good on the third number." Strangely, in spite of his hearing problems, he had the most incredible ear, which often drove those he worked with nuts. There could be an orchestra of a hundred musicians, and if one played a single bum note he'd know exactly who was responsible. "I could have sworn you were here yesterday for rehearsals," he'd say, or he'd ask pointedly, "Where are you working next week?"

Despite his exacting standards, musicians, arrangers, and orchestra leaders loved working with Frank because he was the greatest. There was a force field of energy surrounding him that everybody fed off, and because he expected the best, he brought out the best in people. Those musicians would rather play for Frank than for almost anybody else. Just to be able to say they'd worked with the most important singer of his generation was worth the gig. Gordon Jenkins (whom Frank called "Lefty" because he was left-handed) arranged a great many of Frank's songs, and the two of them really got along. Lefty had been on the periphery of my life one way or another since before my Riviera days. Of a song that Gordon wrote in an autobiographical suite about Frank's life called "Before the Music Ends," he told me, "You're in that one, Barbara." I listened but couldn't hear any reference to me until Gordon explained, "It's in the line *'You won't hear me talking about saving shoes; baby's got fifty-seven pairs!'* "

That wasn't the only song in which I was referred to. Not long after we were married, Frank recorded a number called "I Love My Wife" from the Broadway show of the same name, set in New Jersey, which he sang just for me. Deciding that wasn't good enough, he had Jimmy Van Heusen and David Mack write a number specially for me called "Barbara." He surprised me by announcing it during one of his performances in Las Vegas as "a new song for a special lady," then sang it directly to me from the front of the stage. The first line was, "Where there is sunshine, there is Barbara."

Talk about romantic.

Without a doubt, my happiest times with Frank were spent in the company of friends at home or at play. He was never more relaxed than when he was off duty. As an ardent fan of baseball, he had boxes at the Dodger and Yankee stadiums, which were always great fun to go to, especially when Bobby joined us with whichever girlfriend he had in tow at the time. Frank and Dean Martin even started their own rival baseball teams (although I think they only ever played one game). My husband's team, which included Bobby, Tommy Lasorda, and Pat Henry, was called Old Blue Eyes, and Dean's was called Old Red Eyes. They started playing around three in the morning, and with the score tied at dawn, they went home. Pat said it was the only game that was stopped on account of light.

At Yankee Stadium, Frank would don a baseball cap and bomber jacket and watch the game sitting with the likes of Yogi

Berra. Frank was a great friend of Joe DiMaggio, who married Marilyn Monroe, and was also friendly with O. J. Simpson. I met O. J. once at a disco with his wife, Nicole, who was adorable; it was so sad how that ended. At Dodger Stadium in L.A., Frank would go to the locker room and give a pep talk to the players. Frank would sit on the first-base side, across from Tommy Lasorda in the dugout, eating hot dogs and drinking beer. Tommy was a huge Sinatra fan and had a wall in his office crammed with photographs of Frank. Don Rickles went into that office one day and asked Tommy, "Hey, where are my photos?"

Frank didn't much care for horseracing, which he thought was too slow, but he loved boxing, having been a featherweight fighter like his father, Marty, and his uncle Babe. Sugar Ray Robinson and Muhammad Ali, both of whom I met and loved, were friends. They were sweet and soft-spoken, not at all aggressive. At the famous Ali-Holmes fight in Vegas, we were sitting so close to the ring that I ended up splattered in blood and sweat. Frank also supported Joe Louis, the "Brown Bomber," until the end of his days, visiting him in Vegas and ultimately paying for him to be in the care of our friend Dr. Michael DeBakey in Houston when Joe suffered a stroke.

Home was the one place Frank could completely relax, and we still had a few to choose from. Frank had gifted his remote Pinyon Crest property to a religious order as a retreat, and we'd soon give up the New York apartment. The Coldwater Canyon house was sold after I was followed home one day by two men and Frank realized that I could have been trapped by the gates with no one to help me. The house was on the edge of a deep canyon, and there wasn't even anywhere to turn. I was saved only when I picked up the (broken) car telephone in Frank's Rolls-Royce and pretended to call for help. It was the days before cell phones, but the antenna on the phone went up and the would-be robbers saw that and reversed back down the hill. The dilemma was where we should buy in L.A. once we moved from the canyon. After skimming through a few property listings, Frank announced, "I'm too tired to look for a house. You do it."

"Okay," I replied. "Give me some parameters. How much do you want me to spend?"

"Just find something you like," he said, adding, "but not too big!" I must have viewed a dozen houses before I narrowed it down to three that he agreed to see with me. One was in the district of Holmby Hills, fabulous but enormous. He walked around the property, but there was no reaction from him at all—nothing—so we both got back into the car knowing that it wasn't the one. Then we went to see another in the same area, on Alpine Drive. The house and eight-car garage had burned down, but it was a great location and had a lot of land. As soon as I told him, "We'd have to build," Frank turned around and got back into the car.

I saved the best for last—a magnificent four-bedroom property on Foothill Drive above Sunset Boulevard in Beverly Hills. It had been owned and decorated by the agent Sandy Gallin. The music mogul David Geffen and the designer Calvin Klein had also been involved with choosing art for the place. Best of all, we wouldn't have to do a thing, just move in with our toothbrushes. I fell in love with it. The Universal Studios head, Lew Wasserman, and his wife, Edie, owned the property either side of us, so we had the best neighbors. We also had a lot of friends in that area, including George and Jolene Schlatter as well as Bee and Sidney Korshak. It was perfect. Frank and I walked in with the agent, but he got only as far as the living room. "Is this the one you like?" he asked me.

Hoping to negotiate a deal, I replied rather cautiously, "Well, yes, but it doesn't have a tennis court or a projection room, so it's far from perfect."

Frank grew impatient. "Do you want it or not?" he asked.

I nodded.

"We'll take it," he told the agent, who I'm sure couldn't believe his ears.

Frank walked out without even seeing the whole property. And so it was that we bought the house we referred to thereafter as Foothill. In the woods below our property, Frank discovered a tan-colored dog with all its teeth worn down after eating bark off trees. It was a stray and must have had some collie in it. Frank took that toothless dog to the vet and had his teeth reconstructed. He called it Leroy, after the song "Bad, Bad Leroy Brown," and Leroy lived with us happily until he died, always ready to give us a dentures smile.

Frank once asked me over breakfast, "If you could have a home anywhere in the world, where would it be?"

I thought of the fun times we'd had in Rome and Milan, and how stunning the European countryside was. "Italy," I replied.

Frank almost choked on his coffee. "Are you nuts?" he cried. "They'd kill us!"

"What do you mean?" I asked. "They love you!"

"That's exactly what I mean," he replied. "They'd kill us with love." He was right. I thought of the time we'd gone to the little village where Dolly had grown up near Genoa and had to be escorted through the crowds by armed police. Or the fans who'd rushed forward hysterically each time Frank had stepped from a limo or out of a *ristorante*. Frank was too adored in his ancestors' country ever to live there, I realized with a sigh. My Italian dream would have to remain just that.

Instead, we continued enjoying our friends and family in the comfort of our Italian-style homes—without the danger of being killed. Not that we didn't almost finish off a few of our friends in the process. One night the normally elegant and chic Jimmy Van Heusen was so drunk that Jilly and some of the boys had to carry him to bed. As they pulled him up the stairs, Jimmy's pants came down until his ass was sticking out. He was a big man, and they couldn't lift him onto the bed, so they left him on the floor, and his wife, Bobby, who was a tiny woman, just covered him up with a blanket. The following morning we were sitting around the pool when Jimmy walked out, chic as ever, head high, as if nothing had happened.

When Jack Benny came to stay at the Compound once, leaving Mary at their home in Los Angeles, he tried to keep pace with Frank, Dean, and the rest. There was no way he could win that contest, especially because he was diabetic. By the time we got to Ruby's Dunes restaurant, Jack could hardly stand. The next thing we knew he was facedown in his mashed potatoes. Uncle Ruby helped the boys carry Jack out to a back room while we had dinner. When we'd finished, they carried him to the car and took him home. The last thing Jack said to me as I put him to bed was "Don't tell Mary, Barbara! Whatever you do, don't tell Mary."

First thing next morning, Mary called up and said, "Well, I hear Jack got drunk last night." Somebody had blabbed.

Alan Shepard was with us at the bar one night when Jack walked in. Frank had met most of the Apollo astronauts at various benefits over the years, and Alan was in Palm Springs to play golf in Dinah's tournament. "Oh, my God!" Jack complained to everyone at the bar when he arrived. "I've just got back from Mexico City, and the altitude up there was so high!" We all fell over laughing, and Jack suddenly realized who he was talking to—the first American in space.

Greg Peck and Veronique were frequent visitors too, and Vero is still one of my closest friends. Greg and Frank had always been close, and Frank called him Ahab after his character in *Moby Dick* ("the movie with a fish"), but when Greg's son Jonathan died, in 1975, Frank was one of the first at his side. He did the same for Dean Martin twelve years later when his son Dino was killed in a plane crash. That was one of the best things about my husband—if something went wrong in your life, boom, he was there. And if you had him on your side, it was like having an army at your disposal. Furthermore, he was on your side if you were right or wrong, and that is something very special in a friend; you don't find that so often. Frank was the same with Sammy Davis, Jr., when he lost an eye in a car accident; Frank went to see Sammy in the hospital and then brought him back to Palm Springs to recuperate. Sammy loved Frank, so even though he was depressed, just being with his hero helped get him through that terrible time.

Frank took friendship and loyalty very seriously and believed that true friendship could only be tested in times of need. People just had to get word to him and he'd drop what he was doing and go spend time with them. He'd travel long distances to brighten someone's day, and I went with him to numerous hospitals and homes for retired singers and actors to cheer up old friends. He took me to see Gene Kelly in Santa Monica when he was first sick and to the bedside of John Wayne when he was dying. "The Duke" and Frank had been friends for years and were as close as brothers, even though they were diametrically opposed politically and kidded each other constantly about it. They knew each other from the days when Frank hung out with Humphrey Bogart, Jimmy Cagney, and all those great movie stars, who took a shine to the skinny kid with the sticking-out ears. Frank had already taken me to visit John Wayne at his home in Newport Beach, and I liked him very much. He was a big drinker of tequila and a heavy smoker, but he had a terrific sense of humor and that incredible roar of a laugh.

Frank and Gene Kelly had been in several films together, and for *Anchors Aweigh* Gene taught Frank how to dance outside studio hours. Frank called Gene "the Irish taskmaster" but he never forgot that kindness. Thanks to Gene, Frank could really move. He could even jump up in the air and click his heels together, and he loved to do that. He was also a terrific ballroom dancer, which was terribly romantic, but he didn't dance in public because as soon as he was on the floor, women would ask to cut in. When visiting Gene, I asked his nurse if she'd mind giving me a vitamin shot I needed. Gene laughed at me from his bed. "Sure, Barbara, put all your medical care on my bill and save Frank some money!"

At the Motion Picture Home, Frank took me to meet a couple of comedians he'd worked with decades earlier. His love for comedians knew no bounds. One year he even went out on tour with a bunch of old comics who weren't working so much anymore, people like Charlie Callas, Jan Murray, Richard Stein, Jack Carter, and Norm Crosby. He did it as a kindness to them, but it was a lot of fun for him too. As Burt Lancaster once said, "If you say to Frank 'I'm having a problem,' then it becomes his problem." Frank really had a calling for that.

Generosity came easily to Frank, and not just because he had a lot to give. Sure, he made great money; he knew he always could, and it meant little or nothing to him. He had a heart the size of New Jersey, and he wanted those he cared about to share in his success. There were some who played him for a sucker, of course, and managed to get anything they wanted out of him. Others stole from him more blatantly. Glancing one day at the CCTV monitors, I spotted a bunch of "the guys" who were emptying one of our refrigerators of steaks and whole hams and hiding bottles of wine under their coats before shuffling out. When I showed Frank what they were doing, he shrugged and replied, "They must need it more than we do." He couldn't have cared less, although in his later years it did begin to upset him when people tried to rip him off.

Still, his kindness and consideration always won out. We were at a dinner party one night with Bennett Cerf and Betty Bacall when Frank wandered into a guest room to collect a pack of cigarettes from his overcoat. There he found the producer Arthur Hornblow finishing up a telephone call to a woman. "I hope she's pretty," Frank said softly. Arthur replied that she was; it was his mother, Susie, who was in poor health in Florida but still excited about the latest Yankee scores.

248 LADY BLUE EYES

"What I wouldn't give for one more telephone call with my mom," Frank told him wistfully.

At his suggestion, they called Arthur's mother back and put Frank on the line. "Is this really Frank Sinatra?" she asked. "You sound too much like him not to be. I love your voice."

"Well, I love your voice too, Susie," Frank said. "Tell you what—I'm going to call you every Saturday night at six o'clock, and we'll chew over the Yankees' performance, okay?" He kept his promise and never missed a Saturday evening call to Susie Hornblow until the day she died. For good measure, he sent flowers to her on Mother's Day and to other widowed mothers in the same hospital. Frank added her name to his list of lonely women he'd call on a regular basis. They included a relative of Freeman Gosden's and several single mothers. Few believed them when they claimed that Ol' Blue Eyes was a frequent caller, but they knew the truth and that was all that mattered.

When the Shah of Iran was allowed into America briefly by President Carter for urgent medical treatment, Frank went to visit him in the hospital in New York. The shah had been deposed by then, and his presence on U.S. soil was highly controversial, but that didn't bother Frank—he was always for the underdog. During Frank's visit to the heavily guarded private room, the shah commented on a Bulgari pendant he was wearing around his neck, a birthday gift from me. Frank rarely took it off, but that day he undid the clasp without thinking and handed it to his friend as a keepsake. It was the last time he would ever see the shah alive. In keeping with his philosophy of kindness to widows, Frank made sure to keep in contact with Empress Farah, who eventually settled in Washington, D.C.

Greg Peck certainly never forgot Frank's kindness when his son died, and they adored each other mutually. Greg and Veronique somehow managed to move on from their personal tragedy and became stalwarts of our parties at home and abroad. We had so many laughs with those two, especially at the Compound. Every night was like a Vegas act with our cast of friends. We might have the singer Frankie Randall at the piano, and maybe Liza Minnelli or Dean Martin singing. We had the best comics (natural and professional) with us for days at a time, so the stories, antics, and jokes were never-ending. The Pecks had a hilarious comedy routine they used to perform about baseball, in which Greg would try to explain to his French wife what a "strike" was. We'd laugh until our sides hurt. Greg had a few other tricks up his sleeve too. One night he walked into the bar, his face somber, and said, "Girls and boys, I have an announcement to make. Veronique's left me and I'm very broken up about it. I wanted you to hear it first, but it's over." For a moment, none of us knew what to say. Then he added, "But I've met a girl in Cathedral City. Her name's Trixie, and I've invited her over. Do you mind?"

Cue Veronique, who walked into the room in a dress cut up to her thighs and down to her breastbone, wearing a big black wig, high heels, and fishnet hose. She was smoking a cigarette through a long holder. As Greg announced, "This is Trixie, everybody," she teetered to the bar and ordered a drink in a funny accent. Frank almost fell off his chair. The funniest of all was Walter Annenberg, who was so fascinated he pulled up a chair and sat right next to her. She took a puff of her cigarette and blew smoke into his face out of the side of her mouth. He absolutely adored "Trixie," and we all had a lot of laughs that night.

Vero is still great fun, although the days are over now when she'd be the first to jump at the chance to play tennis or come horseback riding with me. I'd loved horses ever since I'd ridden Pansy the pony as a kid in Bosworth. I had several great animals, including an Appaloosa, which was a present from my old school friend Winnie Markley and her husband.

One of my best horses came from the singer Wayne Newton.

Frank and he were in a show together in Vegas, and after the concert that night Wayne told me that one of his Arabian mares was about to foal at his ranch not far from town. "Do you want to come and watch?" he asked.

"I'd love to!" I replied. When we reached the stables, the vet was already there. Once he told us that the foal was the wrong way around and in distress, I threw my full-length mink onto the straw and forgot about my gown as I jumped in to help. Wayne watched as I assisted the vet in turning the foal, even though he warned me that the contractions could break a man's arm. First one hoof came out, then another, and finally this perfect foal emerged panting and wet as we laughed and cried and hugged each other. Wayne then delighted me further with the announcement "I'm calling her Barbara Ann," adding, "and she's yours." I was over the moon.

A few years later I met the head of Occidental, Armand Hammer, at a party and told him about Barbara Ann. Knowing what a great breeder Wayne was, he offered to fly her to his stud in Florida and breed her with the top stallion in the country. The chestnut foal that was born was named Sinatra Hammer Newton, Sinny for short.

Several of our guests in the desert enjoyed horseback riding too and were only too willing to try out one of my steeds. One customer who wasn't quite so willing, though, was George Schlatter. Poor George was a terrible rider, and everyone teased him about it. To save his face, I decided to lend him my Peruvian Paso, named Tsar d'Oro, which absolutely anyone could ride. I took "Horhay" to one side and told him, "You ride Tsar tomorrow, and I guarantee you'll be the best of them all, even better than Jolene." He came to the stables a little less reluctantly than usual and let me help him up onto that horse. Sure enough, he was fine. Before long he was prancing all over the desert like a king. Jolene couldn't believe it. Neither could R. J. Wagner, who'd seen George ride before. All was going great until George rode Tsar back to the stable, lifted the rein over his head, and got off on the wrong side. With an enormous crash, he fell butt-first onto the dirt while the horse panicked and began dancing all around him. George was hollering and trying to get out of the way until we eventually managed to get him up unharmed. After he'd dusted himself off, he turned to all of us and pleaded, "Whatever you do, please don't tell Frank!"

We drove back to the Compound to find Frank sitting by the pool, his nose in a book. He didn't even look up. He just said, "Hey, Hopalong, why don't you buy your own horse?"

The fun and frolics didn't stop when we went on the road; in fact, in many ways they intensified, because Frank was usually so wound up after shows that he needed to wind down superfast.

We were in Gstaad visiting Roger Moore when Frank got into a late-night argument in a bar with the biggest Arab I'd ever seen. Looking up from where I was chatting with Jolene and George, I suddenly spotted my husband poking his finger in the chest of this man-mountain and thought, Uh-oh.

I nudged Jolene, who nudged George and said, "Your friend's in trouble. Do something."

George almost choked on his drink. "Have you seen the size of him?" he asked. "Frank's not that much of a friend!" We laughed but sent him to rescue Frank anyway. Fortunately George is a big guy too, so he pushed his way between the two men and asked what the problem was. The man, who looked like he wanted to kill Frank, complained about something he'd said. With his back to Frank, George told him, "You're right. My friend is very rude and I'm going to tell him as soon as this is over. But if we get into this beef, we're going to hurt each other, so why ruin our night just because he's a schmuck who's out of line?"

Frank, meanwhile, was standing behind George yelling, "You

tell that son of a bitch!" to which George turned around and replied, "I'm telling him, Frank."

The man countered, "You'll tell him he's rude?" George assured him he would, in between assuring Frank behind his back that he'd sort the man out. "And another thing," started Frank. George said, "No other things, Frank. Please, no." He then turned and offered the aggrieved party a stack of signed Sinatra albums. Eventually, Frank cottoned on to what George was doing, and that tickled him so much, the drama was over. Jolene and I drained our glasses and suggested we leave.

With the help of our friends, I'd try to come up with all sorts of ways to entertain Frank on the road and keep him out of trouble. It didn't always work out. On a tour of the Far East with George and Jolene, Frank had a surprise lined up for me. At the hotel we'd booked months in advance, he'd asked for the best suite, which had an enormous balcony overlooking Hong Kong Harbor. He'd been in it once before and couldn't wait to share its incredible views with me. I knew nothing about that, but I did know Jolene had planned a kimono party in which we were all to dress up and eat Asian food.

Everything started to go wrong when we arrived at the hotel. to discover that a group of Arabs had been booked into our suite before us and ruined it. The manager, who was Swiss, claimed they'd had live animals in there, so it needed to be cleaned and redecorated. The work was almost complete, but the rooms smelled of fresh paint and we couldn't possibly move in. The manager offered Frank an alternative suite and then compounded the problem by explaining that we couldn't have the entire wing as planned because another guest was booked into an adjacent room and refused to move.

Frank hadn't slept for almost twenty-four hours and had been drinking all the way from Japan. That wasn't the time to be telling him bad news. His devoted assistant, Dorothy, always had the next room to ours for convenience, and he wasn't prepared to accept anything less. At Frank's request, Jilly knocked on the guest's door and politely asked him to move to another room at our expense, but the man refused.

"You can't stay in there!" Jilly told him, banging on the locked door. "You have to get out."

The guy yelled back, "Go away! I like my room just fine. I'm staying put."

Frank wasn't in the mood for compromise and told Jilly to get a crowbar. Not surprisingly, as soon as the guest heard that, he called the manager and complained. By this time, Frank was cussing and going crazy at everyone. When the manager called up to the suite about the complaint, Frank pulled the telephone out of the wall and threw it at the window. It bounced off the plate glass and almost hit him in the face. "What kind of a joint is this?" he cried. "I can't even throw a goddam phone through the window!"

In due course, the manager arrived reinforced by members of the Hong Kong police. Frank didn't take to the manager on the grounds that he "sounded like a German." While he launched into a tirade about the war, everybody scattered to hide. George Schlatter, dressed in a kimono, locked himself in his bedroom. I stayed on the periphery waiting for the storm to pass. I knew that if I could just take one step back and view the scene without tension and emotion, it was usually pretty funny. There had always been a sense of danger around Frank. By this time I knew that he wasn't really dangerous, but I also appreciated that not everybody else knew that. As a consequence, I usually ended up the peacemaker, but I was no pussycat either; if I fought back then, boy, watch out.

Mostly, Frank was just acting out, and there was nothing anyone could do until he was spent. The passionate, Italian side to his character that made him such a terrific entertainer also left him prone to mood swings and meant that he had a good cop–bad cop routine. I just had to wait for the good cop to come back.

I sometimes think Frank got a kick out of teasing people anyway. What else was left to him? He'd been everywhere, done everything, met every world leader, and bought everything he wanted. What was left but to wind people up sometimes, mess with their minds, and see what happened?

Unaware of the drama that was unfolding in our suite, Jolene came running in like Pollyanna in a kimono to announce that the food had arrived and her party was about to start. The corridor was lined with waiters bearing trays and trays of delicious Chinese food. Behind them were her guests, also dressed in kimonos. The minute "Injun" looked around the room and realized what she'd stumbled into, she turned right around, sent the food back to the kitchen and the guests to the bar. It was like something from a Broadway farce.

Almost as quickly as Frank's tantrum had flared up, everything was calm. Jilly stopped yelling. The police and the manager left. The guy next door went quiet. Frank sat slumped in a chair in his suit and tie and looked at me in my kimono. "What the hell happened to Jolene's party?" he asked. I called everyone up and assured them it was safe to come back. The waiters who'd been turned away took some persuading, but eventually we had our party—kind of—and ate the food that had now gone cold. Exhausted by the end of it all, I took myself off to bed.

After a while Frank came into the bedroom, pulled off his clothes, and sat on the other side of the bed, staring down at his feet. He looked like an exhausted little boy. Finally he said softly, "Well, there's one thing you won't have to worry about."

"What's that?" I asked, half-hidden under the covers.

"I'll never have an ulcer."

"No," I told him, "but you're a carrier."

THIRTEEN

Making new friends in Africa with Father Rooney.

What Now My Love

In the spring of 1980, Frank was producing and starring in a thriller called *The First Deadly Sin* with Faye Dunaway and was going to be tied up in New York for weeks. Although he hadn't made a film in three years, we both knew the routine, and it was deadly dull—which was the main reason he wasn't crazy about the movie business.

Actors spend so much of their time sitting around and waiting, reading rewritten scripts, learning new lines, rehearsing, and then waiting some more. Known as One-Shot Sinatra, Frank had a reputation for being difficult or impatient on set, but I don't think that was entirely fair. George Schlatter always said Frank's favorite two words were *Jack* and *Daniel's* and his least favorite were *Take Two*. If someone wanted him to do more than one take, they'd better give him a good reason. A lot of people improve as they repeat their lines, but he never did. He felt that it took the energy away from a scene to do it over and over again. He wanted and expected everyone else to be ready so that he could walk in, say his lines, and walk out again. If they called him to the set at 8:00 A.M. but didn't use him for three hours, he'd threaten to abandon the whole project.

Even when he was being his most bullish about movies, though, Frank would still find a way to inject humor into a situation. Once, when a director told him they'd have to shoot over the weekend because they were five pages behind, Frank took the script, tore out five pages, and announced, "Now you're on schedule." On another occasion, when he did a commercial for Budweiser, the director filmed a full dress rehearsal and then handed out notes about how it should be done next time. When he went to Frank's dressing room and found him slipping on his coat, he asked, "Where are you going?"

"I'm getting out of here."

"But the show!"

"I just did the show."

"No! That was the dress rehearsal! We're doing it all again."

"Not me, buster. I can't do it any better than I just did. That's your show."

George always said that what Frank really demanded was only the respect that artists like him should be accorded. He believed that was the way it ought to work, and his attitude was learn your words, know your mark, and be professional. Then we can all go home. Unfortunately, that made him a hard act to book, and in the end I think he may have toughed himself out of the business. He'd always wanted to play something that really stretched him, as he had in *The Man with the Golden Arm* (the film of which he was most proud) as well as with his Oscar-winning performance in *From Here to Eternity*, but the scripts stopped coming and he was never again offered those kinds of roles.

One part he would have really liked was that taken by Dustin Hoffman in the movie *Rain Man* with Tom Cruise. Frank had been talking about playing that sort of character for years, and when he heard of that movie he longed to be the autistic genius that Dustin made his own. If a great part like that had come along—especially if Scorsese had offered it—Frank would have dropped everything to do it. Now Scorsese is said to be making a film of Frank's life, which is kind of ironic. I like Marty, and I trust him to do the right thing.

Even though Frank was busy making his movie in New York, he still needed to know that I was safe and being taken good care of at all times. Ever since his son had been kidnapped, he was paranoid about the security of those he loved. What he didn't want was for me to put myself in any kind of risky situation, but what Frank wanted and what I wanted weren't always the same thing.

The World Mercy charity for the poor in West Africa was something we both supported enthusiastically. Frank had narrated a documentary about its work, and I had organized a benefit in New York at which Julio Iglesias performed. I'd always liked Julio's voice and had never met him, but I made contact and asked him if he would help us out. Fortunately, he jumped at the chance, hoping to meet his hero Frank, and I think he must have been very disappointed when he discovered that Frank wasn't in town. Still, we became friends and I was able to return his favor years later when he wanted to perform on one of Frank's *Duets* albums but his agent said he couldn't make it happen. Julio called and asked me to help, and through pillow talk, I persuaded Frank that it was a good idea—and it was. A few years later, when Julio left his agent for another, the original agent reportedly protested, "But I got you on that Sinatra record!" to which Julio told me he'd replied, "No, you did not. That was Barbara Sinatra!"

The head of the World Mercy charity in America was Father Rooney. He'd been a friend to us both for a long time, ever since we'd met him at one of our parties in New York. A charismatic missionary, he was a very easy man to like. When he asked me if I would like to go to Africa with him to see where our money was being spent, I agreed immediately. Frank thought I was crazy. He didn't want me gallivanting off at all, but I was determined to go.

Hoping there might be safety in numbers, I asked Bee Korshak and my friend Suzy Johnson if they'd go with me, and they both said yes. I knew Suzy from my modeling days, and when she moved to Palm Springs and her marriage broke up, I helped set her up in the best resale shop I know. So the three of us got our shots for yellow fever and a whole host of other unpalatable diseases and set off.

I packed a few clothes, some peanut butter, some cans of pork and beans, and a large bottle of vodka. Then we flew to Dakar in Senegal. On our first night we stayed in a nunnery where we were offered a meager dinner and then went to bed. The next morning my vodka was gone, so I guess the nuns were planning on having a good time. I went to my girlfriends' rooms to see if they were ready for our first day in the bush, and they had me in hysterics. They were rifling through their designer outfits for what they'd imagined would be some sort of elegant safari. "Forget your Chanel and Gucci!" I told them. "All you need is a cotton shirt, comfortable pants, and good walking shoes." When they were finally ready, we set out in a battered old Jeep to travel more than two hundred miles to Mauritania.

Over the next few days, Father Rooney took us on a whistle-stop tour of clinics built by World Mercy, and we also opened a new one. He took us to several other places that had been funded by the Vatican. He carried money from World Mercy in one pocket and cash from the Pope in the other. Needless to say, Father Rooney was extremely popular, so at every camp the villagers pressed forward, crying, singing, and reaching out, desperate to touch him and us. The children were adorable and enthralled by the strange white women in their midst and by the bubble gum I took along. I unwrapped some and showed them what to do with it; they'd clearly never seen anything like it. Several followed us around blowing enormous pink bubbles, although I must confess that some swallowed the gum whole.

That trip to Africa was such a culture shock in every way.

The villages were drought ravaged; they had no pure drinking water and little food. Sickness and malnutrition were endemic. Most of the rivers were contaminated with parasites that caused disease and blindness. I watched worms a foot long being taken out of screaming babies as their mothers held them down. It was so warm, yet the people wrapped themselves up in layer upon layer of brightly colored clothes. Women with babes in arms walked for miles with pots on their head just to get a bucket of water. World Mercy's new, clean wells were transforming lives.

At night, the villagers put on elaborate displays of dancing, and our funny little Irish host with his pale, bald head would leap into the midst of these statuesque people and jump up and down energetically. They'd always prepare some sort of feast for us and offer the "best" parts to Father Rooney. In one village they'd saved an elephant heart for him for two months, without refrigeration. I cried, "You can't eat that, Father!" but he told me he couldn't possibly disappoint them, and then he got sick.

In another village deep in the bush, we were entertained in a grass hut by a chief and his many wives. Sitting cross-legged on a dirt floor, I watched as the number one wife washed some cups in dirty water and then poured hot tea into them from on high. The stream of brown liquid hit each little cup perfectly. I didn't dare risk even tasting it for fear of infection, but I took my cup with a smile, placed it on the floor next to a nun who lived in the village, and whispered, "Will you please drink this for me?" Fortunately, she did.

Just as we were leaving Mauritania, there was a coup d'état. Father Rooney explained that these were quite common in that part of the world and suggested we get to the airport as soon as possible. Despite his apparent calmness, I never saw anyone drive so fast. We managed to get on the last flight out of the country. God only knows what Frank would have said if I'd ended up trapped there. I could just imagine it: "She's stuck where?" I'm sure he had people following us wherever we went, but I don't think even Jilly and his friends could have done anything about the complex politics of Africa.

For our last two nights in Senegal we stayed with some priests and a monsignor and were surprised to find that they lived life to the full. They had plenty of vodka, loud music, and good food. They were a lot of fun and very different from the nuns we'd stayed with at the start of our journey. What an experience. Leaving Africa behind, Father Rooney and I traveled on to Rome, where I was presented with the prestigious Dames of Malta decoration in a Vatican ceremony dating back centuries. Then I was granted a brief audience with Pope John Paul II. Frank had met Pope Pius XII in the 1940s (as had Dolly) and told me how special that was, but I don't think I fully appreciated how much it would mean to me. When I saw John Paul walking down some steps into the chapel where we were waiting alongside dozens of sick and handicapped people, devout Catholics and invited guests, I swear he was bathed in a holy light, the kind I'd been urged to see as a young evangelist in Wichita. It was an incredible experience and one I wish I could have shared with Frank, and with Dolly, for they had been jointly responsible for my becoming a Catholic in the first place.

One by one, His Holiness approached everyone in the room, and when he came over to us I was surprised to see that he had a twinkle in his eye that was verging on flirtatiousness. I bent to kiss the ring on his finger, but he smiled and said, "No, please, you don't have to do that." He held my hands in his instead, and we chatted away as Father Rooney spoke of our recent trip. The Pope was so light in his personality and not at all heavy, as I'd expected him to be. It was such a thrill to meet him. Dear Father Rooney, who'd started as a missionary in Nigeria and was sent to America by his bishop to raise money, befriended politicians and movie stars, singers and priests. He was an incredible man who raised millions for the needy, and I feel blessed to have known him.

Returning home from my audience with the Pope, I was honored with a special award for my fund-raising efforts for a multiple sclerosis charity I'd become involved with. It was presented to me by President Jimmy Carter in the White House. My friends in New York had all been in favor of Carter when he first ran for president and told me he would win, but I'd said to them, "Are you crazy? No one's ever heard of Jimmy Carter!" There was such a machine behind him, though, that he got in. At the presentation in the Oval Office, he kissed me on the cheek, and a photograph of that kiss subsequently appeared in all the newspapers. One of my New York friends called me up and said, "Now you know who Carter is!"

Around the same time Frank was presented with the Variety International Humanitarian Award by our friend Henry Kissinger for his philanthropy over the years. In a televised all-star party for the man they called Mr. Anonymous, Richard Burton described Frank as a "giant." He added, "Among the givers of the world, he stands tallest. He has more than paid rent for the space he occupies on this planet, forged as he is from legendary loyalty and compassion carefully hidden . . . hidden because he has ordered it." Frank was, Richard said, "truly . . . his brother's keeper." The club announced that the money Frank had raised had led to the creation of the Sinatra Family Children's Unit for the Chronically Ill at the Seattle Children's Orthopedic Hospital. What a legacy. There was more to come. The same year Frank was one of five recipients (including his friend James Stewart) of a prestigious Kennedy Center Honor for his lifetime contributions to American culture, given to him at a televised presentation. During a reception afterward at the White House, President Reagan told him, "You have spent your life casting a magnificent and powerful shadow." Two years later, Reagan also awarded Frank the Presidential Medal of Freedom for his humanitarian work.

One of the organizations that had benefited most from

Frank's support was the Memorial Sloan-Kettering Cancer Center in Manhattan, where many friends had been treated. In the early 1980s, he organized a series of benefits for the hospital at New York's Radio City Music Hall featuring stars like Diana Ross and the opera singer Montserrat Caballé. Because of its extraordinary finale, Frank called one show "The Italian Hour." At the top of the bill was a double act starring him and the opera singer Luciano Pavarotti.

Thanks to his heritage perhaps, Frank loved opera and often listened to it very loud when he was painting in his studio. Opera depressed me because it was so solemn and almost always about death and tragedy. I like to smile and I like things that make me smile, but that's not most opera. Frank felt very differently, and Pavarotti was one of his favorite singers. He'd wanted to meet him for a long time, and the feeling was mutual; on several occasions, the Maestro stated that he considered Frank the best singer in the world. When Frank was in New York performing at Carnegie Hall once, Pavarotti called Frank's secretary, Dorothy, to ask a favor. In his broken English, he told her that he desperately wanted to go to the concert but had called the box office to discover the show had sold out. He asked if there was any way she could get him in. Dorothy said, "I think Barbara has a spare seat in her box, Maestro. I'm sure she wouldn't mind if you sat there." I didn't mind one little bit, so Pavarotti came alone and sat next to me, and we smiled and exchanged a kiss, but we couldn't converse because we didn't speak the same language.

Frank appeared onstage and after a couple of songs peered up at our box and said, "Where's my girl? There she is. Say hello to Barbara, everybody." A spotlight dazzled me, but I smiled and waved. Frank said, "I love you. Do you love me?" I nodded. "Then I love you twice," he announced. A great romantic, Pavarotti thought that absolutely marvelous and applauded enthusiastically. He remained riveted through the rest of the performance. By the time Frank took his final bow, Pavarotti's face was wet with tears. Having composed himself, he used gestures and hand signals to let me know that he'd like to go backstage. "Down," he said, pointing and smiling. "Frank. Down."

I waited in the wings with this giant among singers for Frank to emerge from his dressing room. I knew my husband would be nervous to meet one of his heroes too, but I could hardly believe what happened next. In a surprisingly agile motion for such a large man, Pavarotti dropped to his knees, took Frank's hand, and kissed it. Frank looked at me and I looked at him and we both thought, Surely this should be the other way around?

At the Radio City benefit for Sloan-Kettering a year or so later, Pavarotti sang his arias so movingly, mopping the perspiration from his brow throughout with his trademark white handkerchief. Frank was due onstage for the next few numbers, which would include their riveting finale of "Santa Lucia" and "O Sole Mio." There was a momentary delay before Frank walked out, looking like a toothpick compared to Pavarotti. In his hand he was carrying a large white tablecloth with which he pretended to mop his brow. Pavarotti cracked up, and then those two musical legends embraced in a scene of extraordinary warmth. In front of a crowd of six thousand they laughed at each other like two schoolboys in the corner of a playground, oblivious to all those around them. It was the most charming sight to see.

After the show they chatted animatedly in half English, half Italian and bonded somewhere in between. Finally, Pavarotti asked Frank, "Is there anything I can do to help you?"

Frank nodded and frowned. "Yes, Maestro," he replied, suddenly serious. "I've been having trouble with how to end a crescendo, especially a long one. I'd really like to know the proper way to finish."

Pavarotti looked at Frank and placed a bear of a hand on his

shoulder. "'Ats'a easy, Francis," he told him with that twinkly smile
of his. "You just-a shut-uppa you mou!"

Frank was adored around the world, and not just by Italian
opera singers. The Japanese went nuts for him. The English
abandoned their legendary reserve to give him standing ovations.
The Europeans mobbed us. When he performed at the Concert
for the Americas in the Dominican Republic in the middle of a
steamy jungle, the Caribbean crowds were unbelievable. But one
area of the world where he was revered to an almost religious extent was South America—Rio de Janeiro in particular.

There was a false promise offered up by commitment-shy
men all over Brazil: "I'll marry you when Sinatra comes to Rio."
For some reason, Frank had never played Rio de Janeiro, so the
promise was the Latino equivalent of "when Hell freezes over."
Would-be brides would sigh sadly in response, believing that
they'd probably never marry. But in 1980, all that changed. From
the day Frank announced that he'd be touring South America,
starting with Brazil and Argentina, Catholic priests across the
continent were inundated with wedding bookings. The impossible
had happened—Frankie was coming to town.

Not surprisingly perhaps, from the moment we arrived in
Rio we were given a rapturous reception. Having landed at the
airport, we had to be flown by helicopter to a military base because of the crowds. Once we reached our hotel, our motorcade
was surrounded. There were hundreds of fans, yet only a few police officers to hold them behind a small blockade. "Okay, let's
go!" Jilly yelled as we leapt from the car and ran toward the building. No sooner had we stepped a few paces than the crowd burst
through the barricades and swamped us. I was behind Jilly and
Frank was behind me and my face was pressed up against Jilly's
back. The screams around us were deafening. More and more

people started to break through the police cordon to rush at us. I realized that if one of us stumbled, we'd be trampled to death. Reaching a bottleneck near the hotel entrance, we were pushed up against a wall as hands started tearing at our clothes. I was wearing real diamond earrings and thought, Good God! I'm going to lose everything! We were nearly killed in the crush until Jilly and the security guards finally pushed us inside.

A few days later Frank performed at Rio's Maracanã Stadium, one of the largest football stadiums in the world. More than 175,000 people made it an event that went into the Guinness Book of Records as the largest paying audience for a single performer. I was escorted to a seat in a VIP area at the front of the stadium just a few minutes before Frank's show began. I could feel the pressure of the audience anticipation all around me; it created a palpable sensation on my skin. It had been raining hard all day, and his thousands of fans—most without umbrellas—were soaked through from hours of waiting for their hero.

As Frank stepped onto that high center stage, the crowd exploded. I had to cover my ears to protect them from the roar. The fans who had waited a lifetime went absolutely crazy, and the waves of noise that rippled from the far end of the stadium to the stage and back again almost knocked him off his feet. Suddenly Frank looked skyward, and all of us followed his gaze. The rain had stopped. Talk about divine intervention. "*Obrigado.* Thank you," Frank said to the heavens, and the crowd erupted once more. I could tell the man who'd begun his career as a saloon singer in smoky little joints in New Jersey was as overcome as I was by the outpouring of adoration. For a moment he was speechless. The orchestra played the opening bars of "The Coffee Song" with the line, "*They've got an awful lot of coffee in Brazil...,*" but few could have heard a note, except perhaps the millions watching it on television sets across Central and South America. Frank began to sing,

Way down among Brazilians
Coffee beans grow by the billions
So they've got to find those extra cups to fill

and the response was incredible.

I could see he was thrown. Even when the crowd settled down a bit and allowed him to go on, he was overwhelmed. So much so that when the time came to sing "Strangers in the Night," he was completely unable to—the first time I'd ever seen that happen. He stood up there on the stage, eyes welling, as the music carried on without him. Then the most amazing thing happened. Almost every one of the 175,000 people in that arena, many of whom had learned to speak English by listening to Sinatra records, began to sing the words to him, heavily accented. *"Strangers in the night, exchanging glances. Wond'ring in the night, what were the chances..."* Their voices welled as one until the night air was filled with the melody. Tears slid down my face as well as down Frank's. It was one of the most beautiful sounds I ever heard.

Eventually, Frank pulled himself together and joined in. The crowd sang with him for a while, and then they listened in return, enjoying every moment. Halfway through a number, he'd stop so he could listen to their serenade. When he sang the last note of his final song and the roar of the crowd deafened us once more, he put down his mike and waited for a moment, taking it all in. Suddenly, he looked skyward. The rain began again. For the tearful people in that stadium that night, it was the most memorable and magical of moments. I'll certainly never forget it as long as I live.

Because Frank was the kind of man who'd drop everything and rush to the aid of a friend in need, it was natural that Nancy Reagan should call us in March 1981 when someone tried to assassinate Ron. It was not long after Frank had produced and directed the first of Ronnie's presidential inaugural galas and we'd both attended his seventieth birthday party.

We were asleep in Las Vegas when the telephone rang. "Ronnie's been shot!" a distraught Nancy told Frank. "Can you come?" The would-be assassin, John Hinckley, had fired six shots as the president left a speaking engagement at a Washington hotel, seriously injuring three of his aides as well. Having lost JFK to a bullet, Frank was afraid that history was repeating itself. He canceled his performance that night and arranged an immediate flight to D.C. When we arrived at the White House, we were met by Nancy and her family plus a host of others, including Billy Graham, one of Ronnie's closest friends. It was so strange for me to finally meet the evangelist who'd converted my mother and aunts to his particular brand of faith forty years earlier. Reverend Graham was quieter than I'd imagined him to be, soft, sweet, and warm in person and far less of the rabble-rouser I'd expected. He and Frank became Nancy's stalwarts through that difficult time as Ronnie underwent surgery for a punctured lung. Fortunately, the president made a full recovery.

(Later that same year, the world lost Anwar Sadat to an assassin's bullet, something that affected Frank deeply. He mourned the loss of the one he called "the single man of the desert who has stood tall in the sand begging for peace." I could only send my heartfelt condolences to his widow, Jehan, the first lady of Egypt.)

Nancy Reagan was never a close friend, and it had nothing to do with the fact that she seemed to have a crush on my husband. After all, I was quite used to that, and if I'd wanted to I could have flirted right back with hers. What I wasn't so accustomed to was the time and commitment she expected of Frank for the causes she and Ronnie espoused. I felt that she took a little too much advantage of Frank's huge heart. As well as making him director of entertainment at the White House, Nancy appointed him to the President's Committee on the Arts and Humanities and she got him involved in her Just Say No antidrugs campaign, as well as her charitable organizations for children and foster grandparents. She also invited him to the White House frequently to perform at fund-raisers and dinners. Frank was completely unfazed, of course. During long-distance telephone calls and their lunches together whenever they were in the same town, I think he became Nancy's therapist more than her friend.

When he wasn't busy in Washington, Frank continued to entertain his devoted fans and accepted invitations to perform at benefits and concerts around the world. He never stopped raising millions for causes including muscular dystrophy, cerebral palsy, multiple sclerosis, and diabetes, St. Jude's Ranch for Children, the University of Nevada, and the Desert Hospital. At a benefit for the last at what was then known as the Canyon Country Club, he cooked dinner and waited tables at a $1,500-a-plate benefit before slipping into his tux to sing. As a man who had championed the careers of people like Sammy Davis, Jr., Ella Fitzgerald, and Lena Horne, Frank campaigned for civil rights long before it was fashionable. In 1945, he'd made a ten-minute film on racial intolerance aimed at teenagers and called *The House I Live In*, which won an Oscar. He wrote articles and addressed student rallies nationwide with passion and conviction about the importance of equality. Which is why it was a shame when he was criticized for performing in Sun City in Bophuthatswana, South Africa, during the era of apartheid. Having taken a black comedian with him, he announced to the mixed-race audience, "I play to all people of any color, creed, drunk or sober."

President Lucas Mangope was so indignant at the picketing and the controversy that surrounded Frank's visit that he crowned him King of Entertainment in a tribal ceremony that took me straight back to my time with Father Rooney in Africa. My "royal" husband went on to address the Bophuthatswana Senate as I sat watching proudly, and then he became the first white man to receive the tribal homeland's Order of the Leopard. It was just one of many awards he received in his lifetime, most of which he kept in a glass display case. Bobby was with us on that trip and hit it off right away with Eddie Mangope, the president's son. They remained friends until Eddie's tragic death.

Eager to do more, see more, Frank traveled as much as ever, crisscrossing our great country and the globe. As always, friends would join us every now and then, dipping in and out of the tour as it suited them, and we always enjoyed the company. One of them, Dennis Stein, came once accompanied by his fiancée, Elizabeth Taylor, whom I'd introduced him to by sitting them together at a dinner in Los Angeles. Frank and Elizabeth didn't always see eye to eye, and the main problem between them was her lack of punctuality. My perfectionist husband had always been a stickler for timing because of his years of performing. He may have been an impatient man, but he was always professional and his impeccable sense of timing was reflected in his music. If a ticket for one of his shows stated the performance would start at 7:30 P.M., he expected to hear the orchestra strike the first note at 7:29. After so many years of people running around making sure that everything ran like clockwork, his demands were always met.

Unfortunately, Elizabeth was almost always running late. Dennis used to tell her that any event they were going to was an hour earlier than it really was in the hope of at least getting her there on time. One morning halfway through our tour, we were in our suite at the Waldorf getting ready to leave when Dennis came rushing in, clearly a nervous wreck. "What's the matter?" I asked.

"Elizabeth's in the bathtub and she doesn't want to come out yet."

"But our plane leaves in less than an hour!" I said.

"I don't know what to do," groaned Dennis.

"I do," Frank growled. "Leave her there!" Poor Dennis, he

really wanted to come with us, but his girlfriend refused to get out of the tub so we had to leave them behind.

Another time Frank was touring with the singer Pia Zadora, who came on after Don Rickles and warmed up the audience. Pia might have been born in Hoboken, but that didn't automatically qualify her to open for Frank. Her husband, Meshulam Riklis, an Israeli businessman and Vegas casino boss, was determined to make a star of his young wife. She'd had some early success as a pop singer and a child actress, but he sent her to the best music coaches to get her properly trained. One night, as I was about to play gin rummy with Riklis, he asked me if I wanted to bet.

"Sure," I replied.

"What do you want to play for?"

I thought about it for a moment and then replied, "Your plane." Riklis had an even bigger plane than Frank's, which was like an airliner.

"My plane?" he said, but then he nodded. When he lost the game, he agreed that we could use his plane for our next tour, which I was thrilled about. Hoping to save face, he challenged Frank to a game of gin, but my husband hadn't had Zeppo Marx as a teacher. Frank agreed that, if he lost, Pia Zadora could open for him on the tour. And so it was that the little-known singer got possibly her biggest break, opening for Sinatra. She was much better than I thought she'd be, but Pia and Frank were never going to have a marriage of minds. Not least because, whenever Frank finished a show in the middle of a tight tour like the one they were on, he walked offstage and stepped straight into his limo. He made it a rule never to be more than a fifteen-minute drive to the airport because he wanted to be on the plane, sitting down with a glass of Daniel's as we took off. His management team was always trying to persuade him to play venues that were farther than fifteen minutes from an airport, even installing a TV and a bar in his car to keep him occupied, but nothing would change his mind.

One night after a show Pia made the mistake of dawdling to say hello to some people backstage. She and her husband arrived at the airport in their limousine half an hour later to discover that they had missed the flight—*their* flight. They were never late again.

Continuing our tour, we flew to France, and in Paris, Frank performed at the famous Moulin Rouge. I was in the audience with the Pecks and seated next to the French prime minister Jacques Chirac.

Jacques was a tall man and quite flirtatious, as only the French can be. We got along famously. I was wearing a pair of five-carat diamond drop earrings that night, and a dress with a high collar. Just before the concert began, one of my earrings hooked onto my collar and fell off. Realizing that it was missing, I began to search for it in my clothing, on the table, and on the floor. Before long, I had everyone on their hands and knees looking for my diamond, including waiters and waitresses, Greg, Veronique, and Monsieur Chirac.

"Oh dear," I cried after several minutes' fruitless searching. "I'm never going to get that earring back."

The future president of France took me by the shoulders and said firmly, "No one loses anything with me, Barbara. We're going to find it." I smiled and told him that made me feel better. We looked and looked, but the diamond was nowhere to be seen. It seemed hopeless. Then Jacques suddenly caught sight of something glinting in the cuff of his trouser leg. To our astonishment, my earring had somehow rolled into his pant cuff. I was so relieved and happy that we found it, but just as I was thanking him, the music started and Frank's performance began. As we all sat down again, I discreetly pulled off my other earring and put them both in my purse for safekeeping, until I could get the clasps altered to be more secure.

After Paris we flew to London, where Frank was to perform at the "Francis Albert" Hall for the queen in aid of a children's charity whose patron was Princess Margaret. Frank had met the queen and the princess several times before, but I never had and was a little nervous. Once we'd settled in, we went to visit Cubby Broccoli in his London house with our friend Pat DiCicco. A discussion ensued as to how to curtsy to a monarch, so Pat played the queen while we practiced, which was a hoot. Later that night, as we were waiting to meet her at a reception, I felt a tap on my shoulder and turned to see another of our friends, the businessman Kirk Kerkorian. He grinned and said, "Not so bad for two little kids from the sticks, huh?" I had to stop myself from laughing out loud. Not surprisingly in such company, I found the queen rather stiff, although I did meet her again years later at one of the big studios and then afterward at a dinner on the royal yacht *Britannia* moored in Long Beach, where she seemed far more relaxed.

The day before the show, we were invited to dinner at one of the royal palaces, where Princess Margaret would be the hostess. We were led into a large ballroom and informed that the protocol was we were not to sit down unless she did. Annoyingly, she never did, and for some people that was too much. Cubby Broccoli, who was well into his seventies at the time, finally announced, "I can't help it. I've got to sit down!" None of us dared join him even though we were just as tired. After what seemed like an interminable amount of time, we were finally ushered into a long dining room and shown our places. The high-ceilinged room felt freezing cold, and although I'd arrived wearing a brown velvet cape with mink trim, it was taken from me before the dinner and I felt the chill in my strapless dress.

Trying not to shiver, I got chatting with a newspaper editor to my right who was very nice and confided in me that he and the princess hadn't spoken in five years, ever since something appeared in his newspaper about her. "This is the first time I'm back in her good graces," he told me. As the first course arrived and I was disappointed to see that it wasn't a hot dish, I grew colder and colder.

Soon, goose bumps covered my skin. My companion noticed and asked, "Would you like me to turn on the fire?"

"Oh, that would be heaven," I cried. "Thank you!" He jumped up and turned on the log-effect fire a few feet behind me. I could feel the heat of the gas flames immediately and was incredibly grateful. As he came back, I began to thank him again when I was interrupted from farther down the table.

"Turn it *orf*!" Princess Margaret said sharply.

"But Mrs. Sinatra has a chill," my companion countered.

"I said turn it *orf*!"

"Oh my!" he replied. He stood up, got down on his hands and knees, and switched off the one flicker of heat in the room. As he sat back down next to me, he sighed. "Well, that's another five years we won't be speaking!"

Frank's London performance made more money for the princess's charity than it had made in its entire history. Thoughtfully, he had booked the royal box for me, but when we got there I discovered that we were sharing it with Princess Margaret's children, who'd been told at the last minute that they could sit there too. I was a bit teed off because the box had been especially reserved for me and my friends, including Swifty Lazar, Judy Green, Leonora Hornblow, and Ann Downey, but I didn't want to tell their royal highnesses to leave. Princess Margaret, who had a crush on Frank, invited us to Annabel's nightclub after the show for dinner in a private room. By the time we got there, after an evening squashed into the royal box, I was even more teed off and probably a little loaded too. After another drink at the bar, I suddenly announced to Swifty, "I'm not going to her party."

He took one look at me and nodded. "Okay then, we'll have our own."

Frank walked in at that moment, took one look at my face, and said, "What's wrong?"

Pulling "a Frank" on him, I replied, "Princess Margaret is

waiting in the back room for you, but I've decided that I'm not going."

He asked me why, so I told him, adding, "Swifty and I are going to throw our own party back at the hotel. It'll be much more fun." Frank agreed, so we walked out of the nightclub, leaving the sister of the Queen of England waiting for the guests who never showed. In effect, I turned her party *"orf."*

The year Frank was seventy was spent on the road as usual, promoting his latest album, *L.A. Is My Lady*, which he made with the inimitable Quincy Jones. The tour culminated in a concert in the southern states, followed by a private dinner for friends and family. At a time when most people might have considered taking it easy, my husband was still pushing himself, still performing and still delighting his fans—and me. He really loved what he did for a living and often said, "The worst thing you could tell me is that I couldn't work anymore."

I told Jimmy Stewart that one night, and he knew what Frank meant exactly. "That's just the way I am too!" he said. "I never want to quit. I'll do commercials; I'll do anything, but I need to work." Jimmy, whose parents had owned a hardware store in Pennsylvania similar to Blakeley's and who grew up during the Depression, added, "Coming from a poor background, you always fear you might lose it." Bless him, that kind, modest man was a multimillionaire thanks to his shrewd investments, but he did work right into his eighties, and yes, he even did commercials. Anything, as long as it was work.

It hardly seemed possible that Frank was really seventy. As he would say, "That's a lot of bourbon under the bridge, baby." He'd lost so many great friends along the way—Don Costa, Jack and Mary Benny, Nelson Riddle, Yul Brynner, Count Basie, Orson Welles, and Pat Henry most recently—but he was in good health, although the doctors were always warning him about his drinking and smoking, advice he studiously ignored. As a diligent wife, I did try to persuade him to cut back on his drinking several times through our marriage. I also tried to get him to eat less red meat and Italian pasta (even secretly enlisting the help of our chefs), but that was never really going to work. Frank's argument was that he had always taken care of himself and he knew how to pull back when he needed to. In our house Frank was the Sicilian-style *padrone*, a law unto himself, and he'd do whatever he wanted.

Within a year, though, he came to appreciate the damage his diet and lifestyle could do. By November he was suffering acute abdominal pain and almost had to cancel an engagement at the Golden Nugget in Atlantic City. Typically, he went on that night as usual, and none of his fans would have suspected how much he was hurting. The following day he was flown to the Eisenhower Medical Center in Palm Springs, where he underwent emergency surgery to remove a large part of his (infected) lower colon. To allow time for his body to heal, the doctors performed a temporary colostomy and fitted him with a bag, which was something he loathed and detested. Before the six-week rest period was up, he told the doctors he couldn't handle the bag anymore, so he made them open him up and try to fix the problem another way. Sadly, that didn't work at first and they had to perform surgery once more and reverse what he'd made them do. Having joked that if they screwed up he'd have them whacked, one of the first things he asked when he woke up from the anesthesia was, "Are the doctors still alive?"

Frank was never the most patient of patients and he hated getting old, but that colostomy bag really made him feel his age. In defiance of how he was feeling, he went ahead with a television role he'd agreed to months earlier—a part in Tom Selleck's *Magnum, P.I.* series, which was filmed in Hawaii in January 1987. Frank loved *Magnum* and always said if a part came up for him in it, he'd jump at the chance. In the script that was specially written for him, entitled

"Laura," Frank was to play a retired New York cop turned vigilante to find the murderer of his granddaughter. It was an incredibly energetic role for a man of any age, never mind someone in his seventies wearing a colostomy bag. But Frank refused to let that darn bag beat him. In what turned out to be his final major acting role, he did almost all his own stunts, including fight scenes, running up ladders and over roofs, as well as acting his heart out in a tropical shirt. His energy never ceased to amaze me.

Going to Hawaii was always a treat because it was such a fun place. On one of our first holidays there we'd rented two of the singer Willie Nelson's houses in Maui. I'd gone ahead with Suzy Johnson, Bee Korshak, Anne Downey, and Judy Green to set everything up, and when Frank arrived with George Schlatter, we greeted their plane in grass skirts and leis and hired Hilo Hattie (whose music Frank loathed) to serenade him, Hawaiian-style. Grumpily, he walked straight past as if he didn't know us, although he did laugh in the end and even said hello to Hilo Hattie.

When we were in Honolulu for the *Magnum, P.I.* shoot, we met an actor named Larry Manetti. He and Frank got along very well, and as the show was wrapping, Larry told me he wanted to give Frank a farewell gift. He gave us a white German shepherd puppy we named Laura after the show. Then Larry asked, "You wouldn't like a parrot, would you? I live in an apartment and the darn bird's driving my neighbors crazy." I shook my head and told him I didn't know anything about birds except that they were dirty and that I didn't want one. "Oh, all right," he replied, "I'll have it put down." Of course I knew we couldn't allow that, so—like it or not—Frank and I ended up flying home with a two-year-old yellow-naped Amazon parrot named Rocky.

Over twenty years later, Rocky is still part of the Sinatra household. I tried to find him a home, but no one wanted him. He has bitten almost everyone who's ever come near him, including me; I have scars all over my arms and handle him now only with a little ladder. He has no respect for fame or fortune—he's drawn blood on everyone from Frank to the housekeeper. He bit George Schlatter's finger down to the knuckle and wouldn't let go. Frank's road manager, Tony Oppedisano (known as Tony O), used to open the oven door and call, "Here, Rocky, climb in there!" Bobby's frightened of Rocky, and so is most of our staff. Even my husband, who loved all creatures, never warmed to our noisy, green-feathered bird, not least because Rocky crawled out of his cage one day and traversed two rooms with enormous determination just to reach up and sink his beak into Frank's calf. The only people I have ever known Rocky to like (apart from Michael Douglas, Felicia Lemmon, and Dolly Martin) were a chef we once had named Roland and a woman who works for me now named Irena. Rocky especially adored Roland and would ride around in his apron or on his shoulder, but he sank his beak into Roland's neck one day, whereupon Roland refused even to speak to him again. So far, Irena, Rocky's latest crush, remains unscathed.

I have come to the conclusion that Rocky is like a four-year-old with attention deficit disorder. He has tantrums when he gets jealous or if he is moved from a place where he's settled and happy. He makes a racket all day long, he never learned the words to "My Way" despite my patient hours of training, and I can't get rid of him because no one else would want him, so I guess I'm stuck with him for life. When I die, I'll leave him to my enemies.

FOURTEEN

Breaking ground for the Barbara Sinatra Children's Center in Palm Springs on Frank's seventieth birthday, December 12, 1985.

Body and Soul

The highlight of Frank's seventy-first year for me was the fruition of a project very dear to my heart that has continued to be a focus of my life. Having always supported at least one major charity a year, from War Orphans to World Mercy, I'd never quite found the one that seemed perfect for me. That was until the 1980s, when Barbara Kaplan, who played tennis with me at the Racquet Club, approached me about a charity she was trying to establish in Palm Springs.

A mother of three married to Danny Kaplan, head of cardiology at the Desert Hospital, Barbara worked for family counseling services and specialized in child sexual abuse. She and her colleagues had no central base and were forced to give therapy sessions to victims wherever they could find a space—in vacant offices, the basements of banks, or the back rooms of churches. The scheme cost around thirty thousand dollars a year to run but couldn't keep up with demand. When she told me that she hoped to set up a special center where victims and counselors could work in private to break the cycle of abuse, I was impressed but not that interested. I told her, "I'm sorry, but I'm really busy with my other charities, and anyway child abuse doesn't happen to anyone I know. I don't have a connection with this at all."

She refused to give up, though, and kept mentioning it to me each time I saw her. Then one day she told me she was arranging an auction in aid of the charity and asked if I could help persuade some of our celebrity friends to donate art. "Well, I suppose I could do that," I said. Frank offered several of his paintings, and darling Tony Bennett gave us a couple of his much-coveted works (Frank was the first to say that Tony was a far better artist than he). Tony Curtis gave us one or two, and other friends like Kirk Douglas, Dinah Shore, Claudette Colbert, Anthony Quinn, and James Cagney donated sculptures, paintings, prints, and needlework. I persuaded most of our Palm Springs friends to attend the auction with Frank and me at the Sheraton Plaza, which helped draw in the crowds and the money. Don Rickles came along and sat in front of Frank bidding for a Tony Bennett painting his wife, Barbara, really liked. What Rickles didn't know was that every time he put up his hand to place a bid, Frank would raise his hand behind him to place a higher one. Don finally got the painting when Frank stopped bidding, but our comic friend never realized how the price had been bumped up. With that kind of competition, the auction raised more than sixty thousand dollars, so I was very pleased and thought to myself, That went well.

Barbara Kaplan was clever, though. Soon after the auction, she arranged for me to meet some of those who'd benefit from the money we'd raised. Coming face-to-face with those innocent little children who had been so mistreated tore my heart out. That's when I knew I had to get more involved. Those children needed some semblance of sanity in a purpose-built center of their own instead of having their therapy sessions scattered all over town. I knew of an empty building once used for cancer patients, and I approached the hospital that owned it, but sadly things didn't work out with them.

Then I formed a local board to help me get the project running, but we were quickly tied up in red tape. Several people warned me that Palm Springs had had a children's center before that hadn't succeeded. There seemed no way forward until our friend the businessman and racehorse owner Danny Schwartz, who was on our board, said, "Why don't you ask Uncle Walter?"

I knew Walter Annenberg was closely involved with the Eisenhower Medical Center, so I made an appointment with Danny, went over to Sunnylands, and told Walter what I wanted to do. His response wasn't what I'd hoped for. "I started something like this at the Desert Hospital and in London, but both projects died," he told me. "I don't want to go through all that again."

"Okay, Walter. I understand," I replied, trying to hide my disappointment. "You don't have to give me any money, but would you at least help me find a suitable plot?" When he agreed to see if there was any land available within the Eisenhower Medical Center compound, I assured him that, once a site had been found, I'd sell the idea and raise the necessary funds myself. I'd hired an architect to work out how much space we'd need and had the costs broken down per room. In what I hoped would be a state-of-the art facility and outpatient therapy center, there'd be an auditorium and entry hall costing $100,000 each. The other rooms would be as little as $10,000 each, but overall we'd need to raise several million dollars just to get the center built, never mind staffed and operational.

Nelda Linsk, a friend I made when I first came to Palm Springs with Zeppo, in 1958, had recently sold a house to the architect and builder Don Knutson and told me he wanted to get involved in the community. "Great," I said. "Let's set up an appointment." We invited Don to the Compound, and I made sure there was a surprise waiting for him. When he walked into the room and looked around to see Cary Grant, Jimmy Stewart, Gregory Peck, and Frank Sinatra all smiling up at him, his mouth fell open. He didn't know where to look next. Later he asked Nelda, "What does Barbara want from me?" Nelda replied that I'd tell him when I was ready.

Once Walter had arranged for us to have a plot on the campus of the medical center, all I had to do was raise the money. Using all my charm, I persuaded the best in the business—Frank, Dean, Sammy, and Liza—to perform at a benefit. Each table was priced at ten thousand dollars, the cost of one small therapy room. Then I went to see Don Knutson. Just as I was walking out of his house with the plans for the center under my arm, he asked me, "Barbara, what would you rather I do? Buy a table for the concert or a room in the building?"

I paused before replying. "Well, I think you should buy the entry hall, because I know you'll be going to the concert anyway." He didn't respond at first, but as I walked to my car, he cracked. "Okay, okay!" he said. "Then put me down for that." I could hardly believe my ears. Don was the first person I'd asked, and he'd agreed to pay for one of the most expensive areas in the whole center! I was so proud of myself that I hurried home excitedly. I couldn't wait to tell Frank, who listened in silence while I carried on.

Finally he couldn't stand it anymore. "All right! I'm sick of hearing about it. I'll buy the auditorium." That nearly put me away completely.

From then on it was easy. Walter Annenberg asked me how many rooms I'd sold, and when I told him the two largest spaces had been spoken for, he asked me what was the next one down. "The office," I replied. "It's seventy-five thousand dollars."

Walter nodded and said, "I'll pay for it." Not only did he write a check there and then but he and his wife, Lee, continued to contribute to the project for the rest of their lives. So much for not helping. Selling the rest was plain sailing. Our friend the businessman and racehorse owner Danny Schwartz bought four or five of the ten-thousand-dollar rooms. Father Rooney raised the money to buy one and persuaded a bishop from Ireland to fund another. Vince Kickerillo, an old friend and the husband of Mary Miller, a singer signed to Reprise, was more than generous. With the money raised, we found a builder from Riverside and were ready to begin. Frank and I broke the ground on his seventieth birthday in December 1985, confident that the 12,500-square-foot children's center would open the following year.

I was so happy that the project had worked out and hoped that children and staff alike would be able to make good use of the new building. The therapies offered by this not-for-profit organization would be as innovative as the building and become one of America's most comprehensive programs for the victims of abuse. Although I wasn't sure at first, Barbara Kaplan persuaded me to lend my name to the building, which would be known as the Barbara Sinatra Children's Center. But not long after work had started on the site, she and her husband moved away, leaving me in sole charge. I couldn't possibly walk away from a project for which I had become the figurehead.

The center now has around twenty staff annually treating as many as nine hundred children aged between four and eighteen. Funded by more art auctions, galas, and charity golf tournaments than I care to remember, it helps victims of physical, sexual, or emotional abuse or neglect who are referred to us via individuals, the criminal justice system, child protective agencies, churches, and schools. Some have symptoms of depression or anxiety, are self-harming or unusually quiet. Others are more vocal about what has happened. Our pledge is that no child should ever be turned away, regardless of financial status—this key part of our mission statement was Frank's idea. As well as long-term counseling, the focus is on prevention and education to break the cycle of abuse. Our staff produce pamphlets and videos, host forums, and attend conferences, all aimed at prevention as well as treatment.

When we opened, we attempted to treat the perpetrators as

well as the victims, but that approach didn't work out, so we changed the policy to focus solely on the victims. Frank had his own ideas about how to deal with those who abused children. "You can talk to them all you want," he told me, "but let me teach them and they'll never do it again." As I rather foolishly announced at the time, "My husband is from a totally different school. He wants to round up all the men and break their legs. So, he's not allowed in."

The center offers tranquillity and safety to victims—perhaps for the first time in their lives. It is a place of trust, where the healing process can begin. The cheerful entry hall has an inviting play area with giant stuffed animals and several of Frank's most brightly colored paintings. There is another large open-plan area decorated in rainbow colors with an atrium and glass doors leading into private courtyards planted with cacti and other desert plants. The whole atmosphere is of love and warmth. Even the forensic examination room is nonintrusive, with nursery murals on the walls and ceiling enhanced by soft lighting. Special puppets and toy bears are used to help children explain where and how they were touched. There's an interview room with a wall of mirrored glass, where children can be filmed talking with police officers and therapists. Their evidence is then given via video links in court so they aren't forced to face the perpetrators. We worked on changing that law in California, and Sammy Davis was a great advocate. He invited Willie Brown, the speaker of the state assembly, to a cocktail party at his house and let me badger him about the appalling legal situation for abused children. The bill that protected the victims from a further ordeal was passed soon afterward.

My favorite room is a small soundproof space, padded and lined with wipe-clean plastic. The victims can go in there and draw pictures of their abusers on the walls with marker pens before taking a giant paddle and beating them as hard as they like. They can scream and yell and get rid of all their hostility. Every home should have one. I only wished mine had!

As well as helping the victims express their feelings, we work on building their self-esteem so they can move beyond their experiences. That is where my time running the Barbara Blakeley School of Modeling and Charm really came into play. The center has plenty of therapists to help the children from the inside out, but it was my idea to give them confidence from the outside too. In a special auditorium lined with pivoted mirrors, young girls are encouraged to dress up in new clothes and shoes donated by local fashion stores. Once they've been pampered by beauticians who fix their hair and do their makeup, they are persuaded to turn the mirrors around and study their reflections. At first many of them don't even want to look. To see themselves looking lovely is a shock—like hearing your voice on tape for the first time; it isn't at all as you hear it in your head.

Many of these girls think of themselves as cheap, ugly, or guilty of compliance in their own abuse. They feel soiled by their experiences and can't believe how different they look with just a little attention to detail. Seeing their reactions is like watching flowers opening. Suddenly, they lift their heads and put their shoulders back and learn how to carry themselves. Smiles tug at their lips as they finally begin to see their own worth. I knew from mentoring so many young pupils that a sense of self-worth can change everything, and it was wonderful to be able to bring my experiences as the twenty-one-year-old proprietress of a modeling school to these children thirty years later. Just as I had persuaded stores to donate clothes to the models in Long Beach, I cajoled JCPenney and Target to give garments so that each child gets to keep one outfit. For those who feel up to participating, a special fashion show is organized for friends, staff, and family on "graduation day." A child who may have arrived at the center physically or emotionally battered, head low and voice muted, can often be seen months later strutting on a catwalk, turning and posing, confident, grinning, and reborn.

Of course, no amount of makeup or clothing can heal the

deepest emotional or physical scars, and many children we try to help leave as scarred and damaged as when they arrived. A few return to their families only to be abused further. Others grow up and meet or marry abusers, and so the cycle goes on. But from the letters, cards, and follow-up testimonials we receive, we do believe that we are winning.

I think of all the things we manage to achieve with these children, it was the artwork they are encouraged to do which most impressed Frank. The pictures victims draw when they first come into the center are almost always bleak scenes of sinister shapes and angry faces. Some show cigarettes, drugs, or bottles of booze. The artwork they produce toward the end of their therapy couldn't be more contrasting. Those pictures are usually gaily colored images of rainbows and birds flying, hearts, waggy-tailed dogs, butterflies, and blue skies. Sometimes the children scribble their wishes for the future in the margins, revealing their hopes to train as beauticians or models, be teachers, or become counselors. Through art and play as well as the center's invaluable Image Enhancement and Self-Esteem Program, along with its Aunt-Uncle, Grandchild-Grandparent clubs, we try to give the victims the tools to help them overcome their traumas.

Our experiences at the children's center taught Frank and me so much. Some of the horror stories we heard from the children and their families shocked us to the core. The courage of these kids in the face of overwhelming odds taught us both about humility. Their humor in spite of their inner turmoil has been inspirational.

This project, which started as a passing interest for me, has grown into an all-consuming part of my life that, to this day, takes up a great deal of my time and energy. It challenges me in other ways too, because the worst fear I ever had was making speeches, and I was suddenly thrust into a position where I had to make them frequently. It took me a long time and a lot of knee shaking to overcome that fear, but the actress Jill St. John helped me enormously. "When you get up to the microphone, Barbara, stop and take a big, deep breath," she told me. "Hold it for a while, look around, and then you can begin." That helped me a lot, along with the thought that beating my fear was nothing compared to what these children had to beat.

To continue to raise money and awareness for the center, I have shamelessly enlisted the help of friends and family. I've even done the odd commercial, when Frank and I did a photo shoot for Revlon after the company agreed to support our cause. When we became Revlon's first so-called Unforgettable Couple, glossy photos of us appeared worldwide on billboards and in magazines. Our friends Alice Faye, Gregory Peck, and Dick Van Dyke have all presented videos about the work of the center. The latest is called *A Safe Place*. Sammy Davis, Jr., was wonderful with the children and helped us in all sorts of useful ways, as did Kirk and Anne Douglas. R. J. Wagner and Jill St. John have done incredible things for the center. It was Jill who came up with the idea of the Aunts Club, in which friends of the center pay a monthly donation to support a child. (Helene Galen, our new president, had started the Uncles Club.) R. J. even befriended one teenager whose progress he has personally supported ever since without fanfare or accolade—just simple, caring concern.

Casting around for further inspiration to get people involved, I came up with the idea of a celebrity cookbook. Dinah Shore had had so much success with hers, entitled *Someone's in the Kitchen with Dinah*, which stemmed from the cooking segment on her TV show. She asked her friends for recipes to publish, although mine for a tuna boat, featuring tuna, chili peppers, and cheese served inside a scooped-out bread roll, never made it. Already criticized at home for being "the worst cook in the house," I was teed off.

For my *Sinatra Celebrity Cookbook: Barbara, Frank & Friends*, my husband became a willing tester of recipes and volunteered several of his signature dishes, including his marinara and clam sauces,

eggplant parmigiana, "Blue Eyes" Italian chicken, his delicious potato and onion dish, and—of course—his late-night fettuccine special. He and Jilly never let up claiming that I couldn't cook, but I still
think I make the best chili and beans. (I put vinegar in mine, which
gives it a sharper taste and takes out some of the heat.) Undaunted,
I published my recipe for pasta fagioli, which I always claimed was
better than Frank's. Rashly, he made me test that claim one day. He
insisted that we each had to make our own version and offer a blind
tasting to our guests. I am pleased to report that mine won.

In the dedication of our cookbook, Frank was far kinder about
my cooking than he ever was at home. He also wrote warmly of his
memories of Marty and Dolly.

> *My pop would stand at the stove cooking the greatest pasta*
> *sauce any young Italian boy could hope for. One time, I called*
> *in at the last minute and my pop cooked an Italian meal for the*
> *entire Tommy Dorsey orchestra. Some of the sax players had to*
> *eat in the hallway but they still loved the meal. Now that I'm*
> *an adult, two of my favorite things to do are to cook and to eat;*
> *occasionally I do both . . . and always with a beverage!*
>
> *Fortunately, I met the love of my life, a gorgeous young*
> *woman by the name of Barbara Ann. That's when I really*
> *began to appreciate all the finer things in life, including those*
> *that came out of the kitchen. Barbara's talents as a good cook*
> *extend to her graciousness as a hostess by making guests feel*
> *completely wonderful and welcome. The best recipe is a well-*
> *prepared meal, fine wine, and good conversation with people*
> *you know. With these ingredients you can't miss. Barbara and I*
> *have had high tea with Anwar and Jehan Sadat in their Cairo*
> *home; sipped cocktails with Don Rickles and Bruce Springsteen*
> *at La Dolce Vita; gathered our road family after a concert*
> *for supper at an out-of-the-way Italian joint—these types of*
> *occasions are always quite special. As you sample the recipes in*

this book, Barbara and I hope you experience the same warmth
with your loved ones and friends that we do with ours.

Printed between sketches of food by some of the children at the center and a few lighthearted anecdotes from Frank, the list of people who volunteered recipes for our book reads like the index of *Who's Who*. Most of our Palm Springs, Washington, and Hollywood friends willingly contributed, as well as the chefs of our favorite restaurants around the world. Aside from Presidents Reagan, Bush Senior, Clinton, and Ford, we printed recipes from Clint Eastwood (spaghetti Western), Johnny Cash (old iron-pot, family-style chili—for which he said you could use snake meat), Sidney Poitier (the sweetest guy in the world, who gave us his recipe for sautéed broccoli), Neil Diamond (his mother's beef pot roast), Cher (tuna pasta), Farrah Fawcett (her mother's pecan pie), Gene Kelly (potato sandwich), Whoopi Goldberg (Jewish American Princess fried chicken), Jack Lemmon (broiled shrimp), Joan Collins (pasta primavera), and Oprah Winfrey (Oprah's potatoes).

My son, Bobby, who's a terrific cook, gave his recipe for linguine alla puttanesca, or "hooker's sauce," and Katharine Hepburn gave us hers for lace cookies. Julio Iglesias gave up his secret for paella Valenciana, which his father always claimed was what turned him into a great singer. Andy Williams divulged his mother's recipe for rhubarb shortcake, given to him by her on his wedding day. Paul Newman gave us his Italian baked scrod, Dean Martin his delicious caviar-potato appetizers, and Elizabeth Taylor offered her spicy chicken. Frank teased that it was just as well Elizabeth's recipe didn't call for carrots, "because when that lady asks for carats, it could cost you half a mil!"

The recipes came in one by one, on index cards, scrawled longhand on scraps of paper, via telegram, or typed out neatly. Probably the funniest was George Burns's offering for scrambled-scrambled eggs. He wrote:

I haven't cooked in the last 70 years but I think I still remember how to make scrambled eggs. I'm pretty sure you use eggs; put them in a pan (it's better if you break them first). Make sure you move the shells to one side, and then let them cook for about 3 minutes. When it's done, forget the eggs and eat the shells.

The director and producer Freddy De Cordova suggested sardines à la Fred, which went:

Carefully open can of sardines. Pour contents on cold plate. Surround sardines with saltines. Open cold bottle of beer. Pour beer in a glass. Combine sardines with saltines. Wash down with beer. Repeat procedure as required. Serves 1.

Sharon Stone's recipe for pomme du jour read:

Walk to the refrigerator. Open the door. Open the fruit drawer. Take out an apple. Eat it.

Perhaps not surprisingly with such an illustrious cast, the book sold very well and went to a second printing, which was fantastic. I'm not sure how well it would do these days, as everyone is on a diet and this is most definitely not a diet book, but it raised a lot of money and even more laughs.

Aside from selling the cookbook, I help organize a variety of fund-raising events for the children's center—from fashion shows to gala dinners, polo matches to tennis tournaments—but the chief focus of my attention has become the three-day Frank Sinatra Celebrity Invitational Golf Tournament in Palm Springs every February. Now in its twenty-third year, it has featured some of the world's finest celebrity players. Originally billed as "Frank's little party in the desert" and attended by everyone from Perry Como and Sammy Davis to Angie Dickinson and Kenny Rogers, it has earned millions. There are luncheons and a fashion show, pasta dinners, cocktail parties, and auctions. Our guests have included friends like Dennis Quaid and Jack Lemmon with his wife, Felicia, Eydie Gorme and Steve Lawrence, Frank Jr. and Wayne Newton. Those who play golf every year include the television stars Dennis Farina and Joe Mantegna. The highlight is a black-tie gala at which a top celebrity performs. I have been fortunate enough to have Tony Bennett, Julio Iglesias, Quincy Jones, Smokey Robinson, and Barry Manilow perform for us in the past. In 2011, it was the wonderful Tony Orlando. On the final day of the tournament, I host an open house at the children's center for people to come and see where and how the money is spent.

In recent years, the tournament has barely broken even, but in 2010 we moved to the Eagle Falls Golf Course and Fantasy Springs Resort and Casino in Indio, California, which was a huge success. R. J. Wagner and Dick Van Dyke were the cohosts, and the players included Pat Boone, Tom Dreesen, and Elke Sommer. At the gala dinner, I honored "Saint" Wallis Annenberg in a special presentation and speech. Walter Annenberg's daughter has picked up his philanthropic baton and done so much more. I was thrilled when she donated $500,000 to the center. Eagle Falls is owned by the Cabazon Band of Mission Indians. Their involvement came about after Frank opened the new theater at the Foxwoods Resort Casino in Connecticut, one of the biggest in the country, run by the Mashantucket Pequot tribe. Afterward, the tribe sent a delegation to visit the children's center and then persuaded the Native Americans in the Palm Springs area to support us as well. The ripple effect of Frank's good deeds rolls on.

Three years after the children's center opened, the legendary New York Friars Club honored me for my work and for the educational forums on child abuse that I helped set up. Their tribute at the Waldorf was quite the star-studded affair, so I wore quite the gown for it—a dress with enormous pink fabric roses on a green bodice. It was almost as big as a voluminous silk taffeta coat I wore once, which, by the time I'd settled into the backseat of a limousine, left no room for Frank! The "roast" they gave me, hosted by my husband the "Abbott," and attended by my family and friends, was hysterical. Everything from my cooking ability to my humble roots and my penchant for nice rocks came under fire while I sat on a dais and listened to tributes and wisecracks, testimonials and insults in equal measure. Dionne Warwick sang "That's What Friends Are For." Frank and Liza performed for me in an event that he'd personally organized. I had the night of my life.

It wasn't my first experience of a Friars Club roast. Not long after we were married, I'd sat in on the roast given to Frank at the MGM Grand in Vegas, which had to be one of the funniest ever. Telly Savalas, Orson Welles, Don Rickles, Red Buttons, Rich Little, Dean Martin, George Burns, Gene Kelly, and Jimmy Stewart were among the many speakers invited to get a rise out of Frank, who had tears of laughter streaming down his face. Rickles slapped Dean across the face and yelled, "It's morning!" then he pointed me out in the audience as "Frank's new wife—the one with the diamond on her nose!" I laughed until my ribs ached.

My biggest challenge now is how to keep the children's center going after I am gone. To do so I need to find younger blood, which isn't that easy in a town largely for retired people. I only hope that I can find the right individuals to pass the baton on to. What I began all those years ago and what Frank wholeheartedly supported has helped so many children recover from the most heinous of crimes and has given them the opportunity to go out into the world with a restored sense of trust and purpose. Long may it continue.

One of the nicest consequences of the children's center experience for Frank was that it got him interested in painting again after several years of not lifting a brush. After he'd attended the art auction and seen what his friends were up to in their studios, he went home, put on some opera, and picked up his palette. I never thought I'd relish the smell of turpentine again.

From that day, he was on a roll. He invited over a friend who ran an art gallery in Palm Springs, and the two of them painted together every day for two months. He completed several large canvases and donated them to the children's center. He had some of his oil paintings of New York scenes copied onto silk ties to be sold in the menswear department of Bloomingdale's as the Frank Sinatra Neckwear Collection, which raised even more money. Each time one of our parties ended and everyone had gone home or to bed, Frank would wander to his studio at two or three in the morning and paint. He was fascinated by it.

As with his singing, Frank never had any proper art training; he just picked up a few tips along the way. There were no artists in his family; his was a natural talent. My theory is that if you're talented in one area of the arts, then you can do almost anything. Great singers can act. They can often paint and dance; they are naturally artistic. Frank even co-wrote a few songs in the fifties, and he wrote poetry, mostly private things to me, but some of it was really rather good.

His art was mostly abstract in style and often Cubist, with precise blocks of bright colors, carefully delineated. After visiting Japan, he began to copy some of the flowing Oriental styles, daubing black onto red to depict flowers, birds, or symbols. He was, of course, Charlie Neat when it came to his painting; there was rarely any mess. He only ever had one "Jackson Pollock moment" that I knew of. I walked into his studio one day and found him reaching into pots of paint with his fingers and hurling it at the canvas. I don't think he even knew I was there. Watching him lost in a world of his own creativity, I knew that art was another kind of therapy for him.

Frank was also very particular about which artists he liked. One Brooklyn-born artist he admired, Walt Kuhn, specialized in painting circus and vaudeville entertainers. Frank painted clowns too—he called them self-portraits because I think he identified with the masks they wear—but his clowns were never sad or evil looking. He bought two paintings of Kuhn's clowns, but I didn't share his enthusiasm for them because their eyes seemed to follow me around the room. I finally told him, "You know, Frank, I don't like mean art. In fact, I don't like mean anything, and I really don't care to live with those clowns anymore, particularly the one in the television room, which takes up the whole wall." He didn't say anything, but within a day or two they were gone. I saw them for sale in an art catalog a few weeks later. Two gentle landscapes appeared instead, hung in their place.

Frank loved the Impressionists and would sometimes take me to visit their homes or museums when we were in Europe. He also liked artists like Salvador Dalí, who came backstage one night to give us a sketch he'd secretly done of us dining by ourselves. Irving Berlin called Jimmy Van Heusen one day to ask for a picture of me. I sent a photograph, and Irving drew a rather sweet penguin holding a microphone in which the eye of the penguin was cut out and my photo was inserted. It was very interesting. Apparently, Irving loved penguins and drew them all the time. I also have a sketch of us that LeRoy Neiman did, and another by Tony Bennett.

A lot of people painted Frank, but the only portrait he ever commissioned was by an artist he admired named Paul Lewis Clemens, who came from Wisconsin. Paul did a crayon sketch of Frank first. He was sitting on a couch at home, reading a newspaper, completely relaxed. Then Paul completed it in oil, substituting a film script for the newspaper. It captures Frank perfectly in a contemplative mood and is my favorite painting of him, bar none. Frank then asked Paul to paint me, but I was never as crazy about the finished product.

Frank sometimes commissioned paintings of others he cared for and gifted them to the subjects afterward, although he did keep a few for himself. Not long after we were married, I decided to do something about a painting of Mia Farrow that hung in the master bedroom. Digging through my old photographs, I came across a large black and white poster of Zeppo, had it framed, and placed it prominently on my nightstand. "What the hell's that?" Frank asked when he saw it.

"Oh," I replied innocently, "I thought this was a nostalgia room." Frank said nothing, but Mia's portrait vanished the following day. And so, of course, did Zeppo's.

Art was a bond Frank had with many people, even the most surprising. When Bono came to our Palm Springs home, I worried that the forty-five-year age difference between him and Frank, as well as their different styles and musical tastes, might not make for a perfect match. We'd first met the lead singer of U2 when Frank was doing a show in Dublin a year or so before. Everyone at the theater was very excited when they discovered that the members of U2 were in the audience, and the promoters asked Frank to meet them backstage. Frank wasn't pleased and asked, "Well, who the hell are they?" But when the band came to meet him, they completely won him over. They were charming, and I especially liked the Edge, who had a great sense of humor. An hour into Frank's set, he told the audience, "Now I'd like to introduce someone everyone's been talking about." He looked down at Bono and added, "I'm told that you're very important and you make a lot of money, so will you please stand up and take a bow?" Bono stood up, and there was applause, but just as he was about to sit down, Frank added, "You know, since you're so important and you make so much money, why don't you invest some in your wardrobe?"

I needn't have been concerned about their second encounter, at the Compound. Bono came to Palm Springs to appear in a cameo role in the video of Frank's song "L.A. Is My Lady." To Frank's delight, he discovered that Bono was a fellow artist. Thus began a special friendship. Those two singers sat side by side at our bar talking animatedly about the virtues of oil over acrylic, the interpretation of abstract art, and the use of color. It was a joy to watch. Later,

Frank took Bono to his studio and showed him a painting he'd just finished, a vivid yellow swirl of concentric circles. Bono loved it and asked if it had a name. "It's entitled *Jazz* and it's yours," Frank said, taking it off the easel and handing it to him. Bono was thrilled. Later during his stay, in a Mexican restaurant where we all drank margaritas, Bono performed a ballad he'd written for Frank called "Two Shots of Happy, One Shot of Sad." Part of the lyrics went:

> *I'm just a singer, some say a sinner*
> *Rolling the dice, not always a winner*
> *You say I've been lucky, well hell I've made my own.*

Frank thought that was just great.

The following year, when Frank was nominated for a Grammy Legend Award (one of the highest honors the recording industry offers any artist), the organizers asked Bono to present it to him. Flying to New York from Dublin, Frank's new best friend penned his speech, which still, to my mind, sums up my husband the best. Bono stood almost shyly on the stage of Radio City Music Hall and told the audience, "Frank never did like rock 'n' roll. And he's not crazy about guys wearing earrings either. But he doesn't hold it against me in any way." He went on,

> *Rock 'n' roll people love Frank Sinatra because Frank Sinatra has got what we want—swagger and attitude. He's big on attitude; serious attitude; bad attitude . . . Rock 'n' roll plays at being tough, but this guy, he's the boss; the boss of bosses, the man, the big bang of pop.*
>
> *Who's this guy that every city in America wants to claim as their own? This painter who lives in the desert; this first-rate, first-take actor; this singer who makes other men poets; boxing clever with every word, talking like America—fast, straight up, in headlines, coming through with the big* shtick,

*the aside, the quiet compliment. Good cop, bad cop, all in the
same breath. You know his story because it's your story . . .
His voice [is] as tight as a fist, opening at the end of a bar, not
on the beat, over it, playing with it . . . where he reveals himself.
His songs are his home, and he lets you in. To sing like that
you've gotta have lost a couple of fights. To know tenderness
and romance, you've gotta have had your heart broken. People
say Frank hardly talks to the press. They wanna know how
he is and what's on his mind—but he is telling his story through
his songs . . . private thoughts on a public address system.
Generous.*

    *This is the conundrum of Frank Sinatra—left and right
brain hardly talking, boxer and painter, actor and singer,
lover and father, bandman and loner, troubleshooter and
troublemaker. The champ who would rather show you his scars
than his medals. He may be putty in Barbara's hands, but I'm
not going to mess with him. Are you?*

With a final flourish, Bono announced, "Welcome the king of
New York City and the living proof that God is a Catholic."

As Frank took rather shakily to the stage that night, I could
tell he was deeply moved by what had been said and by the roar of
the crowd. He was overwhelmed by the award itself and the kindness of a young man who also found solace in working a canvas.
He spoke of his love for me and for New York and told the audience of his sadness at not being asked to perform. Pulling himself
together and soaking up the adulation, Frank returned to form,
quipping, "This is more applause than Dean had his whole life."

FIFTEEN

Out celebrating with Frank.

That's Life

By the time Frank cracked that joke, dear Dean Martin was in the last year of his life and Sammy Davis, Jr., had already left us. Ava Gardner had died along with many of our closest friends. As Frank once said rather bitterly, "You like people and then they die on you." The eighties and nineties were especially hard on the man who felt like the only one left standing at the bar.

It was while he was standing at Sydney Chaplin's bar on Frank Sinatra Drive in the late 1980s that something bittersweet happened to Frank in the early hours of one particular morning. He was with Tom Dreesen, the young comedian who'd been opening for him for many years. The bar was closing, the bartender was washing glasses, and Frank had his back to the door. Tom looked over his shoulder and saw a station wagon with two women pull up outside. One ran in and asked the barman, "Excuse me, do you have a jukebox in here?" The barman shook his head.

Frank turned around and looked the young woman right in the face. He told her, "I'll sing for you."

"No thanks," she said.

As Frank watched her go, Tom saw his expression and said, "She obviously didn't recognize you."

Frank turned back to the bar and took a swig from his drink. "Maybe she did," he replied.

The final years in the lives of Dean and Sammy weren't easy to witness. Ever since Frank had seen the legendary Billie Holiday throw her talent and ultimately her life away, he was totally anti-drugs and bawled out anyone stupid enough to take them. If his memories of Billie's decline weren't enough, the research he did to play an addict in *The Man with the Golden Arm* turned him off drugs for life. He said kids going cold turkey was one of the most frightening things he'd ever seen. "Jack Daniel's does it for me," he claimed. "That's all I need."

He and Dean had always enjoyed a drink together, although neither of them drank onstage in those days—that was just an act. Even the drinks trolley they wheeled on during their Rat Pack shows was fake; the vodka bottles were filled with water and the whiskey bottles with apple juice. The real stuff came out only after the show, and although Frank joked, "I spill more than Dean drinks," I sometimes saw the two of them in a stupor. Dean was such a sweet guy and so handsome. He worked all the time so he wasn't the greatest father, but then I think Frank wasn't either, although both would have killed for their kids. They carried a lot of Catholic guilt about being absent parents, especially Dean, who had so many kids to feel guilty about. One night he invited Frank home to dinner after a show, but when they got there his wife, Jeanne, was sitting at the table with four children from Dean's first marriage and three from his second, so every chair was taken. Dean turned to Frank and said, "Well, I guess I fucked myself out of a seat."

As Dean got older and wasn't feeling well much of the time, he began to drink more, sitting home alone watching *Jeopardy!* and old Westerns on TV. He had a bad back from years of playing golf and terrible problems with his teeth from all the sugar he consumed—which was a lot. To ease both conditions, he began to rely on pain pills coupled with booze, and the combination took its toll. Around that time, he also started to get sensitive about his age. I was sitting next to Perry Como one night at a birthday dinner for Dean in Washington, D.C., when Perry asked the birthday boy how old he was. Dean said a number and Perry looked surprised. Leaning over, he said to me in a stage whisper, "I can remember when we were all the same age."

Then when Dean's son Dino was killed, in March 1987, he went into a terminal decline. Dino, a thirty-five-year-old military pilot, died when his Phantom fighter jet crashed into Mount San Gorgonio during a blizzard. Frank had mentored a teenage Dino during a successful spell as a pop musician, and we'd both been guests at his wedding to the ice skater Dorothy Hamill, so it felt personal to us too. Just as when Dolly had disappeared in the same area, there were several days when no one knew what had happened and no wreckage could be found. Then came the news—the shocking realization that a loved one had died, and in a horrible way. Dean sank into the deepest despair. At the age of seventy, he closed in on himself; some would say he never recovered. Frank called Dean frequently to ask if there was anything he could do, but he couldn't reach his friend.

With Sammy on the rails because of spiraling debts, Frank finally decided to do something that could help his two pals and proposed a reunion of the three of them doing what they did best. Frank hoped that the twenty-nine-date Together Again Tour, launched at Chasen's restaurant in December of that year, would pay off Sammy's crippling tax bills, distract Dean from his grief, and give Frank a chance to have some fun again with the two men he considered brothers. From the start, though, there were problems. Interrupting Frank at the press announcement, Dean asked, "Why don't we find a good bar instead?"

After lackluster gigs in Oakland, Vancouver, and Seattle, Frank accused Dean of not "stepping up." It was the only time I ever saw Frank being unkind to his "pallie," although I think it was tough love. What he was really upset about was that it was no longer like the good old days. By the time they got to Chicago, Frank told Dean, "You're just not holding up your part of the show, Dag!" He then complained to Dean's manager, Mort Viner.

"Screw this!" Dean said, and went to his room. Late that night he called Kirk Kerkorian and asked him to send a plane. Then he packed up and walked off the tour. We woke in the morning to find him gone. Claiming a flare-up from an established kidney problem, he flew home and admitted himself to a hospital. Before too long, though, Dean went back to what he knew and liked— performing solo in Vegas, where he told his audience, "Frank sent me a kidney. I don't know whose it was."

Frank was deeply disappointed in Dean but determined that the show should go on. He sat down with Sammy and their manager, Eliot Weisman, to discuss who they might get in to replace Dean. One of them said, "You know who would be great for this?" Someone else said, "I'm sure she's too busy." Nobody spoke her name, but they all knew who they were talking about—Liza Minnelli. Sammy told Frank, "Boy, with her between us onstage, that would be an event!"

"No, Sammy," Frank said, "that would be the *ultimate* event."

Fortunately, Liza jumped at the chance to fill in on what was launched at the Crystal Room of the Beverly Hills Hotel as the Ultimate Event. Their sizzling show went on to tour twelve countries and play to over a million people in twenty-nine cities. In one month alone they went to Rotterdam, Stockholm, Gothenburg, Helsinki, London, Paris, Amsterdam, Munich, Vienna, Dublin, Milan, and Oslo. They broke box office records across the United States, Japan, Australia, and Europe. The energy of Sammy and Liza was extraordinary. As Frank stood like a rock in the middle of the stage, singing and cracking jokes, the two of them danced and whirled all around him, performing their hearts out. Their onstage banter was a joy to witness, along with the individual versions of their signature tunes like "Cabaret," "My Way," and "The Candy Man." Sammy did a terrific take on the *Phantom of the Opera* hit "The Music of the Night" by Andrew Lloyd Webber and a very funny Michael Jackson impersonation. Liza sang an extraordinarily moving love song that featured sign language, as well as a great number by Charles Aznavour, who came backstage once to meet everyone. Frank scratched himself all over as he sang "I've Got You Under My Skin" but then stopped joking for a heart-stopping rendition of "One for My Baby (and One More for the Road)." Their three-way rendition of "New York, New York" was surely the showstopper to end all. When Frank, Sammy, and Liza performed their entire routine for me at a benefit in aid of the children's center, I knew nothing would ever top it.

Fortunately, George Schlatter recorded two Ultimate Event shows at the newly restored Fox Theatre in Detroit and his video became a bestseller. Not that George didn't have his problems with the filming.

He had the whole thing set up perfectly. He knew what Frank would be doing and when, and he knew where Liza and Sammy would be. He made sure he knew exactly where I was sitting alongside Jolene, so that he could pan into the audience and get a shot of the two of us. On the first night, Henry Ford, Jr., showed up, and without thinking I told him, "You sit here." I got up to give him my seat. George started filming and was looking all over for me. "Where the hell is she?" he cried, going berserk because I'd given my seat away. The next night he told us, "Wear exactly the same clothes, don't move from those seats, and I'll get the shot." But when he looked through the lens, he knew the shot would never make the final cut. Sitting right behind us was the Mafia boss John

Gotti, known as the Teflon Don, and George couldn't get him out of the shot.

The Teflon Don caused a similar problem for George a few years later but in a different venue when he booked the seats that Jolene and I had sat in the previous night and that George needed us to occupy again for continuity. When George heard they were taken, he told Eliot Weisman, "You've got to get those girls in those seats. I don't care what you have to do, just do it!" The following night, there we were sitting in the seats George wanted us to be in—much to his relief. He told Eliot, "I don't know how you did it, but well done."

Eliot replied, "I didn't do a thing. The Teflon Don was arrested last night." And so he was, along with several others in an FBI raid. He was charged with thirteen counts of murder, racketeering, gambling, and tax evasion. He remained in prison for the next twelve years until his death.

I traveled the world with Frank, Sammy, and Liza as the Ultimate Event took to the road and developed a life of its own. We went to places as diverse as New Orleans and Osaka. Such was the public demand for the three stars that they continued to perform solo as well during that time, coming back together for the show that offered three for the price of one. Everybody wanted to see them. And I mean everybody.

Standing on the side of the stage at the Universal Amphitheatre in L.A. one night, I noticed someone's feet sticking out from under the velvet curtains, where he was rolled up tight. Wandering over to the stranger peering through a gap, I poked him with my finger and made him squeal. Out popped a face I recognized immediately as an old friend of Sammy's. I smiled and said hello.

"Er—hello," replied Michael Jackson in that childlike voice of his. Looking across at Frank in open wonder, he said, "Isn't he great?"

"Yes, he is," I replied, completely unfazed. I was quite accustomed to fellow singers coming to Frank's concerts to study his art, the way he phrased songs, his timing, his choice of numbers, and his presentation. Vic Damone came to stay at the Compound for a couple of weeks once to study Frank and really learned a thing or two. I asked Michael Jackson, "Would you like to stay behind and see him after the show?"

"Oh, I-I'm not sure."

"Well, I know he'd like to say hello to you," I said gently. "You see, I'm his wife."

Michael lowered his head for a moment with embarrassment. At my coaxing, he unfurled himself from the curtains and stood watching the rest of the performance next to me. When Frank exited on the other side of the stage, I walked Michael to the dressing room. As I suspected, Frank was delighted to see Michael, and the two of them sat chatting about the last time they'd met, when Frank recorded "L.A. Is My Lady" with their mutual friend Quincy Jones. After a while, other people started coming in to congratulate Frank, so Michael made his excuses. He squeezed my arm in gratitude and slipped away.

Being on the road wasn't always as charming and magical as that, however. I arrived one night at the Meadowlands arena in New Jersey an hour or so after Frank had gone ahead to prepare for a show he was doing with Liza. As we drove into the parking lot, I noticed that Frank's car wasn't at the stage door.

"Where's Frank?" I asked.

"He left" was the reply.

Confused, I walked backstage, where I could already hear the crowd waiting out front. Tickets had been sold out months in advance, and the place was buzzing with anticipation. I went to Frank's dressing room, and all was as it should be; his hospitality rider had been carried out to the letter. There were his must-have bottles of booze, cartons of cigarettes, bowls of candy, sandwiches,

Italian antipasti, cans of Campbell's chicken soup with rice (his favorite), packets of Luden's cough drops, tea and honey for his throat. An empty glass stood ready to be filled with Jack Daniel's and carried with him onto the stage. He'd tell the audience, "In case you're wondering, this isn't cold tea." He'd also carry a single cigarette and a lighter, which he'd light up for one of his torch songs. His tux was on a hanger waiting to be slipped on at the final moment (never before, in case he creased it), and there was a color television for him to keep up with the news and sports. Everything he asked for from the bars of Ivory soap to the twelve freshly laundered towels was waiting for him, but there was no Frank.

I walked next door to Liza's dressing room and found her having a meltdown. "Oh, Barbara! Frank's gone! I don't know what to do. Should I go on? Or shouldn't I? What do you think? He's not here!"

"What happened?"

Someone explained that Bill Miller, the show's orchestra leader and conductor, had forgotten all the personalized sheet music that night, which meant that the orchestra couldn't play. There was no time to go back to Manhattan and get it. When Frank saw everyone panicking about what they should do, he announced, "You do what you want. I'm leaving."

We'd already arranged to meet for dinner at "21" in New York after the show, so I presumed Frank had gone straight there. I was still dithering about whether to join him or keep Liza from having a nervous breakdown when my friends Judy Green and Ann Downey arrived. Realizing that nothing much could be done, I told them, "I'm leaving."

"Where are you going?" they asked, surprised.

"To '21.' Come and join us."

"But we want to see the show!"

"There is no show," I said, and so off we went to New York, where Frank was waiting at the bar with a drink and a cigarette.

"Bill forgot the damn music," he told me. "What else could I do?"

Back at the arena, a hapless manager had to announce that the show was canceled because of "a technical fault." The fans were offered a refund or a chance to reschedule the next time Frank came to town. Poor Bill Miller never forgot his lead sheets again. The man Frank named Suntan Charlie because he was so pale-skinned had it tough for a while after that, but at least he kept his job. Anyone else would have been fired. Bill had been with Frank since the 1950s, when Frank's pianist walked out on him at the Desert Inn Hotel in Vegas after his wife asked him for a divorce. Frank asked Jilly to help him find someone, and Jilly took him to see Bill, who was playing on a funny little stage up over the bar. Frank, who hired him on the spot, always claimed he found Bill "on a shelf." Not long after they met, Bill's house was destroyed in a mudslide that killed his wife and put him in the hospital with badly broken legs. Not only was Frank a frequent visitor but he settled Bill's medical bills and set him up with everything he needed to make a new start, including an apartment, clothes, and furniture, all hand-picked.

Frank couldn't read music, so he learned everything by ear when Suntan came over to play for him. Listening to each number, Frank would memorize the melody, set the tempo, and work on the phrasing until they got it just right. Everybody loved Bill, especially Liza, Dean, and Sammy, who really appreciated his incredible musical talent.

Sammy was such a sweet little guy and utterly devoted to Frank, who'd first met him as a young fan waiting for Frank's autograph at a stage door in 1945. I became very close to Sammy, who told me a lot about his early life. He was raised out of a trunk while touring in a vaudeville trio starring him, his uncle, and his father. I always thought the cheerful façade he put up stemmed from his tough childhood, but that was also why he was such a fantastic performer—he'd been performing his whole life. During the war he was the only black in his army unit, and his fellow soldiers teased him mercilessly. They even painted him white one night. In the end, he figured the only way he could get them to like him was to perform. He worked the racial abuse he'd suffered over the years into his act, claiming he'd been insulted in places "most blacks never get the chance to see." The trouble with Sammy was that he was on, day and night. We were in Hawaii once, and he came running into our suite wearing tiny briefs, waving his arms around, and shouting, "The natives are restless! The natives are restless!" Then he ran out. Accustomed to his crazy antics, we looked up, laughed, and went back to our brunch.

It was such a shame that Sammy got hooked on cocaine and booze in the seventies, because that's what really changed his relationship with Frank. Having married Altovise, one of his dancers, he turned her on to drugs too so that he'd have some company. That finally did it for Frank with what he called "this coke crap," and he wouldn't even speak to Sammy for three years, which broke his friend's heart. Sammy was also in dire financial straits by then, and although Frank had helped him before, this time he cut him off completely. Sammy asked everyone including me to try to persuade Frank to let him back in, but it was no use. As far as Frank was concerned, Sammy might as well have been dead.

It was Alto and I who finally got them back together, having decided the silence had gone on too long. Just as Frank had gotten Dean Martin and his onetime comedic sidekick Jerry Lewis back together again (by walking onstage with Dean during one of Jerry's muscular dystrophy telethons) and I'd done the same with Billy Wilder and Swifty Lazar (sitting them together at a party), I went to work on Sammy and Frank. I invited the pair of them to a private dinner at Caesars Palace without telling Frank. Fortunately, he wasn't so mad at me that he walked out. He was still tough on his stand, though, and told Sammy how disappointed he was.

"You're the greatest talent there is, and yet you're going to let this shit destroy you?" he asked. Sammy listened tearfully, and he did clean up his act after that—to please Frank, I always thought.

Sadly, Alto didn't, and she ended up having a car accident in which she could have killed someone. Frank, Sammy, and I finally took part in an intervention with her therapist and a friend of theirs named Mark. We went to her house, sat in a circle, and took turns speaking. We told Alto that we loved her but that we'd reserved a room for her at the Betty Ford Center in Palm Springs. Frank told her his plane was waiting, and Mark and I accompanied her to the desert. Sadly, she didn't stay there nearly long enough. We were at some affair a month or so later and she asked me, "Please, Barbara, give me one sip of your martini?" I wasn't aware alcohol was also part of her problem, so I handed her my glass. When she downed it in one gulp, I knew that she was back to her old tricks.

When Sammy started to have problems with his voice and was diagnosed with throat cancer in 1989, Alto couldn't cope. Sammy was so afraid of losing his ability to sing that he opted for radiation rather than surgery, but then the cancer spread and he lost his voice after all. At a televised sixtieth anniversary tribute for Sammy, when everyone knew he was dying, more than thirty stars, including Whitney Houston, Clint Eastwood, Stevie Wonder, Michael Jackson, and Ella Fitzgerald, performed in an Emmy award–winning production. George Schlatter organized it, and knowing how Frank hated hanging around, George suggested he open the show. The only star to turn up with a single member of his entourage (Jilly) agreed, instantly resolving the petty backstage disputes about who should go on first. George told the others, "Put it this way, Sinatra's opening and Ella's closing, so where would you like to be in the lineup?" Frank came out, stood on the stage of the Shrine Auditorium a few feet away from Sammy, and told him, "I want to get my licks in before the rest do." He called him "My brother... the best friend I ever had."

Toward the end of his life, Sammy had a lot of people around who were telling him what to do, how big a star he was, and how he didn't need Frank Sinatra anymore. The two of them were still friends, but they didn't work together and Sammy went out on his own, doing numbers like his popular "Music of the Night" by Andrew Lloyd Webber. We went to visit Sammy several times in the hospital, but then he went home to Beverly Hills to die, so we flew back to L.A. from a concert in Detroit to say good-bye. Sammy had a trach tube in his throat by then and was clearly having trouble breathing. He couldn't even speak anymore; it was tragic. Frank was very emotional, so leaning forward, I touched Sammy's hand and said, "Sam, I thought you'd want to know that Frank's called Andrew Lloyd Webber. He's going to sing all his songs from now on." Sammy thought that was so funny, he almost spat out his trach. A few days later he passed away. Frank canceled four Radio City Music Hall concerts to fly home and grieve in his usual quiet way.

Sammy was buried with a watch Frank had given him. His funeral was presided over by Reverend Jesse Jackson. I sat in the front row with Dean and Frank, and both men wept openly. It was so sad, especially for Frank, who'd lost Chester Babcock just a few months earlier. Altovise was at Sammy's service, but she didn't make much sense. She'd been so attractive, fun, and in great shape before drugs took hold of her. It was not a pretty picture, and although Frank was determined to support her as best he could, sadly, Alto died ten years later.

Like Sammy, Jimmy Van Heusen also couldn't speak before he died, having suffered a catastrophic stroke. We missed his great humor as much as his writing talent. He and Sammy Cahn, who'd written together for years, fell out over something and never made it up. When Frank and I went to visit Jimmy toward the end, he was lying on a couch and could barely manage a facial expression because of paralysis. Frank leaned forward and said, "Sammy Cahn's here, Jim. He wants to see you." Well, Jimmy's face twisted into a grimace then like you wouldn't believe. Bless his heart.

Dear Dean lasted another five years, until respiratory failure claimed him too. That was probably the toughest loss of all for Frank. He said afterward that Dean was "like the air I breathe; always there, always close by." The friend who he claimed brought more fun into his life than anyone else was gone. Frank couldn't face that funeral; he couldn't even talk about it, so I went in his place. Dean's passing, of all of them, meant that the good old days really were over. Those slick young men I'd first spotted across a smoky bar at the Sahara in 1957 would be forever immortalized in film, on CD and vinyl, and their memory still makes me smile. But when they dimmed the lights in Vegas at the passing of Dean and Sammy, it seemed to both Frank and me that those lights would never be quite as bright again.

Frank refused to let life beat him and eventually pulled himself together. Like me, Frank was a survivor. We'd known some tough times, but we were able to say, "This too shall pass."

He never lost his passion for life; in fact, losing people he loved only made him more passionate. His curiosity and interest in everything from the personal problems of his friends to the political crises of the world never waned. When Iraq invaded Kuwait in 1990 and Saddam Hussein seemed to be courting disaster, Frank felt it was his duty and responsibility to write to both Saddam and George Bush. Mr. Fixit never gave up hope that he could fix everything. Needless to say, only President Bush responded to Frank's letters, and the Gulf War was, sadly, not avoided.

One of Frank's ways of getting past sad times was to celebrate, and he never needed an excuse. If there wasn't a reason to throw a party or buy someone a gift, he'd invent one. He loved Christmas so much, with all its twinkling festive lights and message of goodwill to all men, that he had the lights kept on a tree outside his home all year round. "Everybody could do with a little extra Christmas," he'd say.

Birthdays and anniversaries were always the biggest deals, though, and the older he got the more they came to mean to him. We had lots of places we liked to go—favorite clubs and restaurants in almost every city in the world. There was "21" or Patsy's in New York, Café de Paris in London, and Lord Fletcher's or Dominick's in Palm Springs. But probably our most frequent party venue away from home was Chasen's restaurant in Los Angeles, where Dave Chasen, an old vaudevillian, served excellent southern food, including his famous chili, creamed spinach, and "hobo steak." Chasen's had significance for so many of us. Zeppo had asked me to marry him there. Jimmy Stewart threw his bachelor party at Chasen's. Dean Martin, Greg Peck, Kirk Douglas, Bing Crosby, Bob Hope, and Elizabeth Taylor were all regulars. Ronnie Reagan proposed to Nancy in one of the booths. We had our own booth, and when the restaurant eventually closed someone bought it.

Chasen's also served wonderful cocktails, including my favorite Flame of Love martini, which the barman Pepe Ruiz created for Dean Martin when Dean told him he was bored with ordinary martinis. Pepe would pour a dash of Tio Pepe into a chilled glass, then tip it out. He'd light a strip of orange peel with a match and smear the hot oil the flame released around the glass. He'd then fill it with ice and vodka before wiping the rim with more flambéed orange peel. Heaven. Frank immortalized the drink in the song "Nothing but the Best" with the line *"I like a martini and burn on the glass."*

It was in Chasen's that Frank sang "True Love" to me at a party for one of our wedding anniversaries, which was one of the few times he sang at an informal gathering. It was also where

we first met the singer Michael Feinstein when he was just starting out. Michael had been hired to play the piano that night and
thought, What can I do to get Frank Sinatra's attention? Frank
had his back to him at first, but as soon as Michael began to play,
Frank stopped talking and turned around with a look of astonishment on his face. Then he went over to the piano, where Michael
was playing some of Frank's earliest and least known songs.
"Where did you get these tunes from, kid?" Frank asked, incredu-
lous. "You're only fifteen years old!" They were friends from that
day on, even more so when Frank found out that Michael was a
huge Gershwin fan.

Another place we liked was La Dolce Vita on Santa Monica
Boulevard. It was there that Frank and Swifty Lazar got into a
heated argument when they were both well into their seventies and
Swifty was in a wheelchair. Swifty made some remark that Frank
objected to, so, bristling, he told Swifty, "I oughta knock your
damn brains out!"

Swifty, who was such a feisty little guy, pulled himself up to
his full four feet whatever and said, "Yeah? Well, come on then,
I'll take you on, Francis. Let's go outside!"

That was all Frank needed—something to make him laugh.
He slapped Swifty on the back and said, "Swifty, you're probably
the only one I could still beat." Everyone cracked up.

In Palm Springs, we usually dined at the Tamarisk Country Club, Dominick's, or Ruby's Dunes. For my parents' sixtieth
wedding anniversary we threw a huge party at Tamarisk. It was
amazing to me that they had stayed together so long, especially
when they'd had such different dreams. My father could never have
imagined when he was chopping meat at the butcher's counter
in Blakeley's that he'd end up being toasted by Frank Sinatra at a
Palm Springs country club one day. My mother, who never lost her
Rochelle Hudson looks, was far better suited to the life she'd made
for them in the desert.

Sadly, toward the end my father had prostate cancer and other problems, but I hired staff to take care of him. Frank and I were in New York in 1989 when I got the call that his ninety-four years on this earth had come to an end. "I'll be right there," I told my mother, long distance. Replacing the receiver, I told Frank, "My father died. You stay and work and I'll fly home on my own."

To my surprise, he said, "No way, sweetheart! I'll cancel. I'm coming back with you," and he did. I was amazed and touched that he did that, but then he'd always gotten along extremely well with Willis Blakeley and was sad that he'd gone. The funeral was small and private, and Bobby stood up and said a few nice words about his grandfather, which I truly appreciated. As I watched my father buried in the same cemetery as Frank's parents, I felt surprisingly little. My father had never been a very demonstrative man, and he didn't like too much fuss. I loved him, but I'd been closer to Pa Hillis than I had ever been to him. I knew that I'd helped give him and my mother a good, long, and happy life. They had a comfortable home, all that they could possibly need, and the kind of life they might never otherwise have had. Although they never said, I think they must have appreciated that.

My mother, who was twelve years younger than my father, handled his death very well. His last few years had been rough on her, giving her almost no life at all. I'd take her to lunch at the Racquet Club, but despite always complaining that she wanted to get out more, she never liked to leave him for too long. After he died, I told her, "Mother, I have a wonderful life ahead planned for you. You're going to have a lot of fun." I sent her on a cruise with a girlfriend, but by the time she got back she was exhausted. It was too late for her, and she didn't last long after that. She had emphysema and congestive heart failure, but she never stopped smoking and we had the worst fights about it. Then she started to get sick, and I told her, "Mother, you can't get sick because you still have so many more places to go."

Frank and I were abroad when I got the word that she was in the hospital, so we flew home and went to see her, but she could barely breathe. It was the most horrible thing I had ever seen. A couple of days later she was gone. As we buried her in a favorite red dress, true to her code, I reflected on how much of an influence she had been on my life. The woman for whom living in Bosworth, Missouri, was never going to be enough not only got herself out, but got me out too. If she hadn't, I've often thought, how different my life could have been. Without a doubt, Irene Blakeley shaped my destiny.

With people dropping like flies all around us and Frank in his mid-seventies, he showed no signs of taking it easy. In the early 1990s he performed almost every week. Whenever he felt the urge, the singer his band and crew affectionately referred to as the Old Man would pack up, take off, and hit the road.

In July 1990, we celebrated our fourteenth wedding anniversary in London, marking the longest time either of us had been married and the start of a new and even more challenging phase in our lives. Then we flew up to Scandinavia before Frank returned to the States to honor demanding new contracts he'd signed to play at casinos in Vegas and Atlantic City. He continued to do political benefits and fund-raisers, this time for George H. W. Bush (his fourteenth president), when he wasn't promoting his new line of pasta sauces. Frank had done commercials for everything from cars to booze, and as long as he didn't have to hang around on the set too long, he enjoyed the experience. Commercials certainly beat the weeks it took to make a movie and were often equally well paid. George Schlatter was usually the poor guy who got roped into making Frank's commercials—not least because everyone knew that he was one of the few who could handle Frank. But even George had his moments.

When Frank was hired to do a commercial for the Sands

Hotel in Atlantic City, he asked George to go with him to make sure everything ran smoothly. The day before the shoot, Horhay asked the hotel what the commercial would be. They replied, "You tell us. We were told you'd come up with something." George almost passed out. It's bad enough if you're prepared with Frank, but if you're not, you're in trouble, because he looks at you with those two eyes that go right through you, and then he walks away.

George came up to our suite on the morning of the shoot and was clearly agitated, even more so when I told him that Frank had woken in a combative mood. George went away but came back twenty minutes later wearing a hard hat and tool belt and carrying a megaphone. He strode into the bathroom where Frank was shaving and yelled through the loudspeaker: "Now hear this! Would all singers be ready for the shoot in thirty minutes?"

Frank almost had a heart attack. "Jeez, George! What in the hell?" he demanded. Once he'd calmed down, he asked, "So what are we doing?"

George replied, "You don't need to know. Just put on your tux, get down to reception, and get in the limo." Frank was still in a bad mood as they reached the hotel. When he saw the cameras rolling, he didn't know what was expected of him, and he was uncomfortable. The car stopped and the doorman opened the door on the wrong side, so Frank had to slide across to get out. "What's the matter with you?" he growled. There'd be no tip that day. Then the other doorman went to the hotel's front door, opened it, but walked in ahead of Frank, who turned to George and frowned. "What kind of place is this?"

George assured him everything would be all right. Just then, two little old ladies approached Frank and asked for a photograph. Mellowing, he smiled and replied, "Sure," whereupon they handed him their camera and posed, together. Frank wondered what on earth was going on. Before he had time to figure it out, a chorus girl ran up and asked, "Mr. Sinatra, one autograph please?" He shrugged and said okay, so she signed her name on a piece of paper and handed it to him. Standing there staring down at her autograph, he finally got it. This was the commercial. He was already in it, and his reaction was what would make it great. Winking at George, he proceeded on into the hotel and maintained the ruse as the croupier at the craps table handed the dice to the person next to him. Frank tried not to laugh when he was left waiting at the dining room door while others were seated first. Once he realized it was funny, he was completely on board.

George didn't always get such compliance, though. One time in L.A., when he and Frank were doing a commercial for All Nippon Airways, there was trouble before the shooting even began. When George went to meet the men in charge, who claimed not to speak any English, he was told through an interpreter that the shooting would take three days. "Oh, no," he said, shaking his head. "You'll get forty-five minutes."

Those men learned to speak English real fast. "Forty-five minutes!" they cried. "Do you know how much we're paying him?" George assured them that, by using a stand-in, he'd have everything set up so that Frank could just walk on the set and do his part. George arranged everything perfectly, right down to Frank and me being escorted onto the set by some geisha girls. The minute Frank walked in, though, he asked, "Can I go home now?" He changed into his tuxedo and then he said, "Are we almost finished?"

George had some stills taken and then began shooting the commercial as Frank moved closer and closer to the exit. For several minutes, Frank and I had to sit side by side in two airline seats and look as if we were enjoying ourselves with a drink and a laugh. Finally my husband announced, "Okay, that's it."

George told him, "I just need one more shot."

"Not going to happen."

"Frank, without this shot, there is no commercial."

"Do you have a problem with your hearing? You're not going to get it."

George squared up to Frank and said, "Francis, don't make me hurt you."

Frank had to laugh. "What?"

George repeated his threat, so Frank asked, "Would you hurt me, George?"

"If I don't get this shot, yes."

"Okay, let's do it." He did the shot, and then he walked off the set. George looked at his watch; the whole thing had taken precisely forty-five minutes. The commercial was a huge success and won awards, so they offered Frank a small fortune to make another one. He thought about it for a few days, and then he told George, "Well, okay, but this time I don't want to hang around."

Frank grew a full beard for a while, and I didn't like it at first, but we had Little Joe, known as the Hairdresser to the Stars, come in and trim it into shape. For his next commercial, Frank was going to have to shave it off, but he woke up the morning of the shoot and decided he didn't want to. I called George and told him, "We have a problem. Frank doesn't want to shave."

"But he has to!"

"I'm sorry, George. I don't know what you want me to do."

Within half an hour there was a knock on the door. I opened it to find Little Joe, a towel over his arm, holding a cup of lather and a straight razor. "Mr. Schlatter sent me," he said. I directed him to Frank's bathroom, where he told my husband, "Mr. Sinatra, Mr. Schlatter says I have to either shave you or cut you."

Frank laughed and replied, "That's pretty funny. Come on in." But when Frank emerged a few minutes later, he'd had Little Joe shave only one half of his face.

SIXTEEN

Taking a breather between tennis matches.
COURTESY OF THE AUTHOR

Stormy Weather

On December 12, 1990, Frank celebrated his seventy-fifth birthday by performing at the Brendan Byrne Arena in East Rutherford, New Jersey. After the show, I threw a party for him at the Waldorf hotel for a hundred people and we brought people in from all over. It was quite the affair.

Rising to my feet, I quelled my nerves about giving speeches and made a toast. Picking up my glass of champagne, I said, "Frank, darling, to the world you've given your music, but to me you have given the world." I meant every word, and he knew it. Our love for each other was really heartfelt, never more so than as we approached old age together.

To help celebrate his birthday and for what was dubbed his Diamond Jubilee Tour, Frank went back on the road supported by the husband-and-wife duo Eydie Gorme and Steve Lawrence. Liza joined us too on part of that tour. We had so many laughs with Steve and Eydie, who were not only great performers but good friends. Frank called Eydie "Loudie," because she was so loud, but she and I became instant friends. Onstage, she and Steve became

Frank's support act in the true sense of the word. With his sight in both eyes affected by cataracts and his memory suffering the pitfalls of any man his age, he wasn't able to remember every word of every song, nor could he always read from the teleprompters placed strategically around the stage. Whenever he missed a refrain, Eydie or Steve would gently prompt him or sing the words to remind him, and so the show would go on. Frank would often make a joke of his slipup, telling his audience, "You know the words. You sing it!" and they would.

Some of the critics made mileage out of his occasional mistakes, but I doubt Frank's fans noticed. They were just thrilled to be in his company and to hear him still able to hit those long notes effortlessly with a voice that only sounded richer than ever before. The fact that the man whose music they'd grown up with was growing old with them was just another reason to love him even more, especially because he was always so heartfelt when he told them, "Thank you for letting me sing for you."

The positive feedback Frank got from his fans counterbalanced a lot of the negativity about him. Mellowing in later life, he finally came to accept that some people would always say unkind things about him and he couldn't do anything about it. His days of frenetic letter writing and heated meetings with lawyers to threaten legal action were over. He appreciated that most stars get unwanted attention, although he always said he probably attracted more than most because his name ended in a vowel. The Italian connection would dog him long after he'd cleared his name and reputation in congressional hearings and the unremarkable FBI files on him had been published. When he successfully applied for a gambling license (which he never used), because he knew doing so would finally give him a chance to clear his name, Frank was offered a character reference from Ronald Reagan, who called him "an honorable person, completely loyal and honest." I thought it was both brave and loyal for Ron to do that. Kirk Douglas said something similar, and Greg Peck endorsed it with "Frank is one of the finest men and most trustworthy, truthful, and reliable men I have known." None of that cut any ice with those who'd pigeon-holed him as guilty by association with the Mob and refused to let it rest.

Frank never denied knowing some wise guys, but he never actively sought them out. He'd grown up with a lot of them in the early days in New York, and a few were still hanging around, especially when I first came on the scene. I always felt that Jilly had much more of a connection with those guys anyway, and that Frank sometimes accepted them being around for Jilly's sake. Nothing in my background had prepared me for people like that, but I took as I found and they were always very nice to me. That all stopped for a while when Jilly and Frank fell out. I have no idea what Jilly did to tick Frank off, but Frank refused to speak to his best friend for over a year, forcing Jilly to live and work elsewhere. I was sad for them both. Jilly had always been such a true friend to Frank, and he was very supportive of me. I knew it hurt both of them not to see each other, so I got them back together, which made them both a lot happier.

Maybe I was naïve, but it always came as a surprise to me to know that some Mob figure or other had been trying to get closer to Frank, usually because they wanted him to play one of their clubs. I almost fainted when Sidney Korshak told me once, "Did you know that Sam Giancana was planning to move in with you for a while?"

"What?"

Sam Giancana was the boss of the so-called Chicago Outfit. I'd heard his name mentioned all around me, but I'd never met him. Some people said he was nice and some said he was not so nice. "Why on earth would he want to move in with us?" I asked.

Sidney explained that Giancana had some legal problem and was due in court, but he hoped to lie low in Palm Springs instead.

"Why with us, though? We'd never dream of inviting him!"

"That wouldn't make any difference," Sidney replied. "People like Sam Giancana don't wait around for an invite."

"Over my dead body!" I replied (and it may well have been). Fortunately for us both, Mr. Giancana's plans changed.

I'd had my first brush with the Mob shortly after Frank and I were married, and I didn't relish the next. We were in New York and due to have dinner with the former mayor Bob Wagner and several notable New Yorkers when Eliot Weisman and Jilly told me that Frank had been asked if he could stop in somewhere on the way to introduce me to "the Harvard boys." I told them curtly, "No, thank you."

Eliot's face fell. "Well, won't you just go by and shake hands with them?" he asked. "They only want to meet you and pay their respects to Frank's new wife, that's all."

"I don't want to." As far as I was concerned, that was the end of that.

We went for the dinner as planned and had a lovely evening. As we were leaving the restaurant, we walked past the bar, and there was Jilly waiting with a group of men all huddled together waiting to pay their respects. Because I wouldn't go to them, they'd come to me, it seemed. Frank gave me a look and nudged me toward the bar. Jilly flashed me his puppy-dog eyes. The expressions on their faces were like those of hopeful children. I have no idea to this day who those men were, but Frank explained that they controlled venues that he (and many others) had played. They wanted proximity to Frank; they longed to be identified with him. "If I'm working some joint they own and they want their picture taken with me, I let them take it, but that doesn't mean they own me too," he said. With all eyes on me, I finally relented and allowed Frank to introduce me. I really couldn't get out of it with them standing right there, so I shook their hands and said hello, and they were all very respectful and courteous. As we left the bar, I told Eliot and Jilly never to do that to me again, and to their credit, they never did.

Far more irritating than the men in ill-fitting suits were the paparazzi. We'd been chased by them since our first summer in Monaco, and their hunger for us never seemed to be sated. In Europe, especially, the photographers were overly zealous. Eydie Gorme and I were in Rome once, and the minute we left our hotel the photographers followed us closely, snapping away. Goodness alone knows who'd want to see a photo of me buying a new purse.

Being tall, I walk very fast, and Eydie tried to keep up with me, but she's much shorter than I am and her little legs couldn't carry her. Finally, she cried, "Barbara! I can't go any farther!" and she stopped at a café to sit down. Waving good-bye, I made my way back to the hotel. When she eventually joined me, panting, I took pity on her and fixed her one of my famous Bloody Marys, which I make with tequila (not vodka), horseradish, Lea & Perrins sauce, Tabasco, lemon, and lime. Eydie drank a couple and then flopped on the couch.

I'd invited the jeweler Marina B to come to the suite with her wares so that Eydie and I could shop privately, but by the time she arrived Eydie was asleep. Marina had her jewelry in a black velvet roll and looked around for a flat surface. "Where shall I put it?" she asked.

Looking at Eydie, I smiled and said, "Roll it out on her chest. When she wakes up she'll see it." So Marina did as I suggested, and we pored over her jewelry with some girlfriends I'd invited over, but Eydie never woke up. Later, when she spotted my new trinkets, she said, "How come I didn't see it? Where was I?"

"Underneath," I told her.

Steve and Eydie were among the stars who helped salute Frank when he was given a Society of Singers ELLA Award for lifetime achievement at the Beverly Hilton Hotel in Los Angeles.

Others included George Burns (who was ninety but still managed a song), Tony Bennett, Jack Jones, and Peggy Lee, who'd always had a crush on Frank, but then who didn't? That was the last time Frank sang with Ella Fitzgerald, who serenaded him with "There Will Never Be Another You." I loved Ella—she was the best: laidback, easy, and brilliant. Frank had had the greatest respect for the singer known as the First Lady of Song ever since they'd worked together in the fifties. "She has great pipes," he'd say. They were very close even though they didn't get to perform together as much as either of them would have liked. As for me, I just liked the way Ella perspired—she was real. She was also terribly nice and extremely humble and performed some of my favorite songs, like "Have You Met Miss Jones?" and "Miss Otis Regrets."

After making a good recovery from his cataract operations, Frank was in reasonable health and better spirits. We went back to Europe, where he gave another milestone concert amid the ruins of Pompeii. He launched an album of Christmas songs and enlisted old friends like Angie Dickinson to help him man a charity hotline. He sang with another old pal, Shirley MacLaine, in New York. She came to the house so they could rehearse together and he liked her a lot.

So, life was good and our days were filled with the usual fun and frolics—until, that is, the night of May 6, 1992. Jilly Rizzo was about to celebrate his seventy-fifth birthday with a gang of us in Palm Springs. He'd spent the previous day at his house with Tony O, cooking "gravy" for the pasta and preparing for the party Frank had helped him arrange. The house was full of friends, and they were all looking forward to the big event. Jilly? Seventy-five? No one would have believed it.

At around midnight, Jilly decided to go back to the house of his girlfriend Betty Jean and get a (relatively) early night so that he'd be fresh the following day. Betty Jean had taken his car, so he borrowed her white Jaguar XJ and headed home. Just as he was crossing a major intersection on Dinah Shore Drive, a car driven by a drunk smashed into the side of Jilly's Jag at considerable speed. The electronics locked down on impact, and the gas cap was knocked off before the car burst into flames. Unable to open the doors, Jilly was trapped inside and burned to death.

When I first heard the news early the next morning, I couldn't believe it. As George Schlatter said, no one expected Jilly to die of natural causes, but we still didn't expect something like that. On a day when we should have been celebrating his life, we were mourning his death. The biggest trauma for me was wondering how to tell Frank. I let him sleep in as usual until lunchtime, although I was terrified that he might wake early and hear it on the TV news, so I kept going into his room to check. Then, when he finally emerged in his pajamas and was sitting in the den reading the newspaper (which I'd scanned to make sure the story wasn't in it), I wandered in and sat down. Taking a deep breath, I blurted, "Darling, I have some very bad news for you. Jilly's not with us anymore. He was in a horrible accident early this morning, on his birthday. I am so very sorry." Frank sat there in stunned silence. After I told him what happened, he withdrew in just the same way he had with the passing of Dolly and Dean, locking himself away, not speaking and not wanting to be spoken to.

Somehow, he managed to pull himself together enough to be a pallbearer at Jilly's funeral, which was held at the same church where Dolly's service had been. And, boy, was there a cast of colorful characters. I hardly recognized any of them, but there they all were—in their suits and with faces so somber they must have known him for years. For once, there were no cameras and no press. I guess the "boys" arranged that. Frank didn't even notice. He went through the motions of that day, but then he went back to sitting alone with his memories.

I knew one thing that really bothered him was the same thing that had bugged him when Dolly's plane went missing—had Jilly suffered? When he'd heard from the mountain rescue crews looking for his mother that the plane had broken up on impact and Dolly had been killed instantly, he was so relieved. I only wished I could tell him something similar about Jilly, but it didn't seem likely from the information we had. Salvation came in a phone call from a friend who owned a local pizza delivery service.

"Barbara," he told me. "I have something to tell you about the night Jilly died. You must decide whether to tell Frank or not, okay?" He paused. "One of my men was delivering pizza that night and witnessed the accident. He saw Jilly at the window of the car screaming for help."

"Oh, God!" I cried, wondering how this news could possibly help Frank.

"I just want you to know that Jilly died of the smoke before the fire got to him," he said. "That's what the guy saw with his own two eyes. I didn't know whether to tell you or not, but I thought it might help."

I thanked him and put down the telephone. What he'd said helped me to come to terms with Jilly's death, and I was comforted by the fact that he hadn't suffered in the way we'd all imagined. After some private agonizing, I decided the information might help Frank too, but I knew I had to pick the right moment to tell him, because timing was everything. I waited until we were completely alone. He listened in silence. He was quite overcome, but I could tell it helped him too. From that moment, I believe, he was able to pick up the pieces and go on.

Performing was Frank's therapy, so within a few weeks we were back on the road. We started in Europe but then just kept on going for the next two years, delighting his many fans. I think Frank believed that if he stopped working he'd die, so he agreed to a grueling schedule of concerts that had him crisscrossing the globe again and performing back in Vegas as usual every New

Year's Eve. He held a fund-raiser in L.A. for his friend the mayor of Jerusalem, Teddy Kollek, then set off for gigs in Germany, Sweden, and England.

We were home briefly for the funeral of Sammy Cahn, who had written the lyrics to some of the greatest songs Frank ever sang, including "Come Fly with Me," "Love and Marriage," "Three Coins in the Fountain," "High Hopes," and "All the Way." Frank once said the great thing about Sammy's songs was that they really said something. I think he must have felt that, with Sammy gone, his recording career was truly over. Concentrating on his live performances instead, we'd travel on average two weeks in every four.

Whenever we came home, we'd unpack, unwind, and go on a diet after weeks of eating in the world's finest restaurants. I had a surefire diet plan comprising eight hundred calories a day with no fat, sugar, or salt. I still wanted to lose those two pounds I'd been desperate to lose since my teens, and Frank was watching his weight too, with child-size portions of his usual food. When I could I'd escape to the beach with friends like Dinah Shore, Jolene Schlatter, Suzy Johnson, Angie Dickinson, and Bee Korshak, on what we called a "fat farm," where someone supervised our exercise regime and cooked all our food so we couldn't cheat. (Frank sent Jilly and "the Fat Man" Mickey Rudin away once to a special fat farm, and they both gained seven pounds. We found out later that they'd sneaked to the local bus station each night and eaten their way through its vending machines.)

We'd start each day with a long walk on the beach before coming home to play cards and eat healthfully. Walking across the dunes behind Dinah one day, I noticed that her hair was really thin, with her scalp showing through. Dinah had always had such great hair. I knew then that she was going through chemotherapy, but typical of Dinah, she didn't want anyone to know. I hid my shock and figured that if she wanted to tell me, she would. Eventually, she had to, because she got very sick. I was in Europe with Frank, but Angie and

Bee went to Dinah's house every day and sat in her living room just in case she wanted to see them. She never did. That funny, fun gal who so loved life chose to keep her suffering to herself to the end.

I can't recall whose idea it was that Frank record an album of duets with other singers, but I know he didn't like the notion much at first. It wasn't that he didn't want to work with friends like Liza Minnelli, Julio Iglesias, Bono, Aretha Franklin, Tony Bennett, and Barbra Streisand—plus several contemporary artists he'd never heard of—it was more that he didn't think his seventy-eight-year-old vocal cords were up to the job.

He hadn't cut a new album in almost a decade. It was one thing to wow an audience of enthralled fans worshipping at the shrine of Sinatra, people who could be won over by his legendary charm if he hit a bum note. But to lay down some tracks onto a little metal disc that could be played anywhere and listened to with clinical appreciation frightened him. As he once said in an interview, "Once you're on that record singing, it's you and you alone."

Frank had a management team around him by then. It wasn't my place to say anything, though, and I butted out mostly. My husband wasn't exactly a shrinking violet, after all, and I knew that if he didn't think he could do something, then he wouldn't. He was wise like that—he made all the right moves. To begin with, he refused even to consider the duets album and asked his team, "Why would I want to record all those songs again?" Under pressure, he eventually capitulated but warned everyone, "This better be good."

I went with him to the studio at Capitol Records in L.A. for his first session in the summer of 1993. Frank preferred to record at night, when his voice was warmed up, and he also liked to work to a tight deadline, which gave him the stimulus he needed. The plan was that the vocals he recorded that night would be edited and melded in with those of the other stars, who would record their parts later in studios around the world and phone them in on

a new digital telephone line the producer had set up. With typical thoughtfulness, Frank had arranged for flowers and thank-you
notes to be waiting for each of his fellow singers before they cut
their vocals. We walked into the studio to find the musicians and
engineers waiting, along with a film crew hired to record the his-
toric event. There must have been well over sixty people crammed
into that hermetically sealed space. Each of their faces, even those
of the old-timers who'd been with Frank for years and whose children he could name, were full of the usual Sinatra anticipation. A
few minutes after we arrived, though, their idol suddenly turned to
me and announced, "I'm not going to sing tonight."

I looked around the room and saw the shock wave hit. Quietly, I asked him, "Can't you at least do one song?" He shook his
head. "I'm so sorry," I told the producer, Phil Ramone. "Frank's
not going to sing tonight." That was that. We turned and walked
out as the musicians began to pack their instruments away.

The following day we went back in, and Frank was full of voice.

"Are you ready?" the sound engineer asked.

"I've been ready since I was a kid," Frank quipped.

Playing around with tempos and phrasing, changing songs
slightly as he went, Frank was on fire. In one session alone, set up
like a live gig, he recorded nine complete songs, and when it was
done his orchestra gave him a standing ovation. Frank knew he
hadn't been up to it the previous night, and secretly, that bothered him. Rather than lower his exacting standards and appease
the waiting crowd, he decided not to sing at all.

It was during the recording of that first *Duets* album that
Frank was told it would make "I've Got a Crush on You" with Barbra Streisand more personal if he said her name, especially as she'd
sung the line *"Oh, you make me blush, Francis."*

Frank liked and respected Barbra enormously, as did I, but
he was bothered by the request. "I'm not singing to any woman
other than my wife," he declared. Pressed by those who were eager

for him to do it, he finally agreed to record an overdub in Atlantic City replacing the word *baby* with *Barbara*. He told me, "I'm going to pretend I'm singing it to you. It'll be to my Barbara with all the a's, not to the other Barbra." He really was such an old-fashioned sweetheart about things like that.

Frank's confidence in his recording ability had been seriously shaken by his experience with the *Duets* album. Everyone told him he was great, just like they always did, but he knew the truth. He fretted about what the critics would say and fully expected them to feed him to the dogs. He needn't have been concerned. Although his voice wasn't as it had once been, he sang with the kind of emotional honesty and rich resonance that only comes with experience. *Duets* became his bestselling album, smashing *Billboard* records and going multi-platinum. One critic wrote, "Is Sinatra half the singer he was? Actually, he's about three-fifths the singer he was—but that still makes him about twice the singer anyone else is."

Duets was so successful that Frank was encouraged to make *Duets II*, which gave him a chance to record songs with Steve and Eydie, Frank Jr., Lena Horne, Stevie Wonder, Patti LaBelle, Willie Nelson, Neil Diamond, Gladys Knight, and some other great singers. Like its predecessor, the album sold millions of copies and introduced him to a whole new generation of fans. That old Sinatra magic I'd first experienced in Wichita more than fifty years earlier still had as many people as ever under its spell.

In March 1994, my seventy-eight-year-old husband collapsed onstage in Richmond, Virginia. Halfway through "My Way," he turned to Frank Jr. and asked, "Can you get me a chair?" Before Frankie could find one, Frank crashed facedown on the floor as the audience of almost four thousand gasped. The orchestra gamely kept on playing as Tom Dreesen and Frank Jr. ran to his side, loosened his tie, and checked that he was still alive. Frankie must have feared the worst as he looked down into his father's face. There was a doctor in the audience, and he leapt up onto the stage to tend to Frank as people wept. An ambulance was called, but by the time the paramedics arrived, Frank was able to sit in a wheelchair.

Even as he was being wheeled offstage, Frank was blowing kisses and waving to his audience, who were on their feet giving him thunderous applause. He was taken to the hospital, where the doctors diagnosed dehydration in the southern heat, exacerbated by his blood pressure medication. They wanted to admit him and run some tests, and one senior doctor insisted he stay because he didn't want anything to happen to "the great Frank Sinatra" on his watch. Frank listened to what he had to say and then asked, "Are you finished, Doc?" The consultant nodded. Frank turned to Tom and said, "Let's get the fuck out of here!" He got on his plane and flew home.

When I heard that he'd collapsed, I was really shaken. For some reason, I hadn't gone on that leg of the tour. All those years of being stuck to him like glue, watching his every move, enjoying all his triumphs and helping him through his lows, and the one time he was taken ill I wasn't there. I knew how much performing took out of him; he'd lose up to fifteen pounds per tour. I should have been there to make him drink extra fluids before he went on; I might have kept him from dehydrating. What if that had been the end? I would never have forgiven myself.

When I met him at the airport at midnight, I was still scared, but he put me instantly at ease. "I'm fine, beautiful," he reassured me as he accepted my hand to help him down the steps. "It was just too darn hot." He had no intention of resting, and as soon as he was feeling better, he picked up the tour where he'd left off. Over the next few months, he worked as hard as ever, pushing himself to the limit, but I could tell he was increasingly tired. His schedule, which included performances in Hershey, Pennsylvania; Tulsa, Oklahoma; Omaha; Syracuse; Atlantic City; and Foxwoods casino in Connecticut, would have fatigued someone half his age.

He went on to perform in New York as part of a celebration to mark the anniversary of Ellis Island. We were the guests of Malcolm Forbes, who earlier in the day took us all out on his yacht *Highlander*, moored near the Statue of Liberty. I sat at a card table on the deck of that magnificent vessel as it cruised around Battery Park, playing gin rummy with two of the richest men in the world—John Kluge and Charles Wallstadter, owner of the Continental Telephone Company. I only wish I'd been playing for big money, because I beat them. Later that month, we flew to Manila and had dinner with Imelda Marcos, the president's widow, whom we'd first met when her yacht pulled up next to ours in Monte Carlo. She was a real character and a lot of fun to be with. I liked her. Everyone talked about how many shoes she had, but I think a lot of people have just as many—only she blabbed about it.

Back home between shows Frank still needed entertaining, so we had as many houseguests as ever, including the English comic actor and musician Dudley Moore and his statuesque girlfriend Susan Anton. I guess their relationship must have been fairly new, because when they arrived they retired to their room and didn't come out for three days. I had trays of food and several jugs of Bloody Marys sent in, and our other guests, who included the Pecks, the Rickleses, and the Schlatters, sent in empty glasses, dirty plates, and anything else unappetizing, until the couple finally traipsed out with big grins on their faces.

Frank celebrated his seventy-ninth birthday in the desert but then went back on the road. Some commentators began to suggest that he was going on longer than he should, and I was starting to feel the same way. At the beach house one afternoon, he'd been too breathless to get back up the dune after a stroll and I'd had to call a doctor. That great big heart of his was undoubtedly weakening, which was affecting his breathing and his voice. He knew he wasn't always up to it but was once again talked into the concert. Frank was surrounded by a great many people—musicians, valets, riggers, managers, and roadies—whose livelihood depended on his working. He considered them family and didn't want to let anyone down. There was backstabbing from as far down as you could go to as high up as you could go—even his dressers were bad-mouthing each other; it was hysterical. He had some wonderful people on his staff who'd been with him for years and were utterly devoted, but he also had a few who—especially when they saw the Sinatra train running out of steam—wanted to make the most of the time they still had.

Frank usually ignored it if someone stole from him, but he did fire one employee who'd worked for him for over thirty years because he'd been too greedy and everybody knew about it, which made Frank look weak. Eventually, he tired of having to keep tabs on his empire, though, which was especially hard to do when he was on the road. Besides, everything about being on the road had changed. Most of the famous venues he'd played had closed or been torn down. Even the Sands in Vegas was in its death throes (we would watch its demolition in November 1996 from our balcony at Caesars), and the pallies he'd had so much fun with onstage had left him alone in the spotlight.

At the end of his eighth decade, Frank finally admitted that maybe it was time he "took it easy." I was bemused when he told me that and wondered what it would mean for someone so driven. Whatever he decided, though, I wasn't going to miss one minute, so at each performance he continued to give I sat right there, a few feet away, watching his every breath.

There were other tough decisions to be made, one of which was whether or not to leave Palm Springs. I'd felt for some time that we needed to move back to L.A. to be closer to family and friends. Despite his emotional attachment to the Compound, Frank appreciated that we'd have to move from the home that was costing us a lot of money when he wasn't working so much any-more. The Springs had given us the happiest years of our lives, but the town had changed beyond all recognition. Most of our fellow desert rats had either died or moved back to the city. We were having a hard time coping with the brutal summers, and golf was no longer such a draw. The main reason for moving, though, was our age. I wasn't getting any younger either, but Frank was that much older and his health was beginning to fail. The decline was so gradual, but I noticed it long before anyone else did. Whatever was going on, I knew he needed to be near the best medical teams L.A. could offer.

I'd never tried to manage Frank's business affairs, and he would have never taken my advice, but like many wives, I'd sometimes attempt to guide him gently. If I ever wanted to sell him on an idea, I'd lay out the pros and cons and let him think about it. After a while, he'd usually come around to my idea but claim it as his own. Once that happened with the decision to move, we put the Compound on the market and made plans to buy a beach house at Malibu instead.

We finally sold the Compound to a Canadian entrepreneur by the name of Jim Pattison. He was a big Sinatra fan who wanted not only to buy his home but to meet the man. Sadly, the day he came to view the house, Frank was in bed with a cold, so Jim never got to meet him or even see the whole interior. He bought the place anyway—along with almost all the furniture and Frank's beloved train set. We auctioned off many of the things we no longer wanted or needed. I sat in a room high above the bidding floor and watched the auction through one-way glass. There was a frenzy for all things Sinatra, it seemed, and I was amazed by how much people paid for the most mundane of objects. Jim Pattison was bidding by phone from abroad, but there were plenty of rival bidders on the floor, raising their paddles for not much more than knickknacks.

Even though Frank knew that the day would inevitably come, leaving the Compound was rough on him. The original moving date came and went, and Frank remained firmly entrenched, so I asked Jim if we could possibly rent the property for a little longer. He declined but allowed us to stay on as his guests. Then, one morning, Frank decided it was time. He got up, showered and changed, had breakfast, and asked for a car to be brought around to the front. With hardly a word, we walked out the door, sat in the back of the car, and told his driver to "step on it." His twenty or so staff, many of whom had worked for him for decades, lined the driveway as we drove toward the main gate and the exit onto Frank Sinatra Drive. Staring straight ahead, unable to acknowledge their emotional farewell, Frank never once looked back.

SEVENTEEN

*Renewing our wedding vows on our twentieth anniversary
at Our Lady of Malibu.*

You Will Be My Music

My husband didn't retire so much as walk away. The last performance he gave as a solo artist was on the night of February 25, 1995, for the Barbara Sinatra Children's Center celebrity gala. He hadn't sung for a while, but he'd always kept his voice warmed up, and that night—the finale of our golf tournament—he was brilliant, and I mean brilliant like the old days.

Without any fanfare as usual, he walked onto the stage at the Marriott Desert Springs hotel after Tom Dreesen's warm-up, went to the microphone, and launched into "I've Got the World on a String." Bill Miller sat a few feet away, as he had done for so many years, his fingers playing the keys for his friend and boss for the last time. From the moment Frank opened his mouth, he had his audience of twelve hundred guests eating from the palm of his hand. It was almost as if he knew this would be the last time he'd sing in public because he drew on all his experience and strength to give us one of the most memorable performances of his life.

A reviewer in *Esquire* magazine described Frank that night as "on the money." He was certainly in sparkling form, cracking jokes between numbers like "Fly Me to the Moon" and "My Kind of Town." There was no sign of his recent forgetfulness, no unsteadiness in his speech or instability on his feet. He was bright and fully present and enjoying every moment in the spotlight. He was meant to sing only three songs, but he did six and received one standing ovation after another. At the fourth, he joked, "Is it time to go home?" Poignantly, he finished with "The Best Is Yet to Come." As he walked offstage, he told Tom Dreesen, "Don't put away that suitcase!"

Speeding home in the back of the limo, I could barely speak. Finally, I squeezed his hand and asked him, "When are you going to learn to swing?"

Later that year, Frank celebrated his eightieth birthday. We'd been married for nineteen years, yet it seemed like only yesterday that my darling husband-to-be had called me the morning of our wedding to tell me he couldn't wait for me to be his bride. Everyone, it seemed, wanted to mark his milestone birthday. Everyone, that is, except Frank. I thought it would be nice to do something special, but I was thinking more of a quiet dinner with friends, which is exactly what we had when George and Jolene threw us an intimate dinner at their house with the Pecks and the Douglases. FS wasn't going to be allowed to get away with just that, though. The Empire State Building was bathed in blue light for Ol' Blue Eyes's birthday, and plans had been afoot for months for an all-star televised tribute—*Frank Sinatra: 80 Years My Way*. With all proceeds being shared between the children's center and a Los Angeles AIDS charity, stars of screen and stage would perform, including Bruce Springsteen, Tony Bennett, Bono, Ray Charles, Bob Dylan, Greg Peck, Arnold Schwarzenegger, Little Richard, Roseanne, Vic Damone, Angela Lansbury, Patti LaBelle, Tom Selleck, and Natalie Cole, among many others who stepped up at L.A.'s Shrine Auditorium. George was executive producer in charge of the special, which he described as "a loving birthday card to Frank."

Frank was more than a little nervous about the show. He wasn't feeling well, and he didn't know if he wanted to have cameras zooming in on him. I knew that if I could just get him there, though, he'd love it. The night before the show was to be taped, I invited Bruce Springsteen and Bob Dylan to dinner to break the ice, and the three of them got on like a house on fire. Along with several others who'd be performing the next night, they drank, goofed around, and sang together at the piano. It was an incredible evening.

On the night of the show, Frank received a standing ovation just for making an entrance. He joked that it was "for still being alive." He and I sat at a small, spotlit table ringside and watched one great star after another pay their respects. Bruce Springsteen opened the proceedings by calling Frank "the patron saint of New Jersey," and then he sang "Angel Eyes," the number Frank had bowed out with when he'd "retired" all those years before.

Arnold Schwarzenegger, the future governor of California, spoke of Frank's incredible fund-raising, which he estimated had netted over a billion dollars for numerous charities throughout the years. (That night alone added another million.) Ray Charles did a fabulous version of "Ol' Man River," and Tony Bennett sang "(He's) Got the World on a String." There were old movie clips and news footage showing images of Frank's remarkable life. Bono recorded a special video singing "Two Shots of Happy, One Shot of Sad." There was a can-can routine by the Moulin Rouge Dancers, before Bob Dylan (who was going to sing "That's Life" but couldn't get along with it) sang an interesting acoustic number instead called "Restless Farewell," which had the same sentiment as "My Way" and which Frank was visibly moved by when he heard the lyrics. The final verse goes:

> So I'll make my stand
> And remain as I am
> And bid farewell and not give a damn.

Patti LaBelle sang an incredible version of "The House I Live In," the song Frank recorded in the sixties to defuse racial tension, and hers was the only performance that he stood to applaud. The finale, of course, was "New York, New York," in which Frank was invited onto the stage to join in. It was the last time he would ever stand before an audience.

Soon afterward, he told his friend Larry King that he'd never sing again in public. "Those days are just gone," he added. "But I'm very, very happy."

A few days after our twentieth wedding anniversary, in July 1996, Frank and I renewed our wedding vows at Our Lady of Malibu Catholic Church. It was a beautiful day. The traditional Catholic ceremony was attended by Bobby, Steve and Eydie, Peggy Lee, Frank Jr., and many others.

Repeating our marriage vows again seemed to take on even greater significance at that time of our lives and proved to be a deeply emotional experience for us both. In front of a handpicked group of friends, we repeated the sacred words we'd said to each other three times already—in Palm Springs, Florida, and New York—and promised once more to love and cherish each other "till death us do part."

Twenty-four years after we'd first started dating, we were still together, still in love. We had defied all the critics; we'd lost money for those foolish enough to gamble on us not staying together more than a few months. We'd risen above all the attempts of those who tried to break us up. Ours was a deep and lasting love, full of trust and loyalty, and not just on my part. Frank had been hit on by just about every glamorous star in the world but not only had he married me, he'd stuck with me for all those years. This was a man who was perfectly capable of leaving if he grew bored, but he'd stayed—and so had I. Was it easy? Not always. Frank could be quite a handful. Was it calm? Rarely. I never knew what drama each day would bring. But was it fun? Oh yes; a thousand times yes. And romantic too. As I'd promised myself as a restless tomboy back in sleepy little Bosworth, I would never, ever be bored.

After the ceremony, we threw a party for seventy guests in the yard behind our Malibu beach house—the venue of many a memorable Sinatra Summer Pasta Party. We served an Italian dinner, of course, and during the toasts Frank announced gamely, "We're going to do it again in twenty years!" As friends and family stood or sat around in the dunes, Bob Newhart and Don Rickles gave speeches and R. J. Wagner made the toast. An old friend from Vegas, the singer Frankie Randall, stood up and announced that he'd "brought something to the party." As he summoned us to stand by the piano, he performed a song he'd written for our anniversary called "Twenty Years Ago Today." He claimed it was based on Frank's words to me over the many years he'd known us. It was so touching that we had copies of the song made and sent to our friends, and Frankie still performs it for me each time I see him. It goes

It was twenty years ago today that you said you loved me in
*   every single way.*
It seems like only yesterday but it was twenty years ago today.
When I first saw you I knew one day I'd make you mine
My life's valentine; until the end of time.
I've loved caring for you knowing you were by my side.
You were a special gift when you became my bride.
Looking back at all we've shared together, day by day
Expecting the unexpected in everything I'd say
You lovingly adjusted to my ups and downs in life
I've treasured you through all these years
As my lover and my wife . . .
Twenty years from now as I look at you and smile

I'll kiss you and remind you that it's all been worthwhile.
One thing I've learned from you is to cherish what we have
And so I'll live each moment as if it were our last.

Even though we were still so happy together, there was no longer any escaping the fact that Frank was getting old. He never lost his humor about it, though, and he wasn't ready to give up just yet. The person who'd defied the odds from his near fatal birth and lived every day since as if it was his last was not going to go gently into that good night. For his eighty-first birthday, when someone asked him what he wanted, he replied, "Another birthday?"

Once Frank was no longer pushing himself so hard with constant touring and performing, though, his body—and his mind— was finally able to relax. Some claimed that without his music he lost the will to live, but I don't think that at all. It was more a case of admitting his age at last and allowing himself to act it. He stopped wearing his toupee. He grew a beard again; he slept more and didn't exercise as much. His hearing, sight, and balance weren't what they used to be, but his passion for reading and crosswords had never diminished, so he spent more and more time at home, curled up with a dog or three, his nose in a newspaper or book, and a cat on his shoulder. His occasional lazy mornings of slouching around in his pajamas became the norm, and sometimes he didn't bother to get dressed at all.

Sadly, when he felt well enough to go out, the press hounded him with even more fervor than they had before. Whenever we left the house, we'd send out two or three cars in different directions first so that the press couldn't be sure which one to follow. If they followed ours, I kept Frank's head down on the backseat. But as soon as we arrived anywhere, restaurant staff knew there were big bucks to be made if they tipped off the newspapers. No matter how generous Frank had always been with waiters and valet drivers, most seemed unable to resist the chance to make themselves an even bigger tip by picking up the phone. Not surprisingly, perhaps, we chose to stay in rather than run the gauntlet of the media. Because we'd always enjoyed card games and I'd never stopped playing gin rummy with friends like Bee Korshak, Anne Douglas, and Quique Jourdan during the day, I decided to set up a weekly tournament.

Friends would arrive in time for cocktails and canapés, followed by a game of gin rummy or poker, and then dinner. We had eight players every week, including our regulars from the Beach Group, Jack and Felicia Lemmon, Greg and Veronique Peck, Angie Dickinson, Bob Newhart, Dick and Dolly Martin, Dick Van Dyke and his wife Michelle, R. J. Wagner, and Jill St. John. The guest list varied, depending on whether we were at the Foothill house or in Malibu and who was available. We didn't play for big money, but that didn't keep us from being competitive. I'd been able to hold my own in poker ever since Bob Oliver taught me back in Long Beach, but I was playing against a lot of actors whose faces were extremely difficult to read. Fortunately, after one of my potent Bloody Marys or a "Barbara martini," their guard would soon drop.

Our card nights became regular fixtures and something we all looked forward to. They have never stopped to this day. The beauty of the arrangement was that, because we were home with friends, Frank could join us if he felt like it or he could stay in bed or on the couch watching TV in his den. People could take a break from the game and drop in to see him if they wanted, and he'd almost always join us for dinner. If he was having a bad day, we'd leave him be. He had Vine and nurses to help him get around and make sure he took his cocktail of pills. If he was in good form, he'd wander into where we were and say something like "You're all under arrest!" Wearing his pajamas and dressing gown, he'd pull up a chair next to mine and I'd show him my hand. He was such a fine actor that his face would never once change expression; he was unbelievable like that.

Not that he was always well enough to join us. With alarming frequency, Frank was rushed to the hospital because of problems with his breathing, his heart, or high blood pressure. He beat off pneumonia once or twice in spite of the fact that he never stopped smoking; he developed bladder cancer and had ongoing problems with his colon. Each time he was admitted to the hospital, he created such a fuss with anyone who'd listen about wanting to "get the hell out of here" that he'd almost always be released prematurely. Despite his feistiness, in January 1997 he was hospitalized for the third time in eight months with pneumonia after a suspected heart attack. Putting on a brave face, I had to go in his place to launch a limited-edition Artist Label magnum of Korbel champagne, decorated with one of his paintings and sold in aid of the children's center. At the recently closed Chasen's, I told the waiting media and celebrities, including Sharon Stone and David Letterman, that Frank was "doing great" and blithely assured them he was "home with a bottle of bubbly to salute you."

Two months later, on my seventieth birthday in March 1997, Frank was still not feeling great, so I wasn't surprised when he announced that he didn't feel like facing our planned dinner with a few close friends. "Won't you even come out and say hello?" I asked, trying to hide my disappointment.

"I don't want to change out of my pajamas," he complained.

"Okay, then. You won't have to," I told him before calling our guests and informing them it was to be a pajama party. When Frank was wheeled into the room, he had to smile. Everyone was dressed just like him.

Each new time he was hospitalized, the rumors would begin to fly. Tabloid newspapers made wild claims, and friends would call us from all over the world to ask tentatively, "Is Frank all right? We heard he'd died!"

"Tell them not yet," Frank would reply gruffly if he overheard. Sensing his slow demise, the newspapers began to prepare his obituaries and called several of our friends to ask for their tributes. The paparazzi became ever more determined to get "the final picture." We were told that some editors had offered over a hundred thousand dollars for such a shot. I developed some cunning ways of getting Frank in and out of the hospital without being seen. If he was taken in by ambulance, I'd arrange for a sheet to be raised when he was carried out of the house to shield him from view. We had a long driveway at Foothill, but there were still angles to get a shot. My problems didn't end there. Because Frank insisted that the ambulance siren be turned off, we'd have to stop at every red light. The photographers following us would jump off their motorbikes or run out of their cars whenever we stopped and press their cameras to the windows. So I worked out a system of fixing tinfoil to the glass. If we had time to get Frank to the hospital in one of our own vehicles, we'd use the SUV with blacked-out windows and arrive at Cedars-Sinai through a secret route to the basement. Accompanied by security guards, I'd drape a scarf over Frank's face while he was carried upstairs on a stretcher.

Even when he was within the relative sanctuary of a hospital, where he was checked in as Albert Francis or Charlie Neat, photographers would go to extraordinary lengths to snap Frank. They'd check in with some spurious ailment just so they could walk up and down outside his room in the hope that his door might be open. We played cat and mouse with the press for a long time, and of course I couldn't always outwit the photographers, so sometimes they'd get a shot of Frank looking frail and publish it in the cheap rags, but I kept all such photos from him. He was fighting for his life. I was fighting for his privacy. The last thing he needed when he was barely able to catch his breath was a camera in his face. That would have killed him.

Back at the beach house—the place he came to love best of all—I'd let him recover after each scare. He'd sit in the garden wrapped up in a blanket, listening to the ocean. We had a bench up on the dune under a shade, and we liked to sit there side by side and watch the pelicans flying majestically by or see the waves come crashing to the shore. It was a simple pleasure I'd never tired of since the first time I'd seen the Pacific as a starry-eyed teenager. Unfortunately, our fragile peace was increasingly shattered by helicopters buzzing overhead, with photographers hanging out the sides. Some of our neighbors, notably Dick Martin and Steve Lawrence, would drop their pants and moon the choppers. Not to be thwarted, reporters hired boats and dropped anchor a few yards off the beach, right opposite our backyard. One time we even found someone lying under our bench on the dune, his lens directed straight at our bedroom window. Others set up a permanent site on the hill opposite with trucks and camper vans, so if we stepped even one foot out the back door their cameras would click and whir away.

Determined to outdupe them, I planted a row of ficus trees in pots across the front of the patio so that we could at least sit outside to eat and get some sun. I told Frank the trees were for shade, but I think he must have guessed their real purpose. In his growing confusion and with an onslaught of people trying to invade our privacy, he became vigilant about security and insisted that he carry a handgun. He'd even take it out onto the dunes and shield it under a sunhat on the bench next to him. Afraid he might actually shoot someone, I had a member of the staff take the pin out so the gun wouldn't fire.

Keeping my husband alive and his spirits up became my primary focus. So much so that when I broke my back, in January 1996, I decided not to tell Frank. It was six in the morning, and I'd been woken by the crying of our new puppy, a Weimaraner named Shadow. I got up and took her out onto the terrace, but on the way back, she ran between my legs and I tripped and fell down four steep steps, twisting as I crashed to the floor. The pain tore through me, and I could barely move. I cried out for help, but there was no one around. I could see the telephone ten feet away but didn't know how to get to it. In the end, I crawled across the floor, reached the cord, and pulled the phone down on top of me.

The doctors told me that I'd broken my T12 thoracic vertebra along with just about every bone in my right foot. Having had a cast put on my leg up to my knee, I was fitted into a steel brace that held me rigid all day and that I could take off only to sleep at night. It was extremely painful, and I got through each day only with the help of pills. I had to wear that darn thing, which dug into my chest and back, for three months, but Frank never even suspected. I wore loose clothing or a housecoat so that the brace couldn't be seen, and I didn't let on. He was being looked after by nurses around the clock by then, and although he was fully aware, he slept a lot and he couldn't focus as well as he used to, which was a blessing in disguise for me at that time. Even when I went to board meetings for the children's center, I wore high-necked blouses so that no one would spot the brace. I didn't want the news getting out in case Frank saw it on the television or read about it in the newspaper.

I wasn't the only one struggling with the health problems of loved ones. One afternoon in 1996, Anne Douglas was at our house playing gin with me, Bee, and Quique Jourdan when she received a telephone call. Her face turned white; she didn't speak, she just said, "I'll be right there." Kirk, who was eighty, had collapsed with a stroke. I offered to go with her or at least have someone drive her, but she refused and hurried to his side. Kirk was rushed to the hospital and they did the best they could for him, but the stroke was severe and—most cruelly for one so eloquent—it took away his ability to speak. Anne did such a great job taking care of him, though. To begin with, he was depressed and just lay in bed all day doing nothing. Then one day, Anne walked into his room and told him, "Kirk, you're to stop feeling sorry for yourself. You're not going to lie there for the rest of your life, so get off your ass. Your speech therapist will be here in an hour." The treatment worked, and Kirk was soon much more understandable. Before we knew it he'd written a book about his experiences and was performing in a one-man show. That gorgeous young man whom I first met at the Racquet Club in Palm Springs all those years before never lost his drive or his incredible sparkle, largely because of the help and encouragement of his loving wife, who refused to let him go under. She was an inspiration.

In May 1997, Frank was awarded the Congressional Gold Medal, the highest award given to an American civilian. The 105th Congress passed an act to award him the medal "in recognition of his outstanding and enduring contribution through his entertainment career and humanitarian activities and other purposes." It stated that Frank had "touched the lives of millions throughout America and around the world" with more than fifty albums and appearances in more than sixty films, as well as his thousands of concert appearances. It authorized thirty thousand dollars for the striking and designing of a medal in gold with duplicates in bronze.

Of all the awards Frank received, I think this one meant the most to him. Not only had it once been awarded to his friend John Wayne—the Duke—but it was vindication at last, as if he needed that. After all those years of vilification in the press, the fruitless FBI investigations and congressional hearings, the governing body of the United States of America had finally announced publicly that here was a man of the highest character. Sadly, Frank had been rushed back to Cedars Sinai just before the medal was awarded and wasn't well enough to go to Washington, but we watched the House's vote on the bill and he wept unashamedly at the honor.

In a letter to President Clinton on Frank's behalf, I wrote, *"My husband has always been a staunch supporter of this country and is a proud American to his soul. Frank is fortunate to have known every President since his first visit to the White House when he met*

Franklin D. Roosevelt. He came to know and admire Mrs. Roosevelt to her passing . . . On concert tours he is a proud emissary of America."

Bill Clinton wrote back to me expressing his pleasure at authorizing the honor and sent us the pen used to sign the act. *"You have touched the lives of so many people over the years, Frank,"* he wrote. *"Warmest congratulations and best wishes."* (The two men were fond of each other, and Bill had even asked Frank's advice once about the laryngitis that kept making him lose his voice.) The medal went into the glass display case with all the others my husband had received over the years. In typical style, he never showed it off, but it had a prominent place, and once or twice I found him staring at it with faraway eyes, as if the skinny kid from Hoboken could hardly believe that it was really his.

EIGHTEEN

At home with a few of our babies.

Put Your Dreams Away

It was an almost perfect day in Beverly Hills. On the sunny afternoon of Thursday, May 14, 1998, Frank and I sat out by the pool on the grounds of Foothill and had lunch together. He was in his wheelchair, and he didn't finish his favorite food, a grilled cheese sandwich, but he was in good spirits and seemed fine.

In the previous few days he'd accepted visits from a few people, including his former road manager Tony O. They had shared a pizza. I was glad Frank had had more of an appetite that night, as he'd lost weight recently and I didn't want him to lose his strength.

"Remember I'm going out tonight, darling," I told him after our lunch together. "I'm having dinner with the Deutsches, but I won't be late."

"Oh, you still live here, do you?" he said, using one of his favorite one-liners if I'd been out more than usual. Another was "This place ain't doing so good for a hotel!" whenever there was nobody around. The truth was that Frank insisted I go out and have fun whenever I received an invitation. "You go ahead," he'd tell me. "I don't want you sitting here all the time looking at me."

Apart from when I had to go to Palm Springs each spring and organize the charity golf tournament, I really didn't leave him very
often and never alone. If I did have to go out or away, I made sure
he had twenty-four-hour nursing and usually arranged for a friend
or relative to keep him company as well. That night, Armand and
Harriet had insisted I take a break from Frank's constant care.
My spirits had plummeted in recent weeks as Frank became ever
frailer and spoke openly about being tired of life. He was eighty-
two; his further decline seemed inevitable, but I couldn't even
bear to think about it.

The Deutsches had invited me to dinner with some friends at
Morton's restaurant in Beverly Hills, which wasn't far. But I still
felt a little guilty about accepting their invitation. Later that day,
Frank took his usual nap while I showered and changed for dinner. I remember I put on a white pantsuit and pink silk blouse. I
went to his bedroom to say good night but found him sleepy and
a little breathless. The doctors had recently changed the medication for his heart problems, but the new medicine only seemed to
make him weaker. I made a mental note to call them the following morning to see if the dose could be altered. Frank's television
blared noisily in the corner, so I turned it down a notch. Kissing
him gently on the forehead and squeezing his shoulder, I told him,
"Good night, darling. Sleep warm." I left him tucked up in his bed
with a nurse close at hand and made sure Vine had all my numbers
in case she needed to call me. Then I went out. Armand, or Ardie,
as he was always known, picked me up, and as we drove down Sunset I couldn't help but notice the moon that night, low and huge in
the western sky like a peeled orange.

Ardie was older than Frank, but he had all his faculties and
spoke warmly to me about the King Charles spaniel we'd recently given them. When we got to the restaurant, I took a seat
and ordered a drink. As we were chatting, a waiter tapped me on
the shoulder and told me I had a call. Putting down my glass with

a hand that was surprisingly steady, I went to the front desk and lifted the receiver. I heard Vine's voice and flinched. "You'd better come right away. The paramedics are here. They're going to take Mr. S to the hospital."

"What happened?" I asked, because less than an hour before he'd been fine.

I heard her hesitate before she said, "They can't find a pulse."

I don't remember replacing the receiver or going back to where the others were eating dinner, but I do remember telling Ardie, "I have to go."

"Okay," said the man who'd known my husband for more than fifty years. "I'll take you right after dinner."

"No! I have to go now," I told him. Ardie drove at about two miles an hour, so I said I'd take a cab, but he insisted, so I sat in the passenger seat willing him to go faster. By the time I got home, the ambulance had just left, and that's when my fear began to kick in.

"But I always go with Frank!" I cried. "I have to mask the windows with foil!" I imagined him lying in the back, looking and feeling dreadful as photographers took their fill of shots. The thought made me sick to my stomach.

I asked one of our staff to drive me to the hospital immediately, and he must have broken every speed limit to get me there. Running in through the door of the ER, I hurried to the front desk and was directed to where Frank lay on a gurney in a cubicle behind a curtain. Three doctors were working on him. Feeling faint, I tried to blank out what they were doing and focus on my husband's face instead. Gripping his hand, I told him, "Darling, you've beaten worse than this and you can beat this too. You've *got* to fight." His lips were blue, but I saw them move, so leaning closer, I told him again, "You have to fight, Frank!"

He really tried to. He did. He must have clung to life for twenty minutes or more, although it seemed like considerably longer. I didn't leave him for a second, his hand like a bag of bones in mine. Briefly, his eyes flickered open. They were watery but still the same dazzling blue as when he'd first pulled me into his arms and kissed me all those years earlier, stealing my heart. He looked at me for just a moment and opened his mouth to speak. Leaning closer, turning my head to hear, I heard him whisper the words "I can't."

Then his eyes closed forever, and that was it.

That was the end.

The doctors stepped back, and one placed a hand gently on my shoulder.

I shrugged it off and remained by Frank's side, talking to him and stroking his forehead. "Come on, Frank," I told him, "you can do this, darling. You can."

I have no idea how long I stood there, willing him not to be dead, but finally the doctor pulled me away with the words "Barbara, he's gone."

The rest of that night is a blur. There'd been no time. Not to call anyone. Not even to say good-bye. I can't now remember how I got home or who called Bobby and Frank's family for me. Vine probably. Maybe I did. Suddenly, our house was full of people. There was Bee Korshak, George and Jolene Schlatter, Steve and Eydie. Our road and driveway were floodlit as the media gathered. Someone told me that on the news of Frank's passing, the lights had been dimmed in Vegas and at the Helmsley Hotel in New York. The Empire State Building was bathed in hues of blue, and the tower of Capitol Records was to be draped in a black shroud. Blue cocktails were served in bars around the world, and at every address from Hoboken to Palm Springs that held some significance to Sinatra, fans stood vigil with flickering candles.

Everyone kept telling me that they didn't want me to be alone. Well, it was too late for that. With Frank gone from my life, a part of me would always be alone. People tried to reassure me that time would heal my wounds. Most were kind, although some arrived just to take what they could of his, but I didn't care. It didn't matter. Nothing was important to me. Nothing. All I could think about were Frank's final words—"I can't." For the last year of his life, I'd been fighting to keep him alive, keep him with me. That's all I could dwell on as the minutes crawled by that longest of nights.

In the first twenty-four hours after he died, all I wanted to do was what Frank had done in times of grief—curl up somewhere in a corner and block out the rest of the world. But his was no ordinary passing. This was the death of an icon, of someone everyone felt they knew and deserved a piece of. The doorbell never stopped ringing as baskets, wreaths, sacks of mail, and other tributes cascaded into our home. We had so many bouquets we had to lay them on the floor, through the hall, up the stairs, out in the backyard. I sent half of them to the local children's hospital and the rest to Cedars-Sinai, where they lined the corridors and little old ladies shuffled out of their bedrooms to admire the flowers that "Frank sent."

Our street was virtually closed because of the media vans and the vehicles of individuals who flocked into Beverly Hills. A huge crowd gathered outside the gates, many dressed in the kinds of suits and hats that Frank used to wear. Peering out of an upstairs window, I realized that if ever I'd hoped for a small, private ceremony for my husband in the desert church we both adored, I was being naïve. Frank was a megastar. I knew I'd be sharing him with his public from the day we'd started seeing each other. I'd never minded until now; he'd earned all that love, and he deserved it. His farewell could be nothing less than an event, his final performance watched by millions around the world. Akin to a state funeral, it would be televised and closely scrutinized. There would be no quiet corners in which to weep.

Drawing on all my reserves and remembering that, as Mrs. Frank Sinatra, I had to remain dignified, stoic, and do everything in my power to keep my husband's legacy alive, I set about arranging what I hoped would be a fitting tribute to the man I dearly loved and already missed so dreadfully. I soon discovered that arranging such a funeral would be a huge undertaking, strewn with pitfalls. Everyone who was anyone expected an invite, and I—as the gatekeeper—had to say yes or no. The former employee of Frank's whom he'd fired pleaded with me to be allowed to come. He even had his wife go to work on me in tears, which was when I finally cracked. Then there were his two surviving ex-wives to be considered, along with the wishes of his family and the expectations of friends in show business, industry, and politics. Because of the overwhelming number of people who wanted to attend, we had to make it invitation only and arrange for tickets to be issued at a special box office, as if this were his last concert.

As well as trying not to upset anyone and staying true to what Frank would have wanted, I had to organize the entire affair in less than a week. The two-hour funeral Mass at the Good Shepherd Church in Beverly Hills was set for Wednesday, May 20, six days after Frank's passing. I went to see Cardinal Roger Mahony, the archbishop of Los Angeles, who was wonderfully helpful and planned it all with me, from the music to the prayers.

Although it was a closed casket, I wanted Frank to look his best, so I had the staff at the funeral home dress him in one of his finest navy blue suits and a striped tie. Friends and family gathered around his coffin before it was closed to place special mementos inside. He was to be buried with a flask of Jack Daniel's, a roll of dimes, some stuffed toys from his grandchildren, and his favorite candies. Bobby added a packet of Camel cigarettes and his Zippo lighter. My gift to Frank was a gold Bulgari medallion I'd had inscribed and given to him for one of his birthdays. I slipped it into his pocket. The wording, translated into Italian, was: "You still give me a thrill." It was something that held special meaning for us both.

The night before the funeral, we held a candlelit vigil with musical tributes and prayers in the chapel. Dear Suntan Charlie played "In the Wee Small Hours" and other classics. Friends stepped up and offered reminiscences, read poems or extracts from letters Frank had written to them. I stayed for the service but then prepared to go home, leaving some of those closest to Frank standing around his casket talking about him and telling jokes. My parting glimpse was of George and Jolene, Steve and Eydie, Don Rickles, and several others laughing and telling stories about Frank's great humor, generosity, and warmth. I liked the idea of him still being the center of attention, even after he was gone. Frank would have enjoyed that.

The day of the funeral was surely one of the longest of my life. I don't think I slept a wink the night before, and when I arrived at the flower-filled service, I was numb. I'd had official programs printed with a picture of Frank on the cover above the words "Francis Albert Sinatra, born into life December 12, 1915. Entered into eternal life May 14, 1998." Someone handed me one, and I stared down at the photo, still unable to take in that he was really gone. The chief pallbearers included Don Rickles, Eliot Weisman, Bobby, Steve Lawrence, and Frank Jr. Tom Dreesen, who'd first heard Frank singing "Come Fly with Me" when he shined shoes in bars as a young boy and had gone on to "fly" with him for fourteen years, couldn't believe he'd ended up carrying his coffin. Honorary pallbearers included old friends like Tony Bennett, Milton Berle, Ernest Borgnine, Kirk Douglas, Quincy Jones, Gregory Peck, Wayne Newton, and Jerry Vale. It was what Frank would call "a good crowd," with other notable faces including Liza Minnelli, Tony Curtis, Mia Farrow, Anthony Quinn, Sidney Poitier, Larry King, and our good friend John Kluge.

After the introductory rites, there was a musical tribute by

Bill Miller on the piano. "Ave Maria" was sung by the choir, followed by an address and prayers from Cardinal Mahony. There were readings from friends and family, then psalms from the choir and congregation. The homily preceded the communion, which was accompanied by Frank singing "Put Your Dreams Away" with its heartbreaking opening lines, *"Put your dreams away for another day and I will take their place in your heart."* It was the perfect choice. When his voice filled that church, fragrant with the scent of gardenias, there wasn't a dry eye in the house.

Remembrances were made by Kirk Douglas, my beloved Bobby, Gregory Peck, George Schlatter, Frank Jr., and R. J. Wagner, among others. George said afterward that all he could think of was that Frank was going to sit up suddenly and say, "Hey, Crazy? Get off!" George made the congregation laugh when he called Cardinal Mahony "Your Honor" (instead of "Your Eminence") and told them, "When you think how old Frank was in people years, you realize he was awake longer than anyone else. He was eighty-two years old, but he'd been up for most of it!" Tom Dreesen, who also spoke, said all he could think of was Frank saying, "All right, Tommy, it's showtime. Be funny and be brief." After prayers, the choir and congregation sang the hymn "May the Angels Lead You to Paradise."

I arranged for Frank's casket to be covered in a blanket of gardenias, and their heady scent filled my nostrils. It brought back powerful memories of our "True Love" wedding at Sunnylands, and of every anniversary and birthday bouquet he'd presented me with since. The portrait of Frank I loved by Paul Clemens took pride of place on an easel at the front of the church. I sat staring at his face and wondering how I could possibly go on without him. Dean Martin once said, "This is Frank's world; we just live in it," and he was right. Without Frank in my world, what sort of a life would it be?

When it came time for Frank to go home to the desert, back

to the Palm Springs cemetery where his parents, Jimmy Van Heusen, and so many of his friends were interred, I followed his casket out through the church, the cardinal steady at my side. In my hand, I tightly clutched a few of the blessed crucifixes we'd had made to give out to special friends after the service. Holding on to them somehow meant that I hadn't let him go yet.

Emerging onto Santa Monica Boulevard and into the dazzling light of day, I was momentarily blinded. The organ music was fading behind me, and in its place all I could hear was the buzzing of media helicopters low overhead. Looking up, I saw a plane flying across the sky trailing a banner bearing a heart and Frank's name. Another plane was doing intricate loops and skywriting Frank's initials. I felt as if I'd entered some surreal circus arena. Traffic was at a standstill because of all the fans who'd gathered holding up signs and banners saying things like "Goodbye, Blue Eyes," or "We Love You, Frank." They jostled for position with television crews and photographers, their lenses all trained on my face. As I stepped into the cool darkness of the limo, I had never been more grateful for sunglasses.

We followed the hearse to the airport, where Kirk Kerkorian had lent us a plane big enough for Frank's casket and the rest of us. The journey home took no time at all, and when we emerged from Palm Springs airport in a motorcade, hundreds of people lined the streets all the way into town. I don't know how they figured out when we would be passing by or how long they'd been waiting in the heat, but there were so many of them and they stood waiting patiently to pay their respects. Most applauded, some saluted, many waved, and several threw flowers and cried, "Good-bye, Frank!" or, "Welcome home, Blue Eyes!" It was unbelievably moving.

At Frank's simple plot, set flat into the earth of the rolling green lawn of the Desert Memorial Park in Cathedral City, we had the area roped off and tented, and the press kept away. This part was for immediate family only. Frank had chosen the plot years before, when he'd relocated his father Marty's remains there from New Jersey. He bought several at once, for Dolly, for him, and for me. My parents were nearby too, along with dear Jilly and Jimmy.

When Frank died, everyone felt they had a claim and wanted to celebrate his life in their own way. One of those suggested ways was a full military honor guard, including the draping of an American flag over his casket as if he'd been a general or something. President Clinton's permission had already been sought. To me, such a gesture would have been disrespectful of the brave servicemen and women who'd given their lives for their country. Frank was denied military service because of his punctured eardrum. Because he was such a deep patriot, that was something he regretted for the rest of his life, but whenever he could he performed for the military and for servicemen at home and abroad. He had the utmost respect for the armed forces and their traditions, but I knew this wouldn't have been right. I told those who were pressing for it, "We cannot do that. Frank was never in the service, and he wouldn't want it. Besides, we'd be terribly criticized."

In an effort to be conciliatory, I eventually agreed that the flag could be draped over his casket at the interment, away from prying eyes. When the service was over and his casket had been lowered into the earth, a member of the Marine Corps handed me the neatly folded Stars and Stripes from "a grateful nation." I accepted it silently before turning to Frankie. "Here," I said. "I'd like you to have this." My husband's only son seemed deeply touched by my gesture.

For Frank's simple granite grave marker, I'd chosen the inscription FRANCIS ALBERT SINATRA. 1915–1998. BELOVED HUSBAND AND FATHER. Engraved along the top was the song title "THE BEST IS YET TO COME." Lost in my grief standing at his graveside, I felt in that moment that the best had come and gone.

. . .

If I'd hoped for some time for quiet reflection after Frank's funeral, I was to be disappointed. The condolence letters, prayer
cards, and messages of sympathy from around the world swamped
me. People were grieving for my husband whether they'd known
him or not. He'd provided the sound track to their lives, and suddenly, it felt to so many of them, the music had stopped. Although
I was overwhelmed by the volume of letters and cards, the outpouring of love and support touched me enormously. One of the
most memorable notes was from James H. Billington, the librarian
of the United States Congress, who wrote that Frank "taught tol-
erance for all people" and "transcended art." He added, "Sinatra
had no equal and will never be replaced."

I had similar notes from presidents and kings, complete
strangers, devoted fans, and distant relatives. Many claimed that
the world had lost its greatest entertainer and that there would
never be another like Frank. Faced with so many letters, I had
response cards printed and edged in navy blue, each of which I
signed personally. It was a mammoth undertaking, but it helped
me get through each new day. The cards said,

> *Your thoughtful condolence has helped me through this difficult*
> *time. Frank was my love, my friend, and my knight in shining*
> *armor. My husband was a vital and dynamic part of his family*
> *as well as for people throughout the world. He has left a deep*
> *void in so many lives. Through his music Frank will live*
> *forever. May God bless you and hold you dear and as Frank*
> *would say, Sleep Warm.*

For those I knew personally, I also slipped in a poem by Shannon Lee Moseley, which seemed to sum up Frank's life and his
passing. It read:

My life's been full, I savored much;
Good friends, good times, a loved one's touch.
Lift up your heart and peace to thee,
God wanted me now. He set me free.

When Frank rewrote his will in 1991, seven years before he died, he told me some of what he'd decided, but I didn't know everything by any means. He'd always kept the business side of his life separate and had an excellent team to help him. All he promised me was that I would never need to worry about money or have to deal with any unforeseen issues after his death. It was just like the promise he'd made when I'd paid for our marriage license.

After Frank died, our attorney and his executor, Harvey Silbert, came to see me. Fortunately, there was to be no family reading of the will as the bulk of the estate had been divided up years before. Harvey then read me the full contents of the will before handing me a copy. Just as Frank had promised, everything had been taken care of. He left Frankie all his sheet music, which was a nice touch. That was Frank's way. I had more than I could possibly need, yet I would have traded it all in a heartbeat for just one more day with my dearest love.

Life had to go on, and I was busier than ever not just with the children's center but with taking over many of the charitable causes that Frank had supported. Friends were very kind and made sure that I was invited out to dinners and card games, parties and concerts, but I wasn't in the mood to be sociable and preferred to stay home with my memories.

Bobby was a great support, of course, and called or flew in frequently from his home in Manhattan. A successful entertainment lawyer, he had recently become engaged to a pretty Texan named Hillary Roberts, and I secretly longed for my first grandchild. One night about three weeks after Frank died, Bobby agreed to be my date for a quiet dinner with George and Jolene Schlatter at their house a few blocks from ours. Deciding to walk there and back, we set off for what was a relaxed and enjoyable evening. A few hours later, on our way home in the dusk with George and Jolene as our escorts, a car suddenly screeched to a halt at the curb and four men jumped out. Running up to us, they quickly separated us. I couldn't see what was happening behind me, but Jolene must have sensed the danger before we did because she fled into a neighboring driveway, the only one with its gate open.

"Where's the park?" the man who'd cornered me barked into my face. "We're meeting someone there."

"I don't know what you're talking about," I replied, sounding braver than I felt. "There isn't a park around here." He began to argue with me and insisted that I must know the place, but I told him, "I don't know and I'm not even sure it exists. In fact, I'm going to get your license number. There's something wrong with all this." I looked at the plate then but noticed it had a piece of paper taped over it. I moved forward as if to rip the paper off, but I didn't have time because the man grabbed my arm and loomed over me suddenly.

"Give me your purse!"

"You can't have it!" I cried. "Go away!" He jerked it off my arm anyway and pushed me aside. Shaken, I turned to see that Jolene was at the door of the house she'd run to, banging on it and ringing the bell. She yelled, "For God's sake, Barbara, come on in here!"

Instead I turned to see what had happened to our men. George was throwing punches at a guy who was trying to rip his Rolex from his wrist. My blood turned cold when I spotted Bobby lying facedown on the ground without his glasses as another robber bent over him, picking his pockets. My son's glasses lay a few feet away. As soon as I saw that, my anger kicked in. Running at the attacker, I yelled, "You! Stop that! Stop that right now!"

Bobby saw me coming and groaned. "For God's sakes, Mother, get out of here!" In the end, I think I scared the muggers off. They jumped in their car and sped away.

By this time Jolene had gotten an answer at the house, and a little old woman in curlers and a hairnet, dressed in an old robe and using a walker, let her in to call the police. I saw the woman briefly, but everything happened so fast and the police were there so quickly that there wasn't time to thank her. The detectives separated the four of us in her driveway to take our statements while Jolene crawled around in the bushes trying to find the jewelry she'd thrown there when the men first struck. Fortunately, I hadn't been wearing anything special that night.

Standing in the driveway, I watched Jolene's antics as I talked to a couple of officers. When they found out who I was, they wanted me to give a press conference to publicize the attack, but I refused. I looked up and saw the owner of the house again, only this time she looked quite different. Her hair was combed back, she had makeup on, and she was beautifully dressed. She wandered up and asked, "Which one is Mrs. Sinatra?" She smiled and took my hand as if we'd just been introduced at a cocktail party. "How nice to meet you," she said. "My husband once conducted an orchestra for your husband." This was clearly the most exciting thing to happen to her in a while. I couldn't help but smile at her evident enthusiasm. I knew then that Frank was still watching over me somewhere, making sure that, whatever happened, I kept my sense of humor.

Once I got home, Bobby made sure I was settled in and safe before leaving with the promise to call in the morning. I went straight to bed and fell into a deep sleep but was woken an hour or so later by our house alarm clanging. Pulling on a robe, I ventured out of my room to be met by members of my staff, who assured me the police were on their way. Not again! I thought. The squad cars arrived quickly, and officers with dogs searched the house and the grounds but couldn't find anything suspicious, so after a lot of fuss, we all went back to bed. The next morning, though, our gardener disturbed a young man who'd slept in a storage compartment in our garage and came running out. They caught him as he tried to scale the fence. He must have been there all night.

From that moment on, I soured on the Foothill house I'd once fallen in love with. Suddenly, I didn't want to live there anymore. It was too big. I felt too vulnerable living there alone, and without Frank, there didn't seem much point. I felt like a change anyway. I needed to close some old doors and open some new ones. There were too many memories there for me to handle. Not long after the mugging, I put that house on the market and bought an apartment in Westwood, where I am very happy. It has great security, so I feel safe and protected. Around the same time, I decided that it would be nice to go back to Palm Springs for the winters.

To begin with, I rented the old Fred Wilson house in Thunderbird Heights, which was wonderful and had a tennis court but was too big for a place I was only going to use two or three months a year. I knew I needed to find something smaller and more practical. Frank and I had watched a condominium being built right across the street from where we used to live. I'd always teased him, saying, "Whichever one of us goes first, *I'm* going to have a place there." The house I chose had plenty of space to hang Frank's art and entertain friends. Better still, the children's center was a five-minute drive away. Having given up our place in New York, I decided to divide my year equally between the beach, the desert, and the city, a routine I've been keeping up ever since.

Surprisingly, the year I lost Frank ended up being a very good year. To my delight, Bobby married his bride in June in a private ceremony in New York. He was forty-seven years old, so I guessed he must have really listened to me in Neuchâtel all those years earlier when I'd told him not to marry too young.

Then on December 19, 1998, my first grandchild—Carina

Blakeley Marx—was born. I couldn't help but think of her as a gift from above. Just as I was mourning the passing of the man I'd loved more than anything in the world, a new life was created, reminding me of the wonderful continuity of things. Carina is a treasure who continues to surprise and delight me as she grows into a beautiful young girl with a mind of her own. Frank would have been so enormously proud.

Feeling broody, I acquired my own new baby—a handsome Cavalier King Charles spaniel who goes by the name of Sir Winston Sinatra. He is my constant companion and my closest friend. A reminder of happier days with Miss Wiggles and Caroline, he brings me great joy. As with darling Carina, I only wish Frank could have known him, but then I think that maybe he does. I have never been one to dwell on the idea of an afterlife, but something happened after Frank died that did make me wonder. My friend Kathy Hilton (mother of Paris and Nicky) called me up one day after she'd been to see a psychic. The medium apparently told her that Frank had a message for me, which was to "look for the hummingbird" whenever I needed a sign. I was quite taken aback by what she said because only the previous day, when I had been in a quandary about some important decision, I'd asked Frank aloud to "show me a sign." Also, Frank and I had always loved hummingbirds. We had watched a pair make a nest in a cactus right outside our bedroom window at the Compound soon after we were married. We had glowed with parental pride when the eggs hatched and the babies finally learned how to fly away from the cats waiting patiently at the bottom of the cactus.

A day or so after Kathy's call to me, a hummingbird suddenly appeared on the terrace of my Los Angeles apartment. It remained there feeding on the flowers for several minutes as I watched. Living in the penthouse, I had never before seen a hummingbird that high up, and I was astounded. Now, it seems to me, whenever I think of Frank and want some sort of sign from him that I'm making the right decision about something, or to know that he loves me, he sends a hummingbird or two to lift my heart.

Not that I am unhappy—far from it. Frank was the driving force of my life and we lived fast and hard, so it was a big readjustment to the pace without him. Fortunately, I like being alone and have always enjoyed my own company. As Frank used to say, "I don't need any more friends," and it has never once occurred to me to get married again. Anyway, where would I go after Sinatra?

I still have the children's center to worry about and the annual golf tournament to raise much-needed funds. Having put my name to the project all those years ago, I can never walk away from it, and I have no intention of doing so. I just want to make sure that the center and all its wonderful work lives on. I am also involved with the many hospital wings, college halls, clinics, and schools Frank helped fund over the course of his sixty-year career. Tony Bennett and his wife, Susan Benedetto, built a school in Frank's name in Queens a few years after he died, so that is another part of my husband's legacy I am involved with. The Frank Sinatra School of the Arts is in Tony's hometown of Astoria and offers courses in art, dance, music, drama, and film. Tony is the singer Frank handed the baton to; there is no one else around to touch him, and his kind and good spirit shows in his music. He'd always admired Frank so much, and he wanted to do something that he knew Frank would approve of in his name. It is a wonderful facility.

Having spent years listening to Frank taking the time and trouble to call up older women widowed and alone, such as Susie Hornblow, I suddenly found myself one of their number. Only I didn't have a Francis Albert to call me up and make me smile every Saturday night or to send me flowers on Mother's Day. What I began to notice, though, was how many of our male friends stepped into that role—surprising me with telephone calls, visits, and gifts. R. J. Wagner doesn't go two weeks without calling me; neither does Steve Lawrence or Vince Kickerillo (who confessed that Frank asked him to keep an eye on me). Greg Peck used to call all the time until we lost him five years after Frank died. Roger Moore still calls from Europe. George Schlatter picks up the phone just to say hello. Don Rickles rings to crack some new joke. Kenny Venturi, Frankie Randall, Jerry Vale, and so many of those who first met Frank way back when still make an effort to keep me from being too lonely.

Knowing of my lifelong weakness for candy ever since my gummy bean days at Blakeley's General Store, Quincy Jones sends me delicious heart-shaped ginger cookies every Valentine's Day. Others drop into my weekly card games if they're in town. I love to see and hear from them all. There is nothing I would rather listen to than "Frank stories," for—like all those getting on in years—I now get my greatest pleasure from feeding on the memories of the remarkable life I have led as Frank's wife.

EPILOGUE

With my granddaughter, Carina, at the beach house in Malibu.
COURTESY OF THE AUTHOR

The Best Is Yet
to Come

Every year, on the anniversary of my husband's death, I go to the desert cemetery where he is buried and lay some flowers before offering up a quiet prayer. It is always an emotional visit, as is the one I make every year on his birthday to the Good Shepherd Church to light a candle.

Each time I go to the Desert Memorial Park, where I will one day be laid alongside my darling husband, I have to smile because his devoted fans have usually gotten there before me. Frank's grave is one of the easiest to spot among the hundreds in the lush grass carpet. Placed lovingly around his marker are miniature bottles of Jack Daniel's, packets of Camel cigarettes, his favorite candies, posies of flowers, and tiny American flags. One day we will be side by side once more, just as we were for almost thirty years. I guess on my grave people might place candy. Someone asked me what my marker might say, and I thought about it for a moment before laughing and suggesting, "Me too!"

Our friends and family are all buried in that cemetery, so I shall be in the best company; it'll be just like the good old days.

So many of those we had the most fun with over the years are gone now, along with the men in my life—Bobby's father, Joe, and Zeppo. I've outlived them all, and here I am bearing witness to the lives we led and the laughs we had along the way. I think it's probably the laughter I miss the most—especially Frank's jackpot laugh, which was music to my ears.

I am rarely alone when I visit Frank's grave. Photographers and fans often hang around, respectfully keeping their distance as they watch me tell my sweetheart how much I miss him. I sometimes wonder what they think of me, this woman in her eighties keeping vigil for her dead husband. Few know where I came from or how I got there. They know nothing of my life before Frank or how rich it became once I met him. If they only knew the places I've been, the things I've seen, the people I've met on my journey. That was some candy jar! Instead, they watch and they wait, nod a polite hello, and as I am driven away, I see them step forward to better examine my flowers and note. There can never be any privacy for me at Frank's grave.

Although he is dead and buried, Francis Albert Sinatra touched the lives of so many, across all generations, and will always live on in people's hearts. The man with the electrifying personality said once that he wanted to be remembered as someone who had "a wonderful time living life." Well, I too had the most wonderful time, living almost thirty years of that remarkable life as Frank's lover, his best friend, and his bride.

He also said he wished for those who loved him a thousand times more than the joys he'd known in his life. "I wish everybody in the world a lot of sweet things and pleasant dreams," he added, "and soft touching, hugging, and kissing." I was fortunate enough to have had all of that and a thousand times more as Lady Blue Eyes, for which I am eternally grateful.

Sleep warm, Frank. Your memory will always keep me warm, and they can't take that away from me . . .

Index